Best Bike Rides
New York City

Help Us Keep This Guide Up to Date

Every effort has been made by the author and editors to make this guide as accurate and useful as possible. However, many things can change after a guide is published—roads are detoured, facilities come under new management, phone numbers change, and so forth.

We would love to hear from you concerning your experiences with this guide and how you feel it could be improved and kept up to date. While we may not be able to respond to all comments and suggestions, we'll take them to heart, and we'll also make certain to share them with the author. Please send your comments and suggestions to the following address:

Globe Pequot Press
Reader Response/Editorial Department
PO Box 480
Guilford, CT 06437

Or you may e-mail us at:
editorial@GlobePequot.com

Thanks for your input, and happy travels!

Best Bike Rides
New York City

Great Recreational Rides
in the Five Boroughs

MARY STAUB

FALCONGUIDES

GUILFORD, CONNECTICUT
HELENA, MONTANA

AN IMPRINT OF GLOBE PEQUOT PRESS

FALCONGUIDES®

© 2014 Morris Book Publishing, LLC

FalconGuides is an imprint of Globe Pequot Press.
Falcon, FalconGuides, Outfit Your Mind, and Best Bike Rides are registered trademarks of Morris Book Publishing, LLC.

Maps by Trailhead Graphics, Inc. © Morris Book Publishing, LLC
All photos are by the author unless otherwise indicated.

Text design: Sheryl Kober
Layout: Joanna Beyer
Project editor: Ellen Urban

Library of Congress Cataloging-in-Publication Data is available on file.

ISBN 978-0-7627-8445-5

Printed in the United States of America
10 9 8 7 6 5 4 3 2 1

Contents

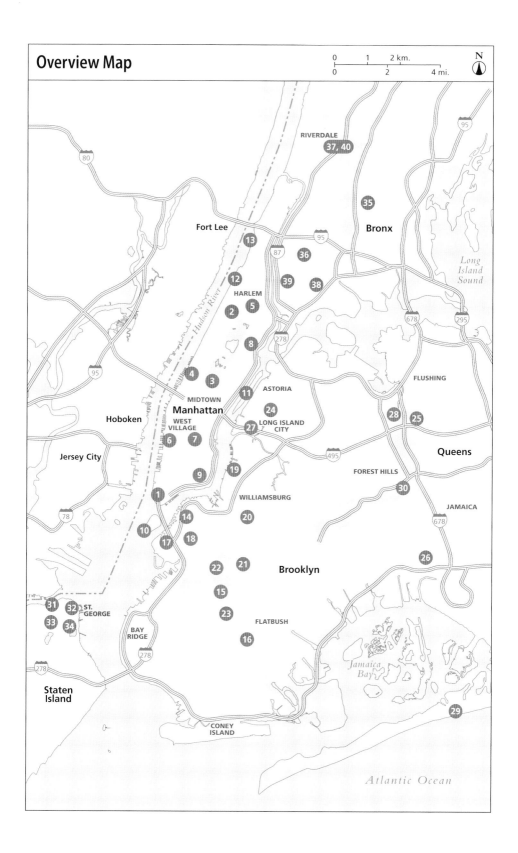

Overview Map

0   1   2 km.

0   2   4 mi.

N

RIVERDALE

37, 40

35

Bronx

Fort Lee

13

95

87

36

12

39

38

HARLEM

2

5

Long
Island
Sound

Hudson River

8

278

678

295

4

3

FLUSHING

11

ASTORIA

MIDTOWN

Manhattan

24

28

25

WEST
VILLAGE

27

LONG ISLAND
CITY

Hoboken

6

7

Jersey City

9

19

495

Queens

FOREST HILLS

30

1

WILLIAMSBURG

95

78

14

20

JAMAICA

678

10

17

18

22

21

Brooklyn

26

15

31

32

ST.
GEORGE

23

33

FLATBUSH

34

BAY
RIDGE

16

278

Jamaica Bay

Staten
Island

278

CONEY
ISLAND

29

Atlantic Ocean

Acknowledgments

The successful outcome of this book owes much to the input, guidance, and support of many experts, amateurs, friends, and family. While I cannot thank them all, I would like to acknowledge at least some of them here.

First, I would like to thank all the people who shared input concerning what routes to ride, roads to ride on, and areas to ride through. Particularly, I am grateful to the people at Bike New York, whose suggestions helped ensure the comprehensiveness of the rides. I would also like to thank all the people who generously shared detailed descriptions of their own favorite routes or organized recreational rides, whether cyclists along the way, bike shop owners, or members of bicycle groups in New York—New York Cycle Club and Weekday Cyclists among them.

Also, a big thank you to the people at Falcon Guides and Globe Pequot Press for giving me the opportunity to work on this project and guiding it into as clear, accurate, and useful a form as possible.

Last, I am immensely thankful for the support and encouragement I received from friends, family, and acquaintances throughout the process. Their interest and enthusiasm greatly enhanced my joy of working on this project.

Introduction: Why Bike New York City?

New York City's commitment to cycling extends back to at least 1894, when the country's first bike lane was inaugurated along Ocean Parkway in Brooklyn. Since then, its allegiance to cyclists has grown in spurts, ebbing and flowing alongside the city's changing economic, social, and political conditions. The past decade, though, has brought a renewed interest in cycling culture. More than 300 miles of bike lanes were added to city streets between 2006 and 2012, with more than 100 miles in Brooklyn, 50 to 70 miles each in Manhattan, Queens, and the Bronx, and the remainder on Staten Island. Additionally, bike stands, covered bike shelters, a bike share program, a "Bike Friendly Business" designation, and a "Bicycle Access Bill" stand testament to the city's dedication to making bicycling a viable option for all types of cyclists, whether recreational, commuter, or competitive. All of this newly implemented cycling infrastructure, together with city-wide cycling advocacy, means that biking New York City is more enjoyable and feasible than ever before.

Additionally, what has long made biking the boroughs so rewarding is the diversity and richness of what you encounter along the way. From waterfront greenways to scenic bridge bikeways to tucked-away parks to wildlife refuges. From historical forts to sloping woodlands to sprawling lawns to constantly changing neighborhoods with rich cultural and ethnic makeups. Cycling is the best way to get to know it all, for it allows you to easily cover much terrain (unlike walking) above ground (unlike subways) while avoiding most traffic congestion (unlike cars). Not to mention the health benefits. Mostly, though, biking provides easy access to tucked-away city spots and a unique perspective on a city you may have lived in all your life, just moved to, or only be visiting temporarily.

About This Book

This book is geared toward anyone interested in exploring all that the city has to offer via bike. The rides were designed to cover the city's best cycling spots and to explore distinct neighborhood landscapes. The aim was to cater to recreational riders looking to expand their cycling repertoire and also to serve urban explorers looking to get to hidden corners of New York City. Lovers of green spaces, waterfronts, scenic views, cultural sites, historic roots, and more should all find multiple routes that speak to them in this book. Recreational riders of almost any level can complete these rides, and no high-tech cycling gear is needed, just common sense, sound health, and a properly equipped, well-functioning bicycle.

Each of the 40 rides in this book is accompanied by all the information needed to successfully complete each ride: a narrative that describes the route and provides texture, whether historical, environmental, cultural, or other; turn-by-turn directions; a map; photographs that illustrate the ride; a list of highlights along the way; en route restrooms; and more. Most rides range from 10 to 20 miles, with shorter options described for some of these rides. Some of the rides are less than 10 miles. These short rides are good first rides to tackle if you don't have much cycling experience. Some routes are between 20 and 30 miles. Additionally, numerous rides are close together or partially overlap, which enables you to link distinct rides to form longer tours. All of the rides are easily accessible by public transportation.

Each ride contains a unique focus, whether waterfront, park space, culture, neighborhood, history, or similar. A ride finder at the beginning of the book provides an easy overview of the different ride types, ride lengths, en route traffic, and more. The front section of the book also contains basic, essential information on city bike laws, bike safety, and city cycling practices. At the back of the book, a list of cycling resources provides you with links to supplementary information about biking in the city, including pertinent maps, bike clubs, and cycling advocacy groups.

Key to icons used in this edition:

 Road Bike   Mountain Bike   Hybrid

Riding with This Book

ORGANIZATION

The 40 rides in this book are grouped according to borough based on the starting point of each ride.

Manhattan: rides 1–13

Brooklyn: rides 14–23

Queens: rides 24–30

Staten Island: rides 31–34

The Bronx: rides 35–40

RIDE PROFILE FORMAT

All of the ride descriptions follow the same format and include the following information:

Brief summary: A brief overview of where you go and what you see on the ride

Start: The starting point for the ride

Length: The length and type of ride—loop, partial loop (mostly a loop, but partially out and back), out and back, one way

Approximate riding time: The time it will take to do this ride at a leisurely pace, including a brief stop (but excluding longer visits to sites along the way)

Best bike: A recommendation for what type of bike to use (overall, any type of bike will serve any of the rides, though)

Terrain and trail surface: The ride's terrain (hilly, flat, etc.) and surface (paved, cobblestones, etc.)

Traffic and hazards: The amount of traffic (none, light, moderate, heavy), tricky intersections, and other hazards (pedestrians, cracked pavement, root protrusions, etc.)

Things to see: A list of some things you will see along the ride

Map: A map that highlights the route, with road names, mile markings, and more

Getting there: A description of how to get to the starting point by public transportation; some of the rides include a description for getting there by car (in general, driving is discouraged for various reasons—environmental, traffic-related, parking difficulties, among others)

Ride profile: A detailed narrative of where the ride goes and what you see

Miles and directions: A turn-by-turn description of the directions with mileage

Ride information: Ride resources and references such as maps used and restroom locations

BEFORE YOU RIDE

Although the ride descriptions in this book should contain sufficient information for you to complete the rides successfully, there are certain steps you should take and points you should consider before heading out:

Make sure that the ride is suitable for you by taking into consideration length, terrain, traffic, other hazards, and location.

Familiarize yourself with the route and its surroundings by looking at an up-to-date *New York City Bike Map* (nyc.gov/bikemap or free at any bike shop) or other map suggested in the ride description.

Be aware that New York City is constantly changing. Where traffic was once moderate, it may now be light. Where a greenway once led, there may now be construction. Bring a current city bike map with you on all rides in case you need to detour along the way.

Check the *New York City Bike Map* for current information on car-free park hours, boardwalk cycling hours, and bridge cycling regulations.

Be aware that, while every effort was made for mileage accuracy and consistency, your mileage may vary slightly from the mileage in this book. There are multiple reasons for this: your route might not mirror the route taken precisely; you might walk your bike along a park pathway to explore something; you might cycle back because you forgot something. These discrepancies can add up. Staying aware and taking note of this as you go along will help keep you on track.

Use the landmarks and road names in the route descriptions, in addition to mileage markings, to help you follow the route.

Use on-road bike lanes where they exist. The route descriptions point out bike lanes only when they are hard to notice (because you'll have to cross a major avenue to access them, for instance).

There are different categories of bikeways in New York City.

- *Greenways* are car-free.
- *Bike lanes* are marked borders reserved exclusively for cyclists along the edge of motor-vehicle roads. You might sometimes find standing cars in these lanes. If so, look behind you before circumventing the car via the main road lane.

- *Bike routes* are marked routes where cyclists share the road with motorists. There is no lane exclusively for cyclists, but signs along the way and arrows on the road alert drivers to cyclists.

If you want to visit any of the sights along the ride, check their websites for opening days and hours.

If you are using public transportation to get to the starting point, make sure the suggested subway is running and stopping at the suggested station. Weekend subway schedules in New York City can be erratic.

Overall, motor vehicle traffic will be lightest on weekend mornings (especially Sundays).

Create a setup so that you can easily view the route's miles and directions during the ride. Fasten them to your handlebar with a cue clip, sheet holder, or similar device.

Make sure your bike is in good condition and properly equipped.

Bring a spare tube, bike pump, tire levers, and multipurpose tool to fix any flats—or other bike problems—along the way. This is especially crucial for rides that go to the city's outskirts, where you won't find bike shops close by.

Most importantly, stay safe and have fun!

GETTING TO THE RIDES

The best way to get to the starting point of the rides is by public transportation or by bike. To take your bike on the public transportation referenced in this book, keep the following in mind:

Subways: Bicycles are allowed at all times for free, but it is highly discouraged during rush hour (circa 7 to 10 a.m. and 4 to 7 p.m. weekdays). Use the service gate to enter, but swipe your MetroCard and turn the turnstyle (in view of the agent) before doing so. Carry your bike up and down stairs or use the elevator. Hold your bike while on the subway. mta.info/nyct/safety/bike

Staten Island Ferry: Bikes are allowed at all times for free. Bicyclists board the ferry on the lower level at both the St. George and Whitehall Ferry Terminals. On the ferry, store your bike in the designated bike storage area (located at different spots on different ferries, but always on the lower level). mta.info/bike

Governors Island Ferry: Bikes are allowed at all times for free. (Ferries run during summer months only.) www.govisland.com/html/visit/biking .shtml

Staten Island Railway: Bicycles are allowed except during peak hours on weekdays: 6 to 9 a.m. going toward St. George. mta.info/bike

PATH: Bikes are allowed except during peak hours: 6 to 10 a.m. going toward Manhattan; 3:30 to 6:30 p.m. going toward New Jersey. www.panynj .gov/path/bicycles.html

Liberty Landing Ferry: Bikes are allowed at all times at no additional charge. (There is a charge for passengers.) Check the schedule for operating dates. www.libertylandingferry.com

Bicycling in New York City

LAWS

Cyclists are subject to the same traffic rules as motor vehicles (and have the same rights, too). By law, you must:

Ride in the street, not on the sidewalk, unless you are under 13.

Ride with the flow of traffic, not against it.

Stop at red lights and stop signs.

Use a white headlight, red taillight, and bell or horn.

Yield to pedestrians.

SAFETY

Additional safety measures you can take for a safer journey include the following:

Wear a helmet.

Don't wear earphones (more than one is illegal).

Keep an eye on parked cars and keep your distance to avoid getting doored.

Take the road on shared lanes; bicycles have the same right to an entire lane as cars do.

Bike defensively, especially near taxis. They swerve often to pick up and let out customers, so keep your distance.

Avoid drivers' blind spots.

Don't swerve.

Look over your shoulder before merging or turning, even on bikeways, where other cyclists might be close behind you.

Use hand signals before making a turn.

Wear brightly colored clothing and sensible shoes.

Use your bell.

Check out the Department of Transportation's Bike Smart guide for more detailed suggestions: nyc.gov/bikesmart. Also check out Biking Rules, by Transportation Alternatives: bikingrules.org.

INFRASTRUCTURE

While the ride profiles for each of the rides contain information on biking permissions and restrictions on bridges and boardwalks, you can find additional information here:

Boardwalks: For current information on boardwalk cycling hours, check the city's parks website for the relevant boardwalk (nycgovparks.org) or the *New York City Bike Map*.

Parks: For up-to-date information on auto-free park hours in Central Park, Prospect Park in Brooklyn, and Silver Lake Park on Staten Island, check the city's parks website for the relevant park. Or check the *New York City Bike Map*.

Bridges: For information on bridge crossings, check the *New York City Bike Map* and resources on the MTA's cycling website: mta.info/bike.

Ride Finder

RIDES WITH HISTORY OR CULTURE

URBAN RIDES

NEIGHBORHOOD RIDES

RIDES WITH BEACHES

EASY RIDES

RIDES WITH HILLS

Author's Note

Researching, riding, and writing this guide has been one of the most fulfilling recreational and professional endeavors I have ever pursued. The project, as so many people have told me, seems like it was made for me, uniquely integrating all of the things I am passionate about.

From being outdoors and riding a bike to exploring diverse neighborhoods. From miles of riverside bikeways along the Hudson and East Rivers to beachfront promenades and bayside greenways in multiple boroughs. From sculpted park spaces to protected natural habitats. From nineteenth-century architecture to avant-garde cultural emblems. From meeting like-minded people to gaining more knowledge about the city's rich cultural, historical, environmental, social, ethnic, and architectural makeup. From recording new perspectives on film to figuring out how to convey the richness of it all in writing.

My hope is that this book will enable others to similarly experience the beauty of biking, discover the marvels of the five boroughs from a new perspective, and have equally fulfilling experiences.

Map Legend

Transportation

Interstate/Divided Highway

Featured U.S. Highway

U.S. Highway

Featured State, County, or Local Road

Primary Highway

County/Local Road

Featured Bike Route

Hydrology

Body of Water

River/Creek

Land Use

State/Local Park, Open Space

State Line

Symbols

Interstate   95

U.S. Highway   1

State Highway   9

Trailhead (Start)   10

Mileage Marker   17.1

Visitor Center   ❓

Point of Interest/ Structure   ■

University/College   🎓

Museum   🏛

Marina   ☸

Church   †

Picnic Area   🛆

Direction Arrow   →

Train Station   Ⓣ

Ferry Terminal   Ⓕ

Lighthouse

Manhattan

The Abyssinian Baptist Church on West 138th Street.

Manhattan is the smallest, most densely populated of the five boroughs, comprising less than a tenth of New York City's overall landmass. Having received about a quarter of all new bike lanes built in the past seven years, the borough is among the best-equipped urban centers for cyclists nationwide. You'll encounter a mix of cycling conditions as you explore the various landscapes the borough has to offer. From sweeping car-free greenways ideal for beginners to urban neighborhoods with stop-and-go traffic, the borough has it all.

Central Park offers miles of car-free biking. Fort Tryon Park showcases the Cloisters and affords expansive views of the Palisades across the Hudson. The Hudson River Greenway runs from the tip of Manhattan at Battery Park to its northernmost point just south of the Bronx, with waterfront views along the way. The George Washington Bridge brings you to one of the region's most popular cycling routes in Palisades Interstate Park. Governor's Island and Randall's Island are great weekend escapes that feel far-removed from New York City. Dense urban landscapes in Chinatown, Little Italy, the Upper West Side, and the financial center bring you face to face with the city's cultural, architectural, and historical roots. The variety Manhattan has to offer guarantees that all cyclists—novice and expert, young and old, commuter and cruiser—will find multiple routes that please them.

The Hudson River

From the birthplace of New York City at Battery Park, this waterfront route travels past sculpted riverside green spots, harbor enclaves, and architectural marvels, and takes you northward to the West Harlem Piers at West 130th Street. It then climbs to the top of Riverside Drive, where you have sweeping views of the river below and can stop off at Grant's Tomb, where Civil War general Ulysses S. Grant rests alongside his wife. The route then returns southward via the riverfront once more, hugging the waterfront along Battery Park City, and ending in Battery Park, where there's much to explore.

Start: The northwest corner of Battery Park, at the intersection of West Street and Battery Place

Length: 18.9 miles out and back (partial)

Approximate riding time: 2.5 hours

Best bike: Hybrid, road, or mountain bike

Terrain and trail surface: The trail is paved throughout. There's one major uphill climb after leaving the West Harlem Piers to get to Grant's Tomb. It then goes downhill from Grant's Tomb to the water along Riverside Drive.

Traffic and hazards: This route travels almost exclusively along the Hudson River Greenway and is thus mostly car-free. On your return journey, a 1-mile stretch toward Grant's Tomb leads along Riverside Drive, with light traffic. Stay especially alert at the top of the hill, when you cross to the left side of Riverside Drive to make a U-turn, following the road southward. Also, the greenway you follow along most of this ride is often crowded on weekend with cyclists, joggers, and inline skaters. (The earlier in the day you go, the lighter the crowds.) Stay alert and yield to pedestrians. Stick to the right side of the Hudson River Greenway, allowing faster cyclists to pass on your left, and stay alert and heed the traffic signal when traversing crossroads along the greenway.

Things to see: Battery Park, North Cove Marina, Hudson River, Hudson River Park, Chelsea Piers Park, Jean Nouvel architecture, Frank Gehry architecture, West Harlem Piers, Grant's Tomb, Riverside Church, Riverside Park, New York City Marina

Map: *New York City Bike Map*

Getting there: By public transportation: Take the 4 or 5 subway to the Bowling Green stop. Go west along the northern edge of Battery Park on Battery Place until you reach the park's northwestern corner at West Street. By car: From the West Side: Take the West Side Highway/West Street south to the Battery Place exit. From the East Side: Take the FDR Drive south to exit 1 at Whitehall Street. Check the Battery Conservancy's map (at www.thebattery.org) for parking garages in the area. GPS coordinates: N40 42.278' / W74 01.006'

THE RIDE

Battery Park offers much to explore—early relics like Castle Clinton and monuments honoring significant New York figures—but save the park for the end of your journey. To start your ride, catch the Hudson River Greenway along the west edge of West Street, going northward toward Battery Park City. You'll soon veer away from the greenway along Albany Street to reach the North Cove Marina, where yachts and motor boats are moored offshore on your left and the gleaming World Financial Center rises on your right. On fair-weather days, the eateries that surround the marina provide outdoor seating, turning the wharf into a bustling enclave where locals and tourists gather. A right onto North End Avenue (next to PJ Clarke's) then returns you to the greenway.

On your left, hug the edge of Hudson River Park, with ball courts, dog runs, and sculpted recreational piers. Farther north on your right, starting at West 14th Street, you can catch glimpses of the Highline, an elevated promenade with sculpted greens that used to be a railway line. The recreational complex of Chelsea Piers soon appears on your left and two architectural gems rise on

Bike Shop

New York's Waterfront Bicycle Shop: 391 West St.; (212) 414-2453
Opposite the Hudson River Greenway at Christopher Street, this waterfront bike shop with a friendly staff will serve all your en route biking needs.

your right—the rounded glass IAC Building by Frank Gehry and a glittery Jean Nouvel-designed apartment complex of angular glass panes. At the north end of Chelsea Piers, you can explore an elaborate parks complex sprawled across multiple piers. Dismount and walk your bike to explore the piers. (Biking is prohibited.) At Pier 66, check out the historic fireboat *John J. Harvey*, built in 1931.

Continuing northward, you'll traverse a major tourist hub at Pier 79, where several tour boat companies house their headquarters. Just beyond, the Intrepid Museum attracts similar throngs. Stay alert for pedestrians as tourists scouting the area often wander onto the greenway. At West 59th Street, as you enter Riverside Park South, the bikeway veers right to run underneath

Riverside Church—a Bastion of Social Engagement and Political Debate

In the early twentieth century, Christian churches and churchgoers in New York City founded Riverside Church amid heated debates concerning the future character and role of their religion. The church was established as an institution that would take a more modern approach to Christianity by becoming more actively involved in the world at large. The cathedral-like establishment was grounded by three core principles—it was to be a large church in a significant New York City neighborhood; the church was to exist in an interdenominational context; the church was to welcome all who believed in Christ.

For the church to be erected, John D. Rockefeller Jr. purchased a swath of land overlooking the Hudson River and contracted architects to travel across Spain and France to gather ideas for the church's design. In the end, multiple cathedrals served as inspiration for the architects' work including the thirteenth-century Cathedral of Chartres, France, for the nave, and the twelfth-century Laon Cathedral, of Spain, for the soaring twenty-two-story spire. Work on the church was started in 1926, but it wasn't completed until 4 years later due, in part, to a fire that destroyed much of the original wooden framework.

In keeping with the church's mission of active engagement in the world, the institution was furnished with classrooms, a library, a gym, and a nursery. Today, Riverside Church continues to have a role in numerous movements for social justice including LGBT support, anti-torture campaigning, HIV-AIDS ministry, and immigrant rights advocacy. The church also continues as a significant center for political and social discourse with noteworthy speakers over the years including Martin Luther King Jr., Cesar Chavez, Nelson Mandela, Kofi Annan, Bill Clinton, and Fidel Castro.

Biking north along the Hudson River Greenway, with the George Washington Bridge in the distance.

(parallel) the highway overhead. Return to the water's edge next to ball fields and head north along a pleasant promenade of benches. Ship masts moored offshore in the New York City Marina can be heard as you approach the Boat Basin Cafe on your right. Continue north along the waterfront Cherry Walk (especially stunning when trees are in bloom) and gaze ahead for views of the George Washington Bridge. When you reach the West Harlem Piers, bike to West 130th Street, where you can grab a snack at the Fairway Market for a short break on the piers.

To continue, head south a short stretch to turn left onto Saint Clair Place, leaving the waterfront behind. Riverside Drive takes you uphill to the right (steep!). There's no marked bike lane on this road, so stay alert. At the top of the hill, make a near U-turn to your right, continuing with the flow of traffic along Riverside Drive. Follow the drive as it veers left again (to head south) toward Grant's Tomb. The site's visitor center is on your right (accessible via stairs going downhill) and the monument itself, with the remains of Ulysses S. Grant and his wife, Julia, is on your left. To explore, lock up your bike and enter on foot.

To proceed en route, continue south along Riverside Drive, passing Riverside Church on your left. Cruise gently downhill along Riverside Drive to

Battery Park

Battery Park is where New York City began. In 1624, thirty families traveling with the Dutch West India Company founded a settlement just near your starting point at Battery Park. Within a year, the Dutch constructed Fort Amsterdam (later named Fort George) at the southern tip of Manhattan, marking the official founding of New York City. After ceding the stronghold to British rule, the fort was later demolished shortly after the American Revolution. Debris from the bastion was subsequently used to expand the landmass at the island's southern tip. Then, in the early 1800s, a new battery was built 200 feet offshore. This fortress, now known as Castle Clinton, was later connected to the mainland through additional landfills. You can visit it at the park's southern tip at the end of your journey.

reenter Riverside Park along a path veering to your right (and into the park) after crossing West 95th Street. Yield to pedestrians throughout Riverside Park, where joggers, dog-walkers, and families abound, and handsomely maintained gardens line the way. Return to the bikeway along the Hudson River up ahead to retrace your route back to Hudson River Park.

After passing Pier 25, turn right to take the waterfront promenade route around Battery Park City. To stay on the bikeway, hug the water's edge (don't go "inland" into Battery Park City proper) and follow the esplanade as it passes the ferry terminal, circles the North Cove Marina, and continues south with views of New Jersey across the water and the Statue of Liberty in the distance. At the southern end of the waterfront esplanade, veer left through Robert Wagner Park to end up on the sidewalk next to Battery Park. Turn right to arrive at your starting point. Now, explore Battery Park at your leisure.

MILES AND DIRECTIONS

0.0 From the northwest corner of Battery Park, use the traffic signal to cross to the north side of Battery Place and catch the Hudson River Greenway, heading north along the west edge of West Street.

0.4 Turn left onto Albany Street, followed by a quick right onto South End Avenue.

0.6 Turn left at Liberty Street and follow the bike path toward the marina. Veer right to go north along the water's edge.

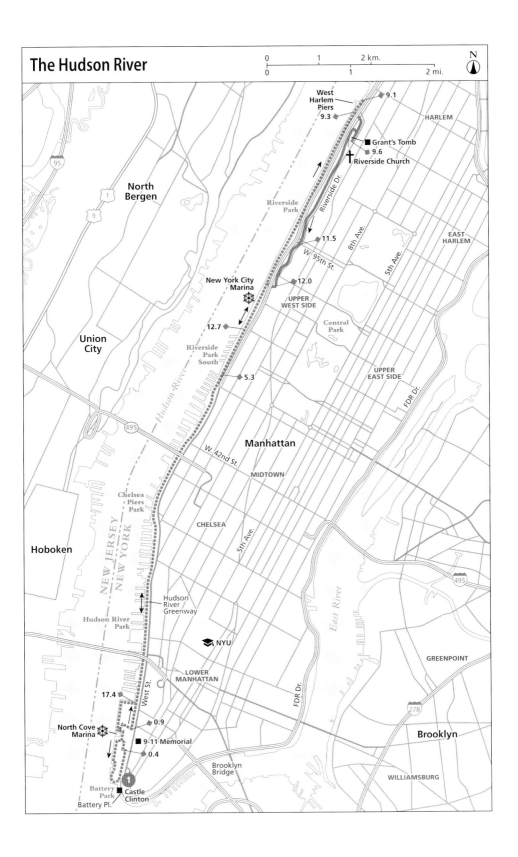

The Hudson River

0   1   2 km.
0   1   2 mi.

N

West
Harlem
Piers

9.1

9.3

HARLEM

Grant's Tomb
9.6
Riverside Church

North
Bergen

Riverside Dr.

Riverside Park

EAST
HARLEM

11.5

8th Ave.

5th Ave.

W. 95th St.

New York City
Marina

12.0

UPPER
WEST SIDE

Central
Park

12.7

Union
City

Riverside
Park
South

UPPER
EAST SIDE

5.3

FDR Dr.

Hudson River

Manhattan

W. 42nd St.

MIDTOWN

Chelsea
Piers
Park

CHELSEA

5th Ave.

Hoboken

NEW JERSEY
NEW YORK

Hudson
River
Greenway

East River

Hudson River
Park

NYU

GREENPOINT

LOWER
MANHATTAN

17.4

West St.

0.9

North Cove
Marina

9-11 Memorial

Brooklyn

0.4

Brooklyn
Bridge

WILLIAMSBURG

Battery
Park

Castle
Clinton

Battery Pl.

0.7 After passing PJ Clarke's on your right (and before reaching the Hudson River), turn right onto North End Avenue, followed by a right onto Vesey Street.

0.9 Before crossing West Street, glance behind you before turning left to cross to the north side of Vesey Street and catch the greenway northward.

5.3 Enter Riverside Park South and veer right to continue along the greenway (the waterfront path is for pedestrians). The bikeway runs parallel to Henry Hudson Parkway overhead.

7.4 Continue north along the Cherry Walk.

9.1 Take a break at the West Harlem Piers at 131st Street. To continue, make a U-turn to return southward on the greenway.

9.3 At Saint Clair Place, use caution as you turn left, crossing the parkway access road. Veer right up ahead, going steeply uphill along Riverside Drive.

9.6 At the top of the hill, cross Riverside Drive, turning right (a near U-turn) to follow Riverside Drive northward (with the flow of traffic). Follow Riverside Drive as it makes a left turn, heading south again.

10.1 Grant's Tomb is on your left.

10.2 Riverside Church is on your left.

11.5 After crossing West 95th Street, veer right into Riverside Park. Yield to pedestrians.

11.7 The bikeway leads slightly downhill before veering left and uphill to access the Riverside Park promenade, continuing south.

12.0 Veer right, going downhill and under the parkway to continue south along the water.

12.7 After the baseball fields, veer left, continuing south along the bikeway.

17.4 At the southern edge of Hudson River Park (before the pedestrian overpass at Chambers Street), turn right onto the waterfront route. Yield to pedestrians.

18.8 Bike through the garden to exit the waterfront route. Turn right along the sidewalk (and bikeway) to return to Battery Park.

18.9 Arrive at starting point and explore the park's sites at your leisure.

RIDE INFORMATION

Local Events/Attractions

General Grant National Memorial: Ulysses S. Grant and his wife, Julia, lie in an open crypt in red granite coffins at this memorial overlooking the Hudson River. 122nd Street and Riverside Drive; (212) 666-1640; www.nps.gov/gegr

The Riverside Church: 490 Riverside Dr.; (212) 870-6700; www.theriverside churchny.org

Restrooms

Mile 2.3/16.4: There are restrooms in the park building in Hudson River Park and water fountains along Hudson River Greenway. Dismount your bike when entering the park area.

Mile 6.2/12.6: There are restrooms in the stone park building in Riverside Park.

The Heights

This ride through the Heights of Manhattan travels from Central Park along historic Saint Nicholas Avenue through Morningside, Hamilton, Washington, and Hudson Heights. You'll travel through the Hamilton Heights historic district, past neo-Gothic spires, and a founding father's home. Then, Fort Tryon Park affords sweeping views of the New Jersey Palisades across the Hudson River and houses the Cloisters Museum and Garden, well worth a visit regardless of your interest in medieval art or architecture. You'll return southward along the Hudson River Greenway, framed by the Hudson River on one side and the towering cliffs of Fort Tryon Park on the other.

Start: The northwest corner of Central Park

Length: 14.3-mile loop

Approximate riding time: 2.5 hours

Best bike: Hybrid, road, or mountain bike

Terrain and trail surface: The route is paved throughout. It goes steadily uphill toward Fort Tryon Park. It goes steeply downhill from there to the Hudson River.

Traffic and hazards: The first half of this route runs along on-road bike lanes on wide city streets, giving cyclists ample space. Traffic here is light on weekends, moderate on weekdays. Stay alert especially at West 162nd Street, where Saint Nicholas Avenue crosses Amsterdam Avenue diagonally. Also, at the north end of your journey, to access the Hudson River Greenway, you have to cross an access road to Henry Hudson Parkway. Stay alert. The second half of the route runs on a car-free greenway.

Things to see: Alexander Hamilton Grange Memorial, Fort Tryon Park, The Cloisters, Hudson River, Palisades, Little Red Lighthouse, Riverside

Church, Barnard College, Columbia University, Hamilton Heights, Washington Heights, Hudson Heights

Maps: *New York City Bike Map*

Getting there: By public transportation: Take the B or D subway to the Cathedral Parkway stop at the northwestern corner of Central Park. This is your starting point. GPS coordinates: N40 48.015' / W73 57.482'

THE RIDE

The first portion of your journey leads northward, with Morningside Heights on your left and Central Harlem on your right. You'll hug the east edge of Saint Nicholas Park, a narrow, steeply sloping park that leads up to the neo-Gothic spires of City College. At the north end of the park, at West 141st Street, you can reach founding father Alexander Hamilton's Harlem home on your left. Stop off to explore the historic house museum if you wish.

Continuing en route, Saint Nicholas Avenue goes steadily uphill through the Hamilton Heights historic district. Follow the bike route as it swings diagonally across the traffic island to your left at West 162nd Street, where Saint Nicholas Avenue intersects Amsterdam Avenue. Continuing northward, Fort Washington Avenue up ahead continues slowly and steadily uphill to Fort Tryon Park. As you travel underneath the George Washington Bridge, you're likely to encounter a flurry of cyclists heading to and from the bridge. This soon brings you to Fort Tryon Park, sitting high on a bluff overlooking the Hudson River. Enter the park via Margaret Corbin Drive, which loops to the north end of the park, where you'll find the Cloisters, a branch of the Metropolitan Museum of Art. Made of architectural components from an amalgam of twelfth- to fifteenth-century religious structures, the Cloisters contains medieval European art. Explore the museum if you wish or find a spot in the surrounding gardens for a break overlooking the Hudson River.

Bike Shop

Victor's Bike Repair: 4125 Broadway; (212) 740-5137
A full-service bike shop in Washington Heights with a loyal following and a staff willing to tackle uncommon bike problems.

To continue, exit Fort Tryon Park to soon go steeply downhill via West 187th Street. A short on-road portion here takes you along the foot of Fort Tryon Park, continuing northward. When you reach Dyckman Street at the

The Little Red Lighthouse at the foot of the George Washington Bridge was built in 1880 and is now a popular cycling stop.

end of the park, use caution as you make a sharp left turn onto Riverside Drive. (Use the pedestrian crosswalk if need be.) At the end of Riverside Drive, use caution once more when the road splits into north- and southbound access roads for the Henry Hudson Parkway. Cross the northbound access road to mount the sidewalk (bikeway) on the right of the southbound access road. Follow the sidewalk as it travels under the parkway. Then dismount your bike, ascend the stairs to your right, and head south on the Hudson River Greenway.

Enjoy the car-free journey southward, with views of the Hudson River on your right and the cliffs of Fort Tryon on your left. The George Washington Bridge in the distance looms ever-larger as you continue south. Just before reaching the bridge, the greenway snakes right and then left to journey underneath the bridge and emerge next to the Little Red Lighthouse. This proud-looking 40-foot-high bastion was built in 1880 (at a different spot) and is a popular resting spot for cyclists.

Continuing southward along the greenway, views of the city skyline greet you in the distance until you reach the West Harlem Piers. You'll then leave the greenway behind at Saint Clair Place to go steeply uphill along Riverside Drive to your right. At the top of the hill, you'll veer onto a quiet, narrow road, Claremont Avenue, which takes you past an array of educational institutions

Alexander Hamilton

After having been orphaned as a young teenager on the Caribbean island of Nevis, Alexander Hamilton came to New York when he was 17 years old to study at what now is Columbia University (then King's College). Thirty years later, in 1802, after playing a pivotal part in the founding of this country, he had this Harlem home built and named after his father's ancestral home in Scotland. Now a national memorial, the historic house museum contains period rooms restored to resemble their Hamilton-era appearance and interactive displays that put the man into context. It also offers sweeping views of Harlem and beyond.

in historic buildings—Barnard College; Bank Street College; the Manhattan School of Music. At West 116th Street you can turn left to visit Columbia University's campus, New York State's oldest college. Alternately (or thereafter), head west on West 116th Street toward the Hudson River once more to return to your starting point.

MILES AND DIRECTIONS

0.0 Bike counterclockwise around the traffic circle and take the second right onto Frederick Douglas Boulevard/8th Avenue's on-road bike lane.

0.6 Just north of West 121st Street, Saint Nicholas Avenue diagonally crosses 8th Avenue. Cross to the north side of Saint Nicholas Avenue. Then swivel left to use the traffic signal to continue northward along Saint Nicholas Avenue.

1.6 Turn left onto West 141st Street. The Alexander Hamilton Grange Memorial house sits at the top of the hill on your left. Visit if you wish. Then, to continue en route, retrace your path down West 141st Street to continue northward on Saint Nicholas Avenue.

2.3 When the road forks at West 149th Street, veer left to stay on Saint Nicholas Avenue.

2.9 At West 161st Street, follow the bike route diagonally across the traffic island to your left. Descend the island on the other side to diagonally cross Amsterdam Avenue, using the traffic signal. Continue north along Saint Nicholas Avenue on the other side.

The Heights

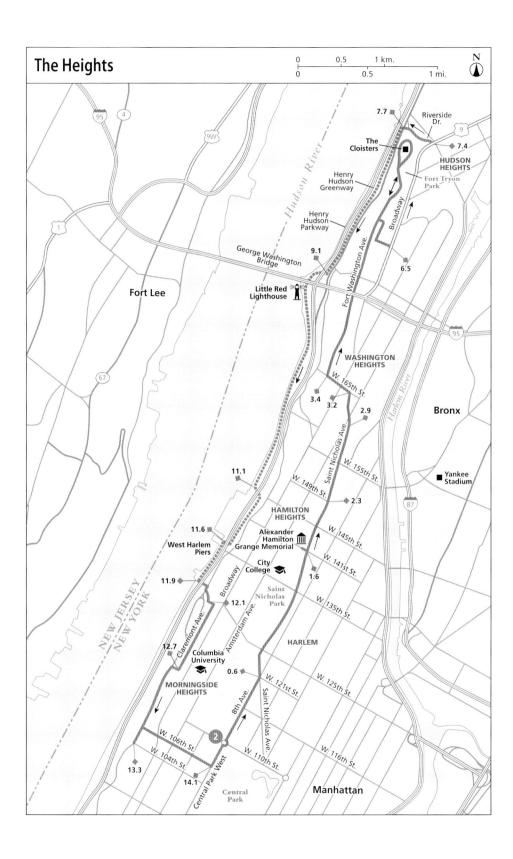

N

| 0 | 0.5 | 1 km. |
| 0 | 0.5 | 1 mi. |

7.7

Riverside
Dr.

9

The
Cloisters

7.4

HUDSON
HEIGHTS

Henry
Hudson
Greenway

Fort Tryon
Park

Broadway

Hudson River

Henry
Hudson
Parkway

6.5

95
4

9W

9.1

George Washington
Bridge

Fort Washington Ave.

Fort Lee

Little Red
Lighthouse

1

95

WASHINGTON
HEIGHTS

W. 165th St.

Harlem River

Bronx

3.4   3.2

2.9

Saint Nicholas Ave.

W. 155th St.

67

Yankee
Stadium

11.1

W. 149th St.

2.3

HAMILTON
HEIGHTS

11.6

Alexander
Hamilton
Grange Memorial

W. 145th St.

87

West Harlem
Piers

City
College

W. 141st St.

1.6

11.9

Broadway

12.1

Amsterdam Ave.

Saint
Nicholas
Park

W. 135th St.

Claremont Ave.

12.7

Columbia
University

NEW JERSEY
NEW YORK

0.6

HARLEM

W. 121st St.

W. 125th St.

MORNINGSIDE
HEIGHTS

8th Ave.

Saint Nicholas Ave.

2

W. 106th St.

W. 110th St.

W. 116th St.

13.3

W. 104th St.

14.1

Central Park West

Central
Park

Manhattan

3.2 Turn left onto West 165th Street.

3.4 Turn right onto Fort Washington Avenue.

4.9 Enter the traffic circle, veering right. Take the first right exit onto Margaret Corbin Drive, entering Fort Tryon Park.

5.2 When the road forks, veer right to continue along Margaret Corbin Drive.

5.4 The Cloisters is on your left. Visit if you wish. To proceed en route, continue along Margaret Corbin Drive, following the road as it loops left to go south. Take a break anyplace along the way.

5.9 Exit Fort Tryon Park; bike counterclockwise around the traffic circle to exit southward onto Fort Washington Avenue.

6.1 Turn left onto West 190th Street and follow the road as it turns right, heading downhill.

6.3 Turn left onto West 187th Street.

6.5 Turn left onto Broadway. At Sherman Avenue, veer left to continue along Broadway.

7.4 Make a sharp left onto Riverside Drive (using the pedestrian crosswalks if you wish).

7.7 Slow down as you reach the end of Riverside Drive at Staff Street. Riverside Drive forks to become the access roads for Henry Hudson Parkway. Cross Staff Street and the parkway's northbound access road to mount the sidewalk (bikeway) on your right along the southbound access road. Go underneath the overpass, dismount your bike, and ascend the shallow steps to your right. Follow the pathway southward onto the Hudson River Greenway.

9.1 Snake right and then left to continue along the bikeway and underneath the George Washington Bridge.

11.1 Follow the bikeway as it veers left and underneath the overpass and then turns right again.

11.6 Turn right and then left, going underneath the parkway to continue south along the greenway past the West Harlem Piers.

11.9 At Saint Clair Place, use caution as you turn left, crossing the parkway access road. Veer right, going uphill on Riverside Drive just ahead. It's steep!

12.1 Turn left onto Tiemann Place, followed by a quick right onto Claremont Avenue.

12.7 To visit Columbia University, turn left onto West 116th Street. Otherwise turn right, followed by a left at the bottom of the hill onto Riverside Drive.

13.3 Turn left onto West 104th Street, followed by a sharp left just after the traffic island onto the east arm of Riverside Drive (going north). Turn right onto West 106th Street.

14.1 Turn left onto Central Park West.

14.3 Arrive at your starting point.

RIDE INFORMATION

Local Events/Attractions

Alexander Hamilton Grange Memorial: Founding father Alexander Hamilton's Harlem home. 414 W. 141st St.; www.nps.gov/hagr

The Cloisters Museum and Gardens: An expansive collection of medieval European art and architecture. 99 Margaret Corbin Dr.; (212) 923-3700; www.metmuseum.org

Restrooms

Mile 1.7: Restrooms are located in the Alexander Hamilton Grange Memorial at West 141st Street.

Mile 4.9 / 5.9: Restrooms are located in Fort Tryon Park, by the cafe.

Central Park

From Central Park's bustling main gateway at Grand Army Plaza, this tranquil ride leads along car-free park drives through the 840 acres that make up Central Park, the city's fifth-largest park system. En route, you can stop off at numerous major park landmarks—from the ancient Obelisk near the Metropolitan Museum of Art to Bethesda Terrace; from the sprawling Sheep Meadow at the park's southern end to the tranquil Conservatory Garden in the north. Explore Belvedere Castle, Strawberry Fields, or the park's grand Mall along the way, and circumnavigate the park once more at the end of your journey because there's always more to see.

Start: Grand Army Plaza, at the southeast corner of Central Park at East 60th Street and 5th Avenue

Length: 7.1-mile loop

Approximate riding time: 1 hour

Best bike: Hybrid, road, or mountain bike

Terrain and trail surface: The trail is paved throughout and mostly flat. It goes uphill a short stretch after the Loeb Boathouse, heading toward the Metropolitan Museum of Art. Later, it goes downhill toward the Harlem Meer at the north end of the park. There's then one steeper uphill climb along the northern edge of the park around North Woods.

Traffic and hazards: The route runs along Central Park's main drives, which are car-free on weekends and certain weekday hours. Check the park's website or the current *New York City Bike Map* for up-to-date information concerning auto-free park hours. Also, stick to the designated cycling lanes along the drives and don't swerve into other lanes even when the park is auto-free as different lanes are for different modes—or speeds—of locomotion. Heading counterclockwise around the park, the innermost lane is for joggers and rollerbladers, the lane to its right is for slow cyclists, and the lane to the right of that is for faster cyclists. Overall, stay alert for pedestrians, joggers, rollerbladers, pedicabs, and horse carriages.

Things to see: Central Park, Carousel, The Dairy, Dana Discovery Center, Delacorte Theater, Conservatory Garden, Shakespeare Garden, Strawberry Fields, The Lake, Bethesda Terrace, Loeb Boathouse, Tavern on the Green, Grand Army Plaza, The Pond

Maps: *New York City Bike Map*, Central Park Map: www.centralparknyc.org

Getting there: By public transportation: Take the N, R, or Q subway to the 5th Avenue/59th Street station. Go north along Grand Army Plaza 1 block to the entrance to Central Park at East 60th Street. By car: If traveling by car, search for parking garages in the area before heading out. You might find space at Narragansett Garage at 124 E. 63rd St., Regency Garage Corp. at 245 E. 63rd St., Renoir Garage at 225 E. 63rd St., or at Distinctive Parking at 35 E. 61st St. GPS coordinates: N40 45.919' / W73 58.392'

THE RIDE

Grand Army Plaza comprises two semicircular plazas that extend north and south of Central Park South. The plaza, whose design was inspired by Paris's Place de la Concorde, is considered the main gateway to Central Park. Bustling with tourists, performers, horse carriages, and street vendors, adorned with the graceful Pulitzer Fountain, and bordered by the famed Plaza Hotel, the plaza makes for a dynamic start to an otherwise tranquil park ride.

Steer your way around pedestrians, horse carts, and ubiquitous pedicabs as you head north into Central Park on the marked bike lane along East Drive. To your left sits Central Park's Pond, envisioned by Central Park's renowned design duo, Frederick Law Olmsted and Calvert Vaux, as an instant escape from the busyness of city life. It serves that same purpose still today, more than a century and a half after

Bike Shops

Innovation Bike Shop: 105 W. 106th St.; (212) 678-7130
The folks who operate this bike shop have more than 20 years racing experience and provide expert service along with pro gear.
Swim Bike Run NYC: 203 W. 58th St. (between 7th Ave. and Broadway); (212) 399-3999
This sports retailer will serve all your biking (running, yoga, triathlon, and swimming) needs. Their services include fittings, installations, adjustments, and maintenance, and they have a good selection of biking gear and accessories.

Views of Central Park's Lake.

initial plans for the park were laid out. Just ahead, you'll pass Wollman Rink on your left, where ice skaters revel in winter and amusement parkgoers rejoice in summer. Stop off along the overhead terrace for some people-watching if you wish before heading on. Just north of Wollman Rink, you'll soon spot the Dairy on your left, one of the park's five visitor centers. In the nineteenth century, this Victorian-style cottage served as serene sanctuary for children and caregivers who would come here for fresh milk and pastries. Stop in for park-related information, maps, and park paraphernalia, or continue straight where you'll soon join the park's main loop, which circumnavigates the entire park. Look to your left for oncoming cyclists before accessing the drive.

At East 72nd Street, East Drive forks, with one arm cutting westward through the park as Terrace Drive and the other arm continuing northward as East Drive alongside the lake. (To know what cross street you're at, find the numbers on the nearest lamppost. The first two numbers reflect the nearest cross street, with 1 being omitted for cross streets in the hundreds.) At the fork, veer left to reach Bethesda Terrace, considered the heart of Central Park. It sits at the northern end of the grand Mall, an extended allée canopied by majestic elm trees on either side. One hundred fifty years ago, this was the go-to spot for displaying one's Sunday best. (Access the Mall from its southern end at the end of your journey.) On your right Bethesda Terrace overlooks

Central Park's Lake and Bethesda Fountain, made famous by many a movie and TV show. You'll be on the terrace's upper level, an excellent lookout point.

Continuing en route, return to East Drive to head north along the east edge of the lake. On your left sits Loeb Boathouse, where you'll find boat rentals, a cafe, and informal birdwatchers' headquarters. Bird sightings are recorded in a notebook on a table inside the boathouse. A short uphill climb after the boathouse brings you to the rear of the Metropolitan Museum of Art on your right and the Obelisk on your left. Continuing onward, skirt the edge of the Great Lawn before reaching the park's 106-acre Reservoir. A 1.58-mile trail loops around the reservoir (which was decommissioned in 1993) and has attracted sightseers, walkers, and runners for decades (Bill Clinton and Madonna, among them). Continuing onward, you'll pass a clearing with baseball diamonds on your left and then reach the access road for the Conservatory Garden on your right. If you wish to visit the gardens, turn right onto the road that exits the park from the north end of the baseball diamonds. When you hit 5th Avenue, dismount and walk your bike along the sidewalk 2 blocks northward to the entrance to the Conservatory Garden at 104th Street. It's one of the park's best-kept secrets, comprising three distinct, smaller gardens—one French, one Italian, and one English in style. To explore, lock up your bike and enter on foot. The garden's tiered hedges, crabapple tree allées, fountains, water lilies, and more make for a soothing break. Then return to East Drive and continue north through the park.

As you near the northern end of the park, East Drive takes you downhill, snaking left and right alongside the Harlem Meer, a man-made lake that's a popular spot for catch-and-release fishing and family outings. Continuing en route and going uphill to the left, you'll brush the edge of the North Woods, the park's most secluded woodlands. Hug the edge of these 40-acre woods as you head south. Pass the park's serene Pool on your right. Lined with benches, weeping willows, and grassy banks, the Pool is another temping rest spot.

South of the Pool, you'll enter the more populated portion of Central Park once more along the western edge of the Reservoir, which brings you to several mid-park landmarks—the Delacorte Theater, Belvedere Castle, and Shakespeare Garden, among them. To visit any of them, dismount your bike and walk it along a park pathway on your left. (Biking is prohibited on park-internal pathways.) Then, continuing southward, you'll pass the Lake on your left, replete with picnickers and boaters during summer months. Then, to visit Strawberry Fields up ahead, the living memorial to Beatles legend John Lennon, veer uphill to the right as you approach the lake's southern end. (To bypass Strawberry Fields, simply stick to West Drive.) At the top of the hill, a pathway leads to Strawberry Fields on your left. To visit the memorial, dismount and enter the grounds on foot (biking prohibited). When you're ready to continue, take the park entrance road at West 72nd Street to reenter the park and access West Drive once more.

The southern leg of your trip takes you past Sheep Meadow, a large, open lawn that today attracts sunbathers and Frisbee players, but that from 1864 to 1934 was the feeding grounds for a flock of sheep. The building that houses the Tavern on the Green (now a visitor center) used to be the living quarters of these sheep and their shepherd. Continuing onward, the road veers left, heading toward your starting point along what becomes Center Drive. After passing the playground on your left, glance to your right to the outcropping overhead where you can spot the rustic pergola that surrounds the Chess and Checkers House. Just opposite the house sits the park's more-than-a-century-old Carousel, which has had three predecessors. The two most recent ones were destroyed by fire. The first, which stood here as early as 1871, was powered by a mule or horse from beneath the Carousel platform. It would start or stop at the tap of a foot.

Up ahead on your left, as you reach the south end of the grand Mall once more, you'll be near the end of your journey. Stop off on one of the benches that line the allée for some enjoyable people-watching along the promenade before returning to your starting point at Grand Army Plaza. Alternately, orbit the park once more before ending your ride.

MILES AND DIRECTIONS

0.0 Enter Central Park via the drive from the northwest corner of Grand Army Plaza.

0.3 The Dairy is on your left.

0.4 Come to a complete stop before joining the main park loop along East Drive. Check for oncoming cyclists to the left before veering to the left side of the road to take the cycling lane and go counterclockwise around the park (heading north).

0.7 At the height of East 72nd Street, the drive forks, with one arm cutting through the park toward Bethesda Terrace along Terrace Drive and the other continuing north along East Drive. To visit Bethesda Terrace, veer left along Terrace Drive.

0.8 Bethesda Terrace overlooks the Lake to your right and offers views of the Mall to your left. To continue en route, turn around to retrace your path to East Drive.

0.9 Turn left onto East Drive, following the bike lane northward and brushing the east side of the Lake.

The Obelisk (nicknamed Cleopatra's Needle)
Commissioned as one of two obelisks in 1450 BC for the ancient
Egyptian city of Heliopolis, the 71-foot obelisk was transferred to
New York and erected in Central Park in 1881. (The other one was
moved to London.) The Egyptian khedive at the time received funds
in exchange for the Obelisk to help modernize the country. After its
arrival on the shores of the Hudson, laborers worked for 112 days to
move it to Central Park. It's the park's oldest man-made object.

1.0 Loeb Boathouse is on your left.

1.4 The Metropolitan Museum of Art is on your right; the Obelisk is on
your left.

2.7 To visit the Conservatory Garden, turn right along the narrow park
entrance road at East 102nd Street. When you reach the park's edge
at 5th Avenue, dismount your bike and walk it 2 blocks north along
the sidewalk to reach the entrance to the Garden at East 104th Street.
Lock up your bike to explore the Garden on foot. When you're ready
to continue, retrace your route to East Drive in the park. Continue
north along the drive. (The 0.5 mile out to the Conservatory Garden
and back are not included in this mileage.)

3.3 You can reach the Charles A. Dana Discovery Center on the banks of
the Harlem Meer by foot on your right. (Biking is prohibited on the
park pathway.) To continue en route, follow the drive as it veers left
to go uphill (west and then south), brushing the edge of the North
Woods. East Drive becomes West Drive.

4.0 The Pool is on your right.

5.2 The Delacorte Theater and Shakespeare Garden are accessible by
foot on your left.

5.3 The Swedish Cottage and Belvedere Castle are accessible by foot on
your left.

5.5 Veer right for an optional trip uphill to Strawberry Fields. Alternately,
continue straight along West Drive. (The mileage remains the same.)

5.6 When you reach the top of the hill, Strawberry Fields is accessible
by foot on your left. To explore, lock up your bike and enter on foot.
When you're ready to continue, remount your bike and catch the

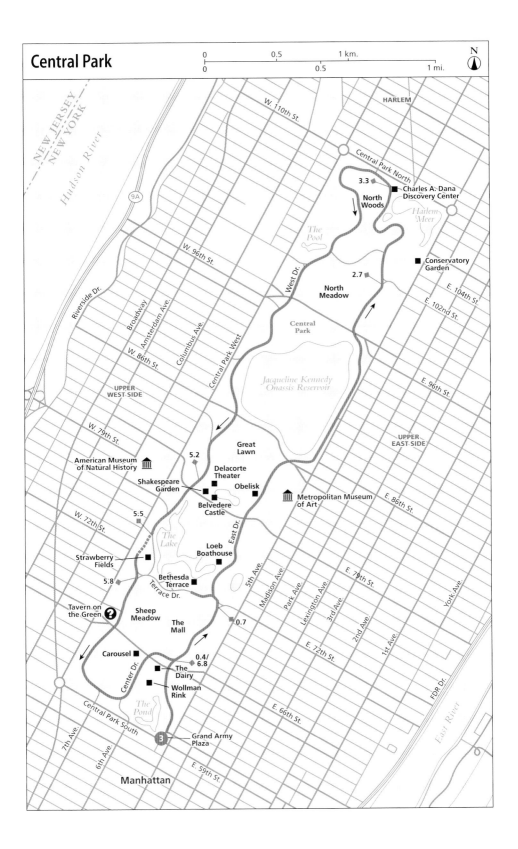

Central Park

0   0.5   1 km.
0   0.5   1 mi.

N

NEW JERSEY
NEW YORK

Hudson River

9A

HARLEM

W. 110th St.

Central Park North

3.3

North Woods

Charles A. Dana
Discovery Center

Harlem
Meer

The Pool

Conservatory
Garden

West Dr.

2.7

North
Meadow

E. 104th St.

E. 102nd St.

W. 96th St.

Central
Park

Jacqueline Kennedy
Onassis Reservoir

E. 96th St.

Riverside Dr.

Broadway

Amsterdam Ave.

Columbus Ave.

Central Park West

W. 86th St.

UPPER
WEST SIDE

UPPER
EAST SIDE

W. 79th St.

American Museum
of Natural History

5.2

Great
Lawn

Delacorte
Theater

Shakespeare
Garden

Obelisk

E. 86th St.

Metropolitan Museum
of Art

Belvedere
Castle

5.5

W. 72nd St.

The
Lake

East Dr.

Loeb
Boathouse

E. 79th St.

Strawberry
Fields

5.8

Bethesda
Terrace

5th Ave.

Madison Ave.

Park Ave.

Lexington Ave.

3rd Ave.

2nd Ave.

1st Ave.

York Ave.

Terrace Dr.

Tavern on
the Green

Sheep
Meadow

The
Mall

0.7

E. 72nd St.

FDR Dr.

Carousel

Center Dr.

0.4/
6.8

The
Dairy

Wollman
Rink

E. 66th St.

East River

The
Pond

Central Park South

7th Ave.

6th Ave.

Grand Army
Plaza

E. 59th St.

Manhattan

park entrance drive at West 72nd Street to the left to rejoin West Drive at the bottom of the hill.

5.8 Come to a complete stop before rejoining West Drive. Check for oncoming cyclists to the left before veering to the left side of West Drive to retake the bike lane, heading south.

5.9 Sheep Meadow is on your left.

6.0 Tavern on the Green is on your right.

6.5 The Chess and Checkers House is on a cliff to your right.

6.6 The Carousel is on your left.

6.8 The Mall is on your left. Dismount to explore and take a post-ride break. Or, if you wish, orbit the park once more. Eventually, return to your starting point at Grand Army Plaza via the park access road just opposite the Mall. As you exit the park along this East Drive access road, use caution. It's bumpy and often crowded with horse carriages, horse dropping, pedicabs, and pedestrians.

7.1 Arrive at your starting point.

RIDE INFORMATION

Restrooms
Mile 0.3: There are restrooms at the Dairy visitor center.
Mile 1.0: There are restrooms at Loeb Boathouse.
Mile 5.2: There are restrooms next to the Delacorte Theater.

The Upper West Side: Grande Dames

Much of the Upper West Side as we know it today was built in a turn-of-the-century building boom from the 1880s to 1920s, when Grande Dame buildings rose throughout the neighborhood. This route crisscrosses the neighborhood, mostly along quiet, residential streets. You'll pass notable grand residences and hotels along the way, hug the edge of Central Park, and stop off on a bluff overlooking the Hudson River.

Start: Columbus Circle, at the southwest corner of Central Park

Length: 7.3-mile loop

Approximate riding time: 1.5 hours

Best bike: Road, hybrid, or mountain bike

Terrain and trail surface: The trail is paved throughout and flat.

Traffic and hazards: This ride travels mostly along residential roads with light traffic and avenues with on-road bike lanes. Moderate urban cycling skills are required as this is a city neighborhood. About 0.6 mile of the route—along Broadway, Amsterdam, and Columbus Avenues—have moderate traffic and no bike lanes. Stay especially alert on these stretches.

Things to see: Soldiers and Sailors Monument, Beacon Theater, American Museum of Natural History, Upper West Side Grandes Dames (Apthorp, Ansonia, Dorilton, El Dorado, Beresford, Belleclaire, Dakota, San Remo)

Maps: *New York City Bike Map*, Landmark West! Map at www.landmark west.org

Getting there: By public transportation: Take the A, B, C, or D subway to the 59th Street-Columbus Circle subway stop. GPS coordinates: N40 46.100' / W73 58.886'

THE RIDE

From Columbus Circle, head north along Central Park West, passing the fifty-two-story Trump Hotel on your left and hugging Central Park on your right. West 71st Street brings you to the Dorilton residences at number 171, completed in 1902 and known for its opulent wrought-iron gateway. Just beyond, the subway house at Broadway and West 72nd Street stems from the same era, as does the Ansonia, 1 block north of here. Occupying an entire city block, the Beaux-Arts–style Ansonia is famous for housing world-class musicians due to its virtually soundproof walls. Opposite the Ansonia, on the east side of Broadway, sits another early-twentieth-century landmark—the Beacon Theater. It's one of the sole surviving Manhattan movie palaces.

After crossing Broadway you'll reach the Belleclaire at 250 West 77th Street. This apartment hotel, completed in 1903, was one of the Hungarian-born architect Emery Roth's earliest New York designs. (He designed most of his New York structures in the 1920s and 1930s.) Then pass the charming West End Collegiate Church at the end of the block to return eastward along West 78th Street. At 2211 Broadway up ahead, another grande dame, the Apthorp apartments, occupy an entire city block.

At the end of the road, cross to the east side of Columbus Avenue to catch the bike lane leading south along the rear of the American Museum of Natural History. This soon brings you to Central Park once more, where the infamous Dakota sits on your left at the corner of West 72nd Street. Completed in 1884, and one of the neighborhood's oldest grand residences, the building entered popular lore when Beatles star John Lennon was shot outside his home here in 1980.

Bike Shops

Bicycle Renaissance: 430 Columbus Ave.; (212) 724-2350
A family-owned and -operated bike shop with a 40-year history. They've long been involved with multiple New York–area tours and road races.

Eastern Mountain Sports: 2152 Broadway; (212) 873-4001
This retailer of outdoor gear and equipment has stores from Maine to Virginia. This New York branch, centrally located at West 76th Street, has bikes and bike accessories for sale, and offers bike services and tune-ups.

Eddie's Bicycles: 490 Amsterdam Ave.; (212) 580-2011
The welcoming atmosphere in this neighborhood bike shop at 84th Street has helped encourage local cycling for more than 30 years.

Heading north along Central Park West, with the San Remo, Beresford, and El Dorado in the distance.

Heading north along the tree-lined western edge of Central Park, you'll pass the imposing twenty-seven-story San Remo, a 1930s-era Roth-relic, at West 74th Street. Skirt the edge of the ornate New York Historical Society and American Museum of Natural History on your left before reaching Roth's Beresford apartments (from 1929) and the storied El Dorado just beyond. West 91st Street then takes you along pleasant residential blocks to Riverside

Drive where, at West 89th Street, the Soldiers and Sailors Monument sits high on a bluff overlooking the Hudson River. The benches along the edge are a great spot for a break.

To continue, head eastward along West 90th Street along a string of town houses to Columbus Avenue. Catch the separated bikeway along the avenue's east edge to go south, passing the American Museum of Natural History once more. A trip to the Upper West Side wouldn't be complete without a jaunt into Central Park, so enter the park along the park drive at West 77th Street, heading toward the park lake. Stop off if you wish and then veer right when the drive splits, hugging the park's western edge and going uphill. Strawberry Fields, a living memorial to John Lennon, occupies a 2.5-acre quiet zone at the top of the hill. To explore the area, dismount and access the site on foot. Biking is prohibited. Then remount your bike and continue south to your starting point at Columbus Circle.

MILES AND DIRECTIONS

0.0 From Columbus Circle, catch Central Park West, going north along the edge of the park.

0.6 Turn left onto West 71st Street.

0.9 Turn right onto Amsterdam Avenue.

1.0 Turn left onto West 73rd Street, followed by a quick right onto Broadway.

1.2 Turn left onto West 77th Street, followed by a right onto West End Avenue.

1.3 Turn right onto West 78th Street.

1.7 Turn right onto Columbus Avenue.

2.0 Turn left onto West 72nd Street.

2.2 Turn left onto Central Park West.

3.3 Turn left onto West 91st Street.

3.7 Turn right onto West End Avenue, followed by a left onto West 93rd Street.

3.9 Turn right onto Riverside Drive.

4.0 Turn sharply left at West 95th Street, making a U-turn to head south on Riverside Drive.

4.3 The Soldiers and Sailors Monument is on your right at West 89th Street.

4.4 Turn left onto West 88th Street.

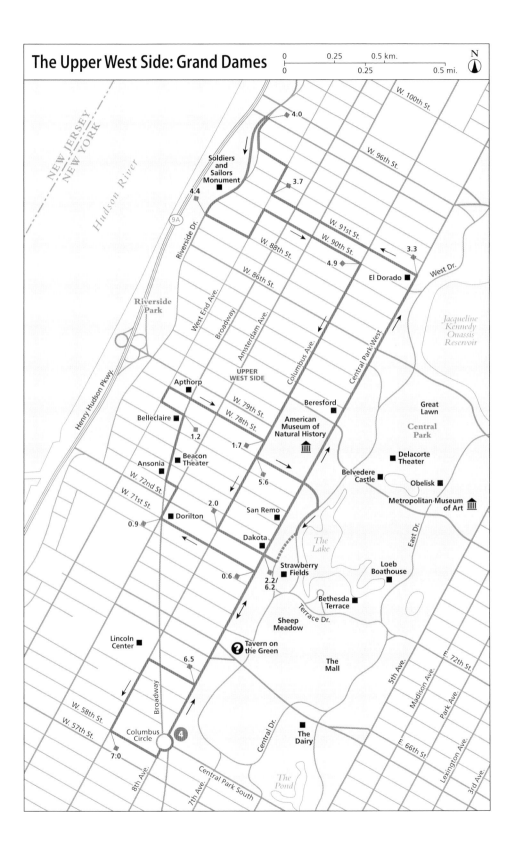

The Upper West Side: Grand Dames

0   0.25   0.5 km.

0   0.25   0.5 mi.

N

NEW JERSEY
NEW YORK

Hudson River

9A

Riverside Dr.

Riverside
Park

Henry Hudson Pkwy.

W. 100th St.

W. 96th St.

4.0

Soldiers
and
Sailors
Monument

4.4

3.7

W. 91st St.

W. 90th St.

W. 88th St.

W. 86th St.

4.9

3.3

El Dorado

West Dr.

Jacqueline
Kennedy
Onassis
Reservoir

West End Ave.

Broadway

Amsterdam Ave.

Columbus Ave.

Central Park West

UPPER
WEST SIDE

Apthorp

Belleclaire

1.2

W. 79th St.

W. 78th St.

1.7

Beresford

American
Museum of
Natural History

Great
Lawn

Central
Park

Ansonia

Beacon
Theater

5.6

Delacorte
Theater

Belvedere
Castle

Obelisk

W. 72nd St.

W. 71st St.

2.0

San Remo

Metropolitan Museum
of Art

0.9

Dorilton

Dakota

The
Lake

Loeb
Boathouse

East Dr.

0.6

Strawberry
Fields

2.2/
6.2

Bethesda
Terrace

Terrace Dr.

Sheep
Meadow

Lincoln
Center

6.5

Broadway

Tavern on
the Green

The
Mall

5th Ave.

Madison Ave.

Park Ave.

E. 72nd St.

W. 58th St.

W. 57th St.

Columbus
Circle

4

7.0

8th Ave.

7th Ave.

Central Park South

Central Dr.

The
Dairy

The
Pond

E. 66th St.

Lexington Ave.

3rd Ave.

The USS *Maine* National Monument

This monument at the center of the Merchants' Square Plaza at the southwest corner of Central Park honors 260 American sailors who died when their ship exploded in Havana harbor in 1898, when Spain still controlled Cuba. Within months the Spanish-American War erupted, eventually leading to Spain's ceder of power over Cuba by the end of the year. While the cause of the explosion is still unknown, remnants of that battleship were reputedly incorporated into the gilded bronze figures sitting atop the pillar. They depict three hippocampi—mythical sea horses—towing a seashell chariot with Columbia Triumphant.

4.5 Turn left onto West End Avenue.

4.6 Turn right onto West 90th Street.

4.9 Turn right onto Columbus Avenue.

5.6 Turn left onto West 77th Street.

5.8 Enter Central Park straight ahead along the drive.

6.0 Veer right to go uphill.

6.1 Strawberry Fields is on your left.

6.2 Exit Central Park to turn left onto Central Park West, heading south.

6.5 Turn right onto West 63rd Street.

6.7 Turn left onto Columbus Avenue, hugging its east edge.

7.0 Turn left onto West 58th Street.

7.1 Turn left onto 8th Avenue to enter Columbus Circle. To get to your starting point on the other side, you might want to use the pedestrian crosswalks to cross 8th Avenue, Broadway, and then Central Park South.

7.3 Arrive at your starting point.

RIDE INFORMATION

Restrooms

Start/end: There are restrooms and water fountains in Heckscher Playground at the southwest corner of Central Park. Walk your bike from Columbus Circle along the footpath northeastward into Central Park.

Harlem Heritage Tour

Founded in the seventeenth century by Dutch farmers, Harlem became a nexus of cultural awakening during the Harlem Renaissance in the 1920s. From the Apollo Theater and Sugar Hill, to Striver's Row and the Abyssinian Baptist Church, this ride takes you past innumerable spots that hark back to Harlem's cultural heyday and continue to define the neighborhood today.

Start: The Farmer's Gate to Central Park, at Central Park North and Lenox Avenue/Malcolm X Boulevard

Length: 11.1-mile loop

Approximate riding time: 1.5 hours

Best bike: Road, hybrid, or mountain bike

Terrain and trail surface: The trail is paved throughout and mostly flat. You'll scale one short, steep hill from Saint Nicholas Avenue to Convent Avenue along West 141st Street. It then goes gently downhill along Edgecombe Avenue.

Traffic and hazards: This route leads along Harlem roads with light to moderate traffic. Only a few of the roads have bike lanes, so considerable city cycling comfort is required. Sunday morning traffic is lighter.

Things to see: Harlem Meer, Studio Museum in Harlem, Apollo Theater, Sugar Hill, Striver's Row, Abyssinian Baptist Church, Schomburg Center for Research in Black Culture, National Jazz Museum in Harlem

Map: *New York City Bike Map*

Getting there: By public transportation: Take the 2 or the 3 subway to the Central Park North (110th Street) station. Go south 1 block on Lenox Avenue to reach Central Park's Farmer's Gate. GPS coordinates: N40 47.887' / W73 57.147'

THE RIDE

The first portion of this journey hugs the edge of Central Park's northeast corner, offering views of the park's Harlem Meer, a man-made body of water whose name stems from the Dutch word for "lake." Going northeast from here, you'll soon reach Marcus Garvey Park, a Harlem mainstay for more than 150 years. Originally called Mount Morris Park, the site became a city park in 1840 and was later named after Marcus Mosiah Garvey, a Jamaican-born advocate of black nationalism and economic independence for African Americans. He moved to Harlem in 1916. To explore the park, dismount your bike and

Bike Shop

Pedal Universe: 2450 Adam Clayton Powell Blvd.; (347) 994-0660
You'll find great deals at this bike shop south of 143rd Street, where they specialize in reconditioned bikes.

The Harlem Meer, in the northeast corner of Central Park.

climb to the top of the hill, where you have a bird's-eye view of the rest of your journey. (Alternately, return to the park at the end of the route to do so.)

Heading west along 125th Street, Harlem's main drag and also called Martin Luther King Jr. Boulevard, you'll pass numerous noteworthy neighborhood institutions. The road often has heavy car and bus traffic, so stay alert. Pass the Studio Museum in Harlem on your left, a promoter of artists of African descent since opening in 1968. Continuing west, the Apollo Theater sits on your right. When it opened as the Hurtig and Seamon's New Burlesque Theater in 1914, African Americans were prohibited from entering both as performers and patrons. After a short period of disuse in the 1930s, the theater reopened in 1934, toward the end of the Harlem Renaissance, and soon became associated largely with black performers and culture.

Up ahead you'll head north on Saint Nicholas Avenue, hugging the foot of steeply sloping Saint Nicholas Park. At the top of the hill you can spot the neo-Gothic spires of City College, founded in 1841 to provide free higher education to all. West 141st Street takes you steeply uphill to Convent Avenue. Along the way on your left sits a historical relic from an earlier era, the Harlem home of founding father Alexander Hamilton. Convent Avenue then hugs the edge of Sugar Hill, now part of the Hamilton Heights historic district. Covering approximately 10 blocks from West 145th Street to West 155th Street, and extending east to Edgecombe Avenue, it was dubbed Sugar Hill to evoke what was seen as the sweet life of Harlem beginning in the 1920s. Today, Convent Avenue is a quiet, residential street with elegant town houses.

A short stretch along Saint Nicholas Avenue brings you to the short, cobblestoned Jumel Terrace, where another vestige of an earlier era sits on your left—the Morris-Jumel Mansion. Built and owned by a British colonel in 1765, it was George Washington's headquarters during the Revolutionary War. Sylvan Terrace, on your right, was the mansion's carriage path and today looks much the same as it did then, with two-story wooden houses on either side.

Edgecombe Avenue then takes you back into Sugar Hill along the edge of an outcropping overlooking Jackie Robinson Park and with sweeping views toward Long Island. Edgecombe Avenue was the favored street of many successful African-American musicians, actors, and professionals in the 1940s. Number 555 attracted musical giants including Count Basie, Duke Ellington, and Roy Orbison. Farther south, at number 409, residents included the writer and nationalist W.E.B. Dubois, US Supreme Court Justice Thurgood Marshall, and civil rights activist Roy Wilkins.

A little farther south, along West 138th Street you'll hit upon Strivers Row after crossing Frederick Douglass Boulevard. The homes on this block were

Strivers Row, along West 138th Street, named after the upward strivers who moved here in 1920s.

largely white-owned until the 1920s, when upwardly mobile black professionals—known as "strivers"—began purchasing homes here. Just beyond, east of Adam Clayton Powell Jr. Boulevard, the Abyssinian Baptist Church sits on your right. It was founded in 1808 by Ethiopian seamen and free Africans in America who wouldn't accept segregated seating in their church at the time.

Heading toward East Harlem along Lexington Avenue, the National Museum of Jazz sits on your right, celebrating innumerable jazz greats who called Harlem home—Duke Ellington, Charlie Parker, and Count Basie, among them. The last stretch of journey then skirts the edge of Spanish Harlem along 2nd Avenue, with idiosyncratic community gardens sprinkled throughout the neighborhood. Pleasant Avenue then leads you north past the site that used to house the city's first integrated public high school, Benjamin Franklin High School. (The spot now houses the Manhattan Center for Science and Mathematics.) One Hundred Eighteenth Street then takes you past Marcus Garvey Park once more (a block north of you) and through Central Harlem's 1-block historic district before you return to your starting point.

MILES AND DIRECTIONS

0.0 Bike east along Central Park North.

0.2 Veer right into the roundabout and turn right onto 5th Avenue.

0.3 Turn left onto East 108th Street.

0.4 Turn left onto Madison Avenue.

1.3 Turn left onto 125th Street.

2.0 Turn right onto Saint Nicholas Avenue.

2.5 Veer left to stay on Saint Nicholas Avenue.

2.8 Turn left onto West 141st Street.

3.0 Turn right onto Convent Avenue.

3.4 Turn right onto West 150th Street.

3.5 Turn left onto Saint Nicholas Avenue.

4.1 Turn right onto West 162nd Street, followed by a right onto Jumel Terrace.

4.2 Turn left onto West 160th Street, followed by a right onto Edgecombe Avenue.

4.5 Diagonally cross Saint Nicholas Avenue, continuing on Edgecombe Avenue.

5.4 Turn left onto West 138th Street.

5.9 Turn right onto Lenox Avenue/Malcolm X Boulevard. The Schomburg Center is just ahead on your right.

6.0 Turn left onto West 135th Street.

6.2 Turn right onto 5th Avenue.

6.5 Turn left onto East 128th Street.

6.8 Turn right onto Lexington Avenue.

6.9 The National Jazz Museum in Harlem is on your right halfway down the block on East 126th Street.

7.0 Turn left onto East 125th Street.

7.2 Turn right onto the bikeway along the east side of 2nd Avenue.

8.1 Turn left onto East 108th Street.

8.2 Turn left onto 1st Avenue.

8.5 Turn right onto East 114th Street.

8.6 Turn left to stay on East 114th Street. Continue straight onto Pleasant Avenue.

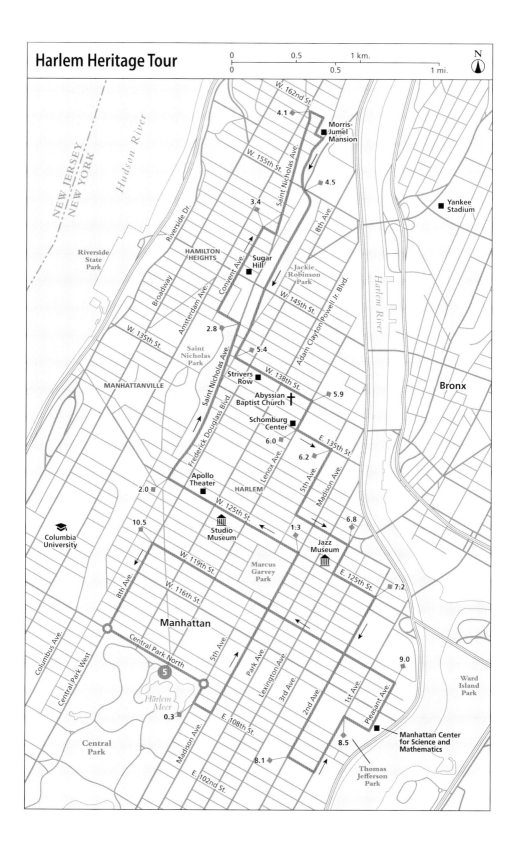

Harlem Heritage Tour

0   0.5   1 km.
0   0.5   1 mi.

N

NEW JERSEY
NEW YORK

Hudson River

Riverside
State
Park

Riverside Dr.

HAMILTON
HEIGHTS

Broadway

Amsterdam Ave.

Convent Ave.

W. 162nd St.

4.1

Morris-
Jumel
Mansion

W. 155th St.

Saint Nicholas Ave.

4.5

8th Ave.

Yankee
Stadium

3.4

Sugar
Hill

Jackie
Robinson
Park

Harlem River

W. 145th St.

Adam Clayton Powell Jr. Blvd.

W. 135th St.

Saint
Nicholas
Park

Saint Nicholas Ave.

Frederick Douglass Blvd.

2.8

5.4

MANHATTANVILLE

Strivers
Row

W. 138th St.

Bronx

Abyssian
Baptist Church

5.9

Schomburg
Center

6.0

Lenox Ave.

E. 135th St.

6.2

5th Ave.

Madison Ave.

Apollo
Theater

2.0

HARLEM

W. 125th St.

6.8

Columbia
University

10.5

Studio
Museum

1.3

Jazz
Museum

7.2

E. 125th St.

W. 119th St.

8th Ave.

Marcus
Garvey
Park

W. 116th St.

9.0

Ward
Island
Park

Manhattan

Columbus Ave.

Central Park West

Central Park North

5

Harlem
Meer

0.3

5th Ave.

Park Ave.

Lexington Ave.

3rd Ave.

2nd Ave.

1st Ave.

Pleasant Ave.

Manhattan Center
for Science and
Mathematics

8.5

Central
Park

Madison Ave.

E. 108th St.

8.1

Thomas
Jefferson
Park

E. 102nd St.

9.0 Turn left onto East 119th Street.

10.5 Turn left onto Frederick Douglass Boulevard.

10.7 Go counterclockwise around the traffic roundabout. Exit to your right onto Central Park North, hugging the north edge of Central Park.

11.1 Arrive at your starting point.

RIDE INFORMATION

Local Events/Attractions

Abyssinian Baptist Church: An important social, political, and religious institution in the neighborhood since 1808. 174 W. 136th St.; www.abyssinian.org

Alexander Hamilton Grange Memorial: Founding father Alexander Hamilton's Harlem home. 414 W. 141st St.; www.nps.gov/hagr

Apollo Theater: Harlem's famous performance venue. 253 W. 125th St.; (212) 531-5300; www.apollotheater.org

Morris-Jumel Mansion: Now a historic house museum, the mansion's exhibits shed light on developments from the colonial era to today. 65 Jumel Ter.; (212) 923-8008; www.morrisjumel.org

National Jazz Museum in Harlem: A jazz museum in a spot where many former jazz greats resided. 104 E. 126th St.; (212) 348-8300; www.jazzmuseumin harlem.org

Schomburg Center for Research in Black Culture: A public library research branch dedicated to research into African-American life. 515 Malcolm X Blvd.; (212) 491-2200; www.nypl.org/locations/schomburg

Studio Museum in Harlem: A museum dedicated to the works of artists of African descent. 144 W. 125th St.; (212) 864-4500; www.studiomuseum.org

Restrooms

Start/end: There are restrooms in the Charles A. Dana Discovery Center along the shore of the Harlem Meer at the northeast corner of Central Park.

The Village's Heyday

This tour ambles along quaint residential streets and past historic hot spots from the Village's heyday when intellectuals, writers, and artists called it home. The route passes numerous former residences of Village icons and, with its narrow lanes and a mazelike street system, forces you to slow your pace. An optional tour to Chelsea travels through Chelsea's arts district and the cobblestone roads of the Meatpacking District, where designer boutiques sit next to outdoor cafes. Stop off at the High Line if you wish before ending your journey.

Start: The Washington Square Arch, also known as the Triumphal Arch

Length: 10.0-mile loop (5.9-mile loop without Chelsea option)

Approximate riding time: 2 hours (1 hour, abbreviated option)

Best bike: Hybrid, road, or mountain bike

Terrain and trail surface: The trail is mostly paved. A few blocks in the Meatpacking District are rough cobblestones, where a bike with wide tires will serve you best. The terrain is flat.

Traffic and hazards: This route runs along on-road bike lanes and quaint, historical lanes in Greenwich Village. Where there are bike lanes, traffic is moderate. Where there are none, traffic is very light. All of the avenue intersections have heavy traffic, so stay alert. The ride requires some city cycling comfort.

Things to see: Washington Square, Washington Mews, Greenwich Village, Chelsea, High Line, Meatpacking District, Stonewall Inn

Map: *New York City Bike Map*

Getting there: By public transportation: Take the A, B, C, D, E, F, or M subway to the West 4th Street subway stop. Bike north on 6th Avenue a couple of blocks until you hit West 8th Street. Turn right onto West 8th Street, heading east, and then right onto 5th Avenue. Fifth Avenue leads to the Washington Square Arch. GPS coordinates: N40 43.876' / W73 59.822'

Washington Square's landmark arch was built in 1889 for the centennial of George Washington's inauguration as first president. Originally made of wood, the arch was replaced by this marble structure just a few years later. From the arch, your journey leads east along the Greek-Revival–style buildings that line the north edge of the park, and which housed the first of this route's noteworthy denizens. Check out numbers 7 and 3, where the writers Edith Wharton and John Dos Passos once lived, respectively.

> ## Bike Shops
>
> **Echelon Cycles:** 51 8th Ave.; (212) 206-7656
> Owned and operated by veteran racer Pablo Castro and two cycling friends, this full-service bike shop has top brands and accessories.
> **Hudson Urban Bicycles (HUB):** 139 Charles St.; (212) 965-9334
> This full-service bike shop specializes in cruiser, specialty, and vintage bikes.

Then head north on University Place, with New York University buildings and college hangouts lining the road on either side. On 5th Avenue, going south, you'll next have frontal views of the Washington Square Arch as you approach the square from the north. On your right, notice the Breevort Apartments at West 8th Street (11–15 5th Avenue). It's the site of the former Breevort Hotel, which housed many infamous artist-activists in its prime—from the playwright Eugene O'Neill to the reporter Lincoln Steffens to the modern dance icon Isadora Duncan. Just south of here on your left, the cobbled Washington Mews are lined by Victorian-style former stables that were converted to houses in the early twentieth century. Here, too, resided John Dos Passos, as well as the artist Edward Hopper.

After leaving Washington Square Park, you'll head north on 6th Avenue toward the Jefferson Market branch of the public library. The building it resides in, with its angular clock tower, served as courthouse in the 1870s. Then, heading west from 6th Avenue, you'll enter a maze of quiet residential streets that make up the most charming section of the Village. An intricate network of one-way streets here defies the laws of the rest of New York City's city block system, making it easy to get lost. Christopher Street soon leads you through the birthplace of the gay rights movement, most notably the Stonewall Inn. During the legendary Stonewall Inn riots of 1969, the inn's patrons protested against continued city-sanctioned police harassment, thus launching a nationwide movement for LGBT equality.

Up ahead, Bleecker Street, a main Village drag, leads past an eclectic mix of boutiques and cafes. Turning right onto Barrow Street, you'll travel

The heart of the Village, at Commerce and Barrow Streets.

along quaint alleyways that appear frozen in time. Many of the buildings that remain standing today played an important role throughout Village history. Chumley's, a Prohibition-era speakeasy whose literary patrons ranged from William Faulkner to John Steinbeck, Allen Ginsberg, J.D. Salinger, and Simone de Beauvoir, sat at 86 Bedford Street. It closed in 2007, but a reopening may be in the making. Just around the corner from here, at 59 Grove Street,

Thomas Paine lived and died. Continuing onward, check out the city's narrowest building, at 57½ Bedford Street. It was the home of playwright and poet Edna St. Vincent Millay, who played a pivotal role in the creation of a Village theater on Commerce Street, which is now the Cherry Lane Theatre.

At the west edge of the Village, you'll note a change of scenery as tiny town houses give way to towering lofts after crossing Hudson Street. You'll then return to the heart of the Village and Bleecker Street along quainter roads. Use caution as you approach 7th Avenue from the south. You'll diagonally cross the avenue to then go south along its west edge a short spurt and make a quick right turn onto Leroy Street (Saint Luke's Place) for a final stretch of Village biking before reaching Chelsea. (Heading north on Hudson Street here, you have the option of bypassing Chelsea and returning to Washington Square Park via West 10th Street. If doing so, skip ahead in the route description.)

Hudson Street leads northward past a flurry of cafes and restaurants before crossing West 14th Street into Chelsea. Up ahead you'll reach the High Line, a former elevated railroad that's been transformed into a park. Bike north along 10th Avenue, with the High Line overhead. This soon brings you to the neighborhood's most picturesque block along West 20th Street. The entire block is occupied by the stately redbrick buildings of the General Theological Seminary, where church leaders have been formed since 1817. Opposite the seminary, from 406 to 418 West 20th Street, sit some of Chelsea's oldest brownstones, built in the 1840s and known as Cushman Row.

Continuing onward, you'll enter Chelsea's gallery district along West 29th Street, where you'll pass countless galleries on a short jaunt through the district. (Stop off at any if you wish.) Continuing onward, the Chelsea Market on 9th Avenue is a great place to grab a snack-to-go to carry to the High Line a few blocks south of here at Gansevoort Street, a cobblestone road that leads into the Meatpacking District. To check out the High Line, dismount and lock your bike. Then climb the stairs to the High Line, which stretches north to West 30th Street. Pick a spot on a bench along the way for a short break before returning to Washington Square Park via the West Village once more.

MILES AND DIRECTIONS

0.0   Bike east along Washington Square North.

0.1   Turn left onto University Place.

0.5   Turn left onto West 13th Street.

0.6   Turn left onto 5th Avenue.

The Village's Heyday

0   0.25   0.5 km.

0   0.25   0.5 mi.

N

Hudson River

12th Ave.

11th Ave.

9A

6.6

W. 30th St.

W. 34th St.

6.9

CHELSEA

W. 29th St.

Penn Station

The High Line

10th Ave.

11th Ave.

7.3

W. 26th St.

6.1

5.3

W. 23rd St.

Manhattan

9th Ave.

8th Ave.

7th Ave.

Avenue of the Americas

W. 20th St.

5.7

5.1

Chelsea Market

MEATPACKING DISTRICT

4.7

W. 18th St.

FLATIRON DISTRICT

6th Ave.

5th Ave.

7.9

Gansevoort St.

Hudson St.

W. 15th St.

W. 14th St.

9.0

W. 13th St.

Washington St.

Bank St.

WEST VILLAGE

Greenwich Ave.

0.6

2.4

Perry St.

Charles St.

2.6

W. 10th St.

University Pl.

E. 13th St.

8.7

Stonewall Inn

GREENWICH VILLAGE

0.5

Broadway

8.4

1.4/2.9

1.1

Christopher St.

Waverly Pl.

West St.

2.2

7th Ave.

1.8

3.1

Barrow St.

6

3.6

W. 4th St.

9A

Leroy St.

3.8

Washington Square Park

Washington Pl.

9.8

4.0

Bedford St.

W. 3rd St.

Washington Square South

Houston St.

Bleecker St.

NYU

NOHO

0.9 Turn right onto Washington Square North to head west. The bike lane runs along the south side of the street.

1.1 Cross 6th Avenue (Avenue of the Americas) and grab the bike lane along the west side of the avenue, heading north.

1.2 Turn left onto Christopher Street.

1.4 Turn left onto Bleecker Street.

1.5 Turn right onto Barrow Street, followed by a right onto Bedford Street.

1.6 Turn right onto Grove Street.

1.8 Make a sharp right onto 7th Avenue.

2.0 Turn sharply right onto Bedford Street, followed by the second left onto Commerce Street, and a left onto Barrow Street.

2.2 Turn right onto Greenwich Street.

2.4 Turn right onto Perry Street.

2.6 Turn left onto West 4th Street, followed by a left onto West 11th Street, and a left onto Bleecker Street.

2.9 Turn right onto Christopher Street.

3.1 Turn left onto Washington Street.

3.3 Turn left onto Morton Street.

3.6 Turn right onto Bleecker Street.

3.7 Turn right onto Carmine Street, followed by a right onto Bedford Street.

3.8 Cross 7th Avenue, using the pedestrian signal, and head south. Make a quick right onto Leroy Street (Saint Luke's Place).

4.0 Turn right onto Hudson Street.

4.2 To bypass Chelsea, turn right onto West 10th Street and skip to mile 8.7. Otherwise, continue straight on Hudson Street, veering right onto 8th Avenue up ahead.

4.7 Turn left onto West 15th Street.

5.1 Turn right onto 10th Avenue.

5.3 Turn right onto West 20th Street.

5.7 Turn left onto 8th Avenue, catching the greenway on the west side of the avenue.

6.1 Turn left onto West 29th Street.

6.6 Turn left onto 11th Avenue.

6.9   Turn left onto West 26th Street.

7.3   Cross 9th Avenue to catch the greenway southward along the east side of the avenue.

7.8   Veer left to continue along the bikeway as it veers onto Hudson Street.

7.9   Turn right onto Gansevoort Street.

8.0   To access the High Line, lock up your bike at Washington Street and climb the stairs to the High Line. To continue, remount your bike and go south on Washington Street.

8.4   Turn left onto West 10th Street.

8.5   Cross Hudson Street and continue eastward. (This is your pick-up point if you bypassed Chelsea.)

8.7   Turn left onto West 4th Street.

8.9   Turn right onto Bank Street.

9.0   Turn right onto Waverly Place.

9.2   Turn right onto Stonewall Place, and then veer quickly left to catch Grove Street. Follow this with a left onto Sheridan Square / West 4th Street. Veer right on West 4th Street so that Sheridan Square is on your left. West 4th Street becomes Washington Square South.

9.8   Turn left at the east edge of Washington Square Park, followed by a left onto Washington Square North.

10.0   Arrive at your starting point.

RIDE INFORMATION

Restrooms
Mile 5.1/7.8: There are restrooms in Chelsea Market on 9th Avenue at West 15th Street.

7

Early East Side Ethnic Enclaves

Several days a week, Union Square, at the starting point of your journey, hosts one of the city's largest farmers' markets, where regional farmers peddle produce much like earlier settlers did via pushcart on the streets of the Lower East Side in the nineteenth century. Some of these early pushcart enterprises grew into thriving businesses that continue to serve the community today. This ride tours through the vibrant neighborhoods of the East Village, the Lower East Side, Chinatown, and Little Italy, passing several such longstanding establishments—cafes, eateries, bars, and merchants— along the way. It's a great ride for anyone interested in the city's early ethnic enclaves, a taste for Old World specialty foods, and some urban cycling savvy.

Start: The northeastern corner of Union Square

Length: 7.3-mile loop

Approximate riding time: 1.5 hours

Best bike: Hybrid, road, or mountain bike

Terrain and trail surface: The trail is paved throughout except for 1 block on Broome Street, which is cobbled. The terrain is flat.

Traffic and hazards: While most of this ride follows bike lanes and bike routes, it's still a deep-city route. Streets are narrow and traffic— although slow—can be heavy. Throughout the journey, stay especially alert along the avenues, where autos travel more quickly. Urban cycling comfort is thus beneficial.

Things to see: Union Square, McSorley's Old Ale House, Cooper Union, The Original Vincent's, Alleva Dairy, Caffe Roma, Seward Park Library, Essex Street Market, Yonah Schimmel Knish Bakery, Russ & Daughters, Katz's Delicatessen, Tompkins Square Park

Map: *New York City Bike Map*

Getting there: By public transportation: Take the 4, 5, 6, N, Q, R, or L subway to the Union Square station. Exit the station at the north end. GPS coordinates: N40 44.198' / W73 59.361'

From Union Square, your journey begins by heading south across East 14th Street, often considered the northern boundary to downtown Manhattan. Stay alert on Broadway, where traffic can be heavy, as you pass the storied Strand Bookstore on your left. It opened at a nearby spot in 1927. East 10th Street then leads along residential blocks into the East Village. This soon brings you on East 7th Street past McSorley's Old Ale House, opened by an Irish-born immigrant, John McSorley, around 1860. At the end of the block, you'll brush up against Cooper Union, established in 1859 by McSorley's close friend, Peter Cooper, as an institute of higher learning where all incoming students received full scholarships. The school's landmark foundation building sits at the north end of Cooper Square, across 3rd Avenue. Its modern counterpart, completed in 2009, forms a striking architectural contrast just south of East 7th Street.

Proceeding southward, you'll approach Houston Street along 2nd Avenue, where you'll merge left to continue straight. Use caution here as this intersection gets heavy traffic. Entering the Lower East Side on the other side, you'll skirt the edge of Sara D. Roosevelt Park, with ball courts and playgrounds stretching south toward the Manhattan Bridge. A short stretch of cobblestones along Broome Street then brings you into Chinatown and Little Italy. Heading south on Mott Street, one of Chinatown's main drags, Asian

Bike Shops

Bicycle Habitat: 244 Lafayette St.; (212) 431-3315
Founded in 1978 by early cycling advocates who encouraged the city to implement some of its earlier bike-friendly features (the Manhattan Bridge and Queensboro Bridge bikeways, for instance).
Busy Bee Bikes: 437 E. 6th St.; (212) 228-2347
A great neighborhood bike shop that has used, new, rental, and custom bikes.
Landmark Bicycles: 43 Avenue A; (212) 674-2343
Known for vintage Schwinns, Raleighs, classic cruisers, and specialty frames.
NYC Velo: 64 2nd Ave.; (212) 253-7771
A full-service bike shop that's a great place to get input on local rides or relax in the rider relaxation area.
REI SoHo: The Puck Building, 303 Lafayette St.; (212) 680-1938
A nationwide seller of outdoor recreation goods and sporting gear, with a bike shop where you can get tune-ups, overhauls, custom fittings, and more. Make an appointment with their bike shop staff for personalized attention.

The Union Square Greenmarket.

grocers and bakeries line the way until you reach a long-standing, family-owned Italian eatery, The Original Vincent's, at the corner of Hester Street. In 1904, a young Sicilian couple opened a small clam bar at this spot and, proving successful, soon moved into a small storefront. They named the spot after their son Vincent. Today, one of the couple's relations, also named Vincent, continues to serve locals and tourists Old World Italian food.

Continuing onward, Mulberry Street leads through the heart of Little Italy, with Italian restaurants lining the way. The Italian American Museum, on your left at Grand Street, sits in what was once Banca Stabile, a bank that in the late nineteenth century served newly arrived Italian immigrants. Crossing Grand Street, you'll pass Alleva Dairy on your right, another early Italian establishment. This *latteria* was founded just a few blocks east of here in 1892 by Pina Alleva, an immigrant from a small town near Naples. It is reputedly America's oldest Italian cheese store and now run by Alleva's grandson. Stop off to pick up some Italian delicacies if you wish before continuing northward through Little Italy. At Broome Street, you'll hit upon another Old World remnant, Caffe Roma, which began as a popular saloon in the 1870s. A decade or two later, the spot was transformed into a *pasticceria* by a pair of Neapolitan brothers. They later sold it to a fellow Neapolitan, Vincento Zeccardi, whose grandson continues to serve traditional Italian coffee and sweets—Neapolitan tiramisu, *pignoli*, biscotti—today. Some of the interiors endure from its early years as a saloon.

East Houston Jewish Eateries

When the Eastern European rabbi Yonah Schimmel arrived on the Lower East Side in the early 1900s, he soon realized that he'd never make ends meet through rabbinic duties alone—the overpopulated neighborhood had more than enough rabbis already. And so, Schimmel let his thriftiness flourish and began selling mashed potatoes wrapped in dough from a pushcart—knishes. By 1910, the Lower East Side's population had peaked at 550,000. (According to city estimates, in 2000, by contrast, a mere 197,000 people lived on the Lower East Side, including the East Village and Chinatown.) At that time, Schimmel's knishes were more popular than ever, enabling him to open shop at 137 E. Houston St., where his knish bakery continues today in the hands of his descendants. Although much of the bakery closely resembles what it looked like more than a decade ago, the eatery's offerings have expanded considerably. In addition to the traditional knishes baked by Schimmel over a century ago, customers can also choose from a rotating cast of innovative knishes—jalapeno, salmon, or pizza, to name a few.

A few blocks east sits Russ & Daughters, a historic seller of smoked fish, caviar, dried fruits, and other specialty foods. Similar to Schimmel's, Russ & Daughters began as a street enterprise. Joel Russ, an Eastern European Jew, began a horse-and-carriage herring business on the Lower East Side after arriving in the United States in 1900. By 1914, the business was successful enough to enable Russ and his wife, Bella, to open shop in a storefront on Orchard Street. A few years later, they moved the store to its current location, where it has continued in operation in the hands of multiple generations of Russes since. The community welcomed the change when Russ's three good-natured daughters—for whom the store is named—began assuming mercantile duties around 1930. (Russ himself was known for having a terrible temper and frequently threw customers out for saying the wrong thing.)

Katz's Delicatessen, just 1 block east, is perhaps the most legendary of early Lower East Side spots. Established nearby on Ludlow Street by the Iceland brothers in 1888, the deli was taken over by Willy Katz and his cousin Benny in 1910. The cafeteria-like deli has been serving traditional New York delicatessen—pastrami, corned beef, tongue, and, more recently, turkey and roast beef—ever since. Upon entering the brightly lit eatery, customers receive tickets and then call their order across a cafeteria counter before taking seats at one of innumerable self-serve tables with old-fashioned relics lining the walls.

Up ahead, Mott Street then returns you to Chinatown, bringing you to another main Chinatown drag along Grand Street. You'll cycle past an array of Chinese seafood, fruit, and vegetable merchants, as well as street vendors selling everything from pork buns to dumplings to fish balls. As you traverse Sara D. Roosevelt Park, you'll pass handball courts on your right, bustling with activity until late at night. Farther south beyond that, you might catch glimpses of a large-scale exercise gathering—people come together for communal Tai Chi, fan dance, and similar sessions at all hours of the day (or night).

East of the park you enter what was the epicenter of immigrant life in the late nineteenth century—the Lower East Side. You'll pass Harris Levy, a long-standing merchant of linens and fabrics, at 278 Grand St. Founded in the late nineteenth century by a young immigrant couple who began hawking wares from a rented pushcart, the family-owned and -operated importer today sells fine linens, tablecloths, comforters, and the like. Continuing onward, a protected greenway along the median of Allen Street brings you deeper into the

The storefront of the Yonah Schimmel Knish Bakery, established on East Houston Street in 1910, when the Lower East Side's population peaked at 550,000.

Early East Side Ethnic Enclaves

Lower East Side. Pass another long-standing neighborhood retailer, Mendel Goldberg Fabrics, up ahead at 72 Hester Street, also founded in the late nineteenth century. This former merchant of notions today continues in the hands of its founder's grandson and great-granddaughter and specializes in high-end fabrics. Next, you'll reach Orchard Street, a main pushcart passageway in the nineteenth century, but today lined with trendy stores and boutiques on the ground floors of former tenement dwellings.

Grand Street then brings you toward a newer section of Chinatown. The area surrounding East Broadway was once home to a large Jewish community, but today the neighborhood attracts mainly Chinese immigrants. The Seward Park Library, a four-story redbrick building in the park on your right along East Broadway, stands testament to this development. Serving a mostly Jewish clientele when it opened in 1909, it today stocks an extensive selection of Chinese materials. From the southwest corner of Seward Park, you'll then return northward toward the East Village. Along the way, stop off at the Essex Street Market on your right to pick up some fresh produce or ethnic specialties for a break toward the end of your journey in Tompkins Square Park up ahead. Before getting there, you'll pass a host of Jewish eateries with a history along East Houston Street—Yonah Schimmel Knish Bakery, Russ & Daughters, and Katz's Delicatessen (see sidebar for descriptions)—and then reach Tompkins Square Park, an East Village backbone, off Avenue A. Take a break here before returning to your starting point at Union Square.

MILES AND DIRECTIONS

0.0 Go south on Union Square East, hugging the east edge of Union Square. Continue straight onto Broadway after crossing East 14th Street.

0.4 Turn left onto East 10th Street.

0.7 Turn right onto 2nd Avenue. Although there's a separated bike path along the east edge of the avenue, you might want to stick to the west side, so you can easily turn right again a few blocks south.

0.8 Turn right onto East 7th Street.

1.0 Turn left onto 3rd Avenue.

1.2 Turn left onto East 2nd Street.

1.3 Turn right onto 2nd Avenue. Second Avenue forks up ahead, with traffic headed south taking the central lane. Merge left to continue along the bike lane going south. Stay alert as cars turning right will be on your right, and cars going straight will be on your left.

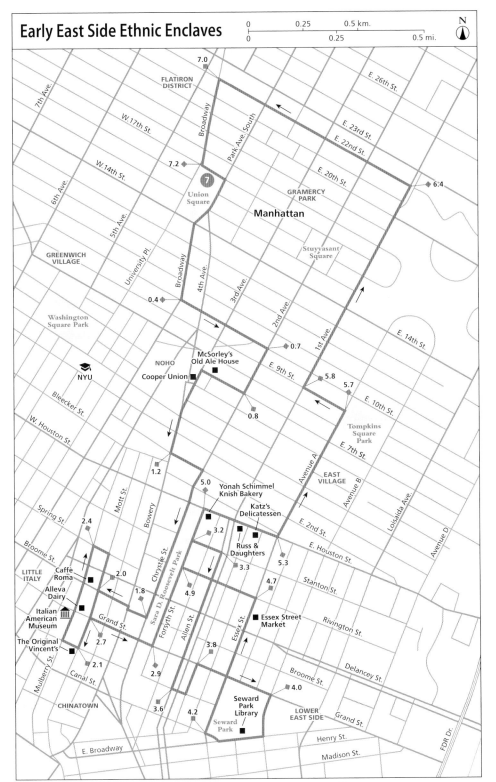

Early East Side Ethnic Enclaves

0   0.25   0.5 km.
0   0.25   0.5 mi.

N

7.0

FLATIRON
DISTRICT

E. 26th St.
E. 23rd St.
E. 22nd St.
E. 20th St.

7.2

⑦
Union
Square

GRAMERCY
PARK

6.4

Manhattan

GREENWICH
VILLAGE

Stuyvesant
Square

0.4

Washington
Square Park

E. 14th St.

0.7

NOHO

McSorley's
Old Ale House

NYU

Cooper Union

E. 9th St.

5.8
5.7

E. 10th St.

Bleecker St.

0.8

W. Houston St.

Tompkins
Square
Park
E. 7th St.

1.2

EAST
VILLAGE

Spring St.

5.0

Yonah Schimmel
Knish Bakery

2.4

Katz's
Delicatessen

E. 2nd St.

Broome St.

3.2

E. Houston St.

LITTLE
ITALY

Caffè
Roma

2.0

Russ &
Daughters

5.3

Alleva
Dairy

1.8

3.3

4.7

Stanton St.

Italian
American
Museum

Grand St.

4.9

The Original
Vincent's

2.7

Essex Street
Market

Rivington St.

2.1

3.8

Canal St.

2.9

Delancey St.

Broome St.

4.0

3.6

4.2

Seward
Park
Library

CHINATOWN

LOWER
EAST SIDE

Grand St.

Seward
Park

E. Broadway

Henry St.

Madison St.

FDR Dr.

McSorley's Old Ale House

One of the bar's claims to fame is that then-Congressman Abraham Lincoln stopped at the watering hole when he came to New York for his infamous Cooper Union speech in 1860. Not much at the saloon has changed since then, with almost all the paraphernalia that lines the walls dating back to at least 1910, when McSorley died at age 87. One difference is that McSorley's today serves women as well as men. The spot was a men-only affair until 1970, when it became illegal to prohibit women from entering. McSorley's maxim had been that it would be impossible for men to drink in peace in the presence of women.

1.4 Cross East Houston Street and continue straight onto Chrystie Street, continuing along the bike lane.

1.8 Turn right onto Broome Street.

2.0 Turn left onto Mott Street.

2.1 Turn right onto Hester Street, followed by a right onto Mulberry Street.

2.4 Turn right onto Spring Street, followed by a right onto Mott Street.

2.7 Turn left onto the bike lane on Grand Street, hugging the southern edge.

2.9 Turn left onto Forsyth Street. A separated bike lane hugs Sara D. Roosevelt Park on your left.

3.2 Turn right onto Stanton Street.

3.3 At Allen Street, cross to the median to catch the separated bike lane going south (right).

3.6 Turn left onto Hester Street, followed by a left onto Orchard Street.

3.8 Turn right onto Grand Street onto the bike lane.

4.0 Turn right onto Clinton Street.

4.1 Turn right onto East Broadway. Veer right after passing the gates to Seward Park Library, hugging the edge of Seward Park on your right.

4.2 Turn right onto Essex Street.

4.7 After passing the Essex Street Market on your right, turn left onto Rivington Street.

4.9 Turn right onto Forsyth Street, where the bike lane hugs the edge of the park.

5.0 Turn right onto East Houston Street. East Houston has heavy traffic so stay alert.

5.3 Turn left onto Avenue A, catching the on-road bike lane along the eastern edge of the road.

5.7 Turn left onto East 9th Street.

5.8 Cross 1st Avenue and then turn right onto the on-road bike lane on 1st Avenue, hugging the west side of the road.

6.4 Turn left onto East 21st Street.

7.0 Cross Broadway to catch the on-road bike lane heading south on Broadway along the western edge of the road.

7.2 Cross East 17th Street to turn left onto the bike path that hugs the northern edge of Union Square.

7.3 Arrive at your starting point.

RIDE INFORMATION

Local Events/Attractions

Alleva Dairy: 188 Grand St.; (212) 226-7990; www.allevadairy.com

Caffe Roma: 385 Broom St.; (212) 226-8413

Essex Street Market: 120 Essex St.; www.essexstreetmarket.com

Katz's Delicatessen: 205 E. Houston St.; (212) 254-2246; katzsdelicatessen.com

McSorley's Old Ale House: 15 E. 7th St.; (212) 473-9148

The Original Vincent's: 119 Mott St.; (212) 226-8133; http://02de1be .netsolhost.com/index.htm

Russ & Daughters: 179 E. Houston St.; (212) 475-4880; www.russanddaughters .com

Yonah Schimmel Knish Bakery: 137 E. Houston St.; (212) 477-2858; knishery .com

Restrooms

Mile 5.7: There are restrooms in the park building in Tompkins Square Park.

Randall's and Wards Islands

This route travels along the East River from the Upper East Side's Carl Schurz Park to Randall's and Wards Islands, where you can explore miles of waterfront bike paths, playing fields, wetlands, and more. The main route then traverses the Queens-bound arm of the RFK Bridge (formerly Triboro)—which affords thrilling views of the city—and returns along Astoria's waterfront through Queens. A shorter version of the route returns directly to Manhattan from Randall's Island. Both versions of this mellow journey afford ample river views.

Start: Carl Schurz Park, where Gracie Square/East 84th Street meets the East River Esplanade

Length: 14.8-mile loop (main route) / 8.7 miles out and back (short option)

Approximate riding time: 2.5 hours (main route): 1.5 hours (short option)

Best bike: Hybrid, road, or mountain bike

Terrain and trail surface: The trail is paved throughout and leads mainly along separated bikeways. It's mostly flat except for the bridges, which ascend and descend slightly.

Traffic and hazards: The short option leads almost entirely along separated greenways, with no traffic. A short stretch on Randall's Island follows an on-road bike lane, but separated bikeways are planned for this spot in the future. The main route leads along on-road bike lanes from the RFK Bridge in Queens through Astoria, where traffic is light along most of the way. Take note that, according to city regulations, you must walk your bike along the RFK Bridge pedestrian platform into Queens.

Things to see: East River Esplanade, Carl Schurz Park, RFK Bridge, Randall's Island, Wards Island, Icahn Stadium, Astoria Park

Maps: *New York City Bike Map*, Randall's Island Park Alliance Map: randalls island.org, Randall's Island Park Map: gardensrandalls.wordpress.com

Getting there: By public transportation: Take the 4, 5, or 6 subway to the 86th Street stop. Bike south on Lexington Avenue 2 blocks to turn left onto East 84th Street. After 5 blocks East 84th Street becomes Gracie Square. Continue straight along the pathway to access the East River Esplanade. GPS coordinates: N40 46.392' / W73 56.672'

THE RIDE

Carl Schurz Park is a little-known gem of a park, with a waterfront esplanade offering splendid views of the East River, the Roosevelt Island Lighthouse, and Randall's and Wards Islands, your destination for this journey. From here, bike northward along the esplanade, skirting Gracie Mansion and multiple well-kept gardens along the way. On your right, you'll pass the mouth of Hell Gate, a narrow tidal strait that separates Astoria, Queens, from Randall's Island. A small greenway bridge up ahead soon leads you across the East River onto Randall's and Wards Islands. Formerly two separate islands, the terrain has been conjoined over the years through a landfill made up of construction debris from Man-

> ### Bike Shop
> **LIC Cycles:** 25-11 Queens Plaza N; (718) 472-4537
> At the foot of the Queensboro Bridge, this full-service bike shop sells everything from road to hybrid to fixed gear to BMX bikes in most major brands.

hattan building projects. The area now serves multiple leisure groups, from after-school programs to city sports leagues, all of whom make ample use of the more than sixty playing fields that dot the islands.

Heading north along the Harlem River Greenway, you'll pass horse stables on your right and the Manhattan Psychiatric Center obscured behind the trees. The greenway then bends right, brushing a marshland on your left, and bringing you to Central Road, where a bike lane leads you northward and from Wards to Randall's Island. After the bus stop, veer right to continue along the bikeway that runs northward underneath (parallel to) Hell Gate Bridge, a century-old railway bridge still in use today. From here, descend to the right to catch the Sunken Meadow Loop, a path that hugs the northeastern edge of the island and circumnavigates the Sunken Meadow ball fields. Go counterclockwise along the loop

Views south across the East River from Randall's Island.

and veer to the waterside pathway as soon as you can. Riker's Island (due east) and Queens (due south) are both visible across the water. And up ahead, as you return westward, the Bronx sits just a few arms' lengths across the water.

A brief spurt on the bikeway beneath Hell Gate Bridge brings you to Central Road once more. Catch the road to go underneath the Bronx-bound arm of the RFK Bridge, where a bikeway picks up on your right alongside Bronx Shore Road. Circle the northwestern corner of the island, currently undergoing revitalization, before heading south under the Manhattan-bound RFK Bridge arm and back toward a more sculpted part of the island. Stick to the waterfront whenever the bikeway splits and enjoy views of the Manhattan skyline and East River shoreline across the water. Check out the Rock Garden at the ferry dock—it combines Eastern and Western rock gardening traditions—and continue toward the Icahn Stadium and wetlands. Dismount your bike and walk it across the wooden boardwalk up ahead, traversing a salt marsh. Then remount your bike on the other side (you're on Wards Island once more) and continue south. After passing the greenway bridge, you'll reach the southwestern corner of the island, where waterside benches make for a lovely breakpoint.

To continue, bike underneath the Queens-bound RFK Bridge arm and descend onto the road (the bikeway ends) and through the parking lot. Here, you can either follow the main route toward Queens or split off to the left to return to the picnic area and Manhattan, retracing your outbound route. To continue to Queens, continue straight at the fork and catch Hell Gate Circle to your left. The pedestrian ramp to the RFK Bridge is on your left up ahead. Dismount and walk your bike across the bridge, scaling four short sets of stairs along the way. The narrow pedestrian platform soars high above the bridge roadway, offering exhilarating views.

When you reach Queens, remount your bike to head to the Astoria waterfront and south toward the Queensboro Bridge. Skirt the edge of Astoria Park, catch the waterfront promenade next to the Astoria Houses playground at 1st Street up ahead, and continue south on the on-road bike lane on Vernon Boulevard. Pass the Socrates Sculpture Park and Rainey Park on your right before reaching Queensbridge Park at the foot of the Queensboro Bridge. Catch the greenway to your left at the southern end of Queensbridge Park, heading east alongside the public housing development on your left. (The bridge will be on your right.) Then grab the bikeway across Queensboro Bridge at Crescent Street, keeping to the right side of the path and staying alert for oncoming bikers. At the end of the bridge, slow down. The bikeway turns sharply right and onto East 60th Street. Head east to access the waterfront esplanade via the ramp up ahead and return to your starting point.

MILES AND DIRECTIONS

0.0 From Gracie Square, bike north along the East River Esplanade, with Carl Schurz Park on your left.

1.1 Access the ramp for the greenway bridge to Randall's Island.

1.4 After descending the bridge, turn left at the roundabout, catching the paved bikeway northward along the water.

2.0 Continue straight through the roundabout.

2.1 Turn left onto Central Road.

2.4 Veer right to continue along Central Road.

Randall's Island Wetlands

There are more than 9 acres of salt and fresh water wetlands on Randall's Island, much of which serves to soak up heavy metals and other pollutants in the surrounding waters, thereby improving the water quality of the East River and Long Island Sound. The park alliance that serves the island collaborates with schools and youth programs to bring local kids into the wetlands and closer to nature.

2.5 After passing the bus station, access the bikeway on your right to continue north, below (parallel to) Hell Gate Bridge.

2.7 Descend from the bikeway to your right at the orange park building to access the Sunken Meadow Loop. Turn right to go counterclockwise along the loop, orbiting the Sunken Meadow ball fields.

3.3 Veer right to access the waterside bikeway, hugging the edge of the water, with the East River on your right, the ball fields on your left.

3.7 Turn left to go south along the bikeway.

3.8 Descend from the bikeway, going northwest on Central Road toward the Bronx-bound RFK Bridge.

3.9 Access the bikeway on your right underneath the bridge. Continue northwest.

4.4 Pass underneath the Manhattan-bound RFK Bridge. Follow the bikeway south along the waterfront, keeping to the waterfront when the path splits.

4.9 Dismount your bike to walk it across the wooden boardwalk across the salt marsh to your right.

5.0 Turn right from the roundabout to continue along the river.

5.9 The benches at the southern tip of the island are a lovely rest spot. To continue, stick to the waterfront when the path forks and follow the path underneath the Queens-bound RFK Bridge.

6.2 When the bikeway ends, descend from the pathway onto the road and bike uphill toward and through the parking lot.

6.5 When the road forks after the parking lot you have two options. You can either follow the main route to Queens via the RFK Bridge or return to Manhattan directly, retracing your outbound route across the greenway bridge. To bypass Queens, veer left at the fork. (Follow the option directions at the end of the main route directions.) To follow the main route to Queens, veer right at the fork.

6.6 When you reach the crossroad just ahead, turn left onto Hell Gate Circle. Follow the road as it veers right.

6.9 Access the pedestrian ramp for the RFK Bridge to your left. Walk your bike across the bridge. (Biking prohibited.)

8.4 At the foot of the stairs at the end of the bridge, turn left onto Hoyt Avenue.

8.7 Turn left onto 21st Street, followed by a right onto Astoria Park South.

9.0 Turn left onto 14th Street.

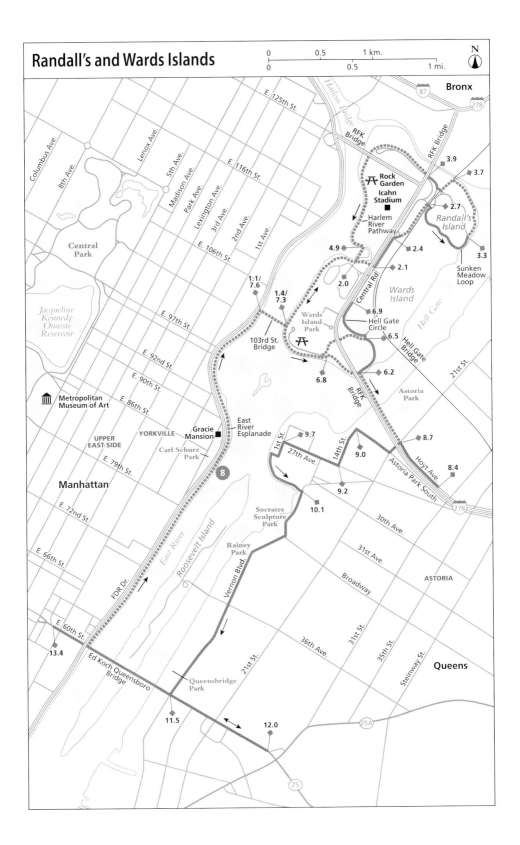

Randall's and Wards Islands

0   0.5   1 km.
0   0.5   1 mi.

N

Bronx

87

278

E. 125th St.

Harlem River

RFK Bridge

RFK Bridge

3.9

3.7

Rock Garden

Icahn Stadium

2.7

Randall's Island

Harlem River Pathway

Lenox Ave.

Columbus Ave.

8th Ave.

5th Ave.

Madison Ave.

Park Ave.

Lexington Ave.

3rd Ave.

2nd Ave.

1st Ave.

E. 116th St.

E. 106th St.

4.9

2.4

2.1

3.3

Sunken Meadow Loop

Central Park

2.0

Central Rd.

Wards Island

Hell Gate

1.1/ 7.6

1.4/ 7.3

Wards Island Park

6.9

Hell Gate Circle

6.5

Hell Gate Bridge

21st St.

Jacqueline Kennedy Onassis Reservoir

E. 97th St.

E. 92nd St.

103rd St. Bridge

6.8

6.2

E. 90th St.

E. 86th St.

Metropolitan Museum of Art

RFK Bridge

Astoria Park

E. 79th St.

YORKVILLE

Gracie Mansion

East River Esplanade

8.7

8.4

278

UPPER EAST SIDE

Carl Schurz Park

9.7

1st St.

27th Ave.

14th St.

9.0

Hoyt Ave.

Astoria Park South

Manhattan

8

E. 72nd St.

9.2

30th Ave.

Socrates Sculpture Park

10.1

E. 66th St.

East River

Roosevelt Island

Rainey Park

31st Ave.

Broadway

ASTORIA

FDR Dr.

Vernon Blvd.

E. 60th St.

13.4

Ed Koch Queensboro Bridge

Queensbridge Park

21st St.

36th Ave.

31st St.

35th St.

Steinway St.

Queens

11.5

12.0

25A

25

9.2   Turn right onto 27th Avenue.

9.7   Turn left onto 1st Street, followed by a right next to the playground to follow the waterfront bike lane. At the waterfront, turn left along the esplanade.

10.1   At the end of the esplanade, turn right onto Vernon Boulevard.

11.5   Queensbridge Park is on your right. At the end of the park (and before passing underneath the Queensboro Bridge), turn left, crossing Vernon Boulevard and accessing the bikeway to the right of the public housing projects. (The bridge is on your right.)

11.8   Cross 21st Street and turn right to cross Queens Plaza North and continue alongside on the bikeway along the south edge of Queens Plaza North (continuing east).

12.0   At Crescent Street, turn sharply right to access the bridge bikeway.

13.3   Slow down as you approach the end of the bridge. The bikeway makes a sharp U-turn to your right.

13.4   Exit the ramp onto East 60th Street, crossing 1st Avenue. Bike toward the water.

13.6   Access the waterfront esplanade via the ramp and bike north along the esplanade. (Push your bike up the ramp when you reach the stairs.)

14.8   Arrive at your starting point.

Short Option: Return Route Bypassing Queens (continuing from mile 6.5)

6.5   Veer left to hug the edge of ball field 70, heading underneath the Queens-bound arm of the RFK Bridge once more.

6.8   Veer left to access the waterfront bikeway at the park building. Turn right onto the bikeway to head west, retracing your outbound route.

7.3   Turn left to access the greenway bridge across the river.

7.6   In Manhattan, head south along the East River Esplanade.

8.7   Arrive at your starting point.

RIDE INFORMATION

Restrooms
Start/end: There are restrooms and water fountains in Carl Schurz Park.
Mile 6.0: There are restrooms at the park building near the picnic spots.
Mile 11.5: There are restrooms and water fountains in Queensbridge Park.

Three Bridges Tour

This East River waterfront tour leads across three bridges, through three boroughs, and visits two East River parks—East River Park in Manhattan and East River State Park in Brooklyn. Most of the journey runs along greenways and bike lanes, including almost 4 miles of car-free bridge biking across the Queensboro, Pulaski, and Manhattan Bridges. The ride is a great option for anyone who enjoys river views and discovering what connects—and distinguishes—some of the boroughs.

Start: Under the Manhattan Bridge, where Pike Street hits the waterfront

Length: 15.3-mile loop

Approximate riding time: 2.5 hours

Best bike: Hybrid, road, or mountain bike

Terrain and trail surface: The trail is paved throughout. The ramps on and off the Manhattan, Queensboro, and Pulaski Bridges ascend and descend. Otherwise the route is flat.

Traffic and hazards: The ride leads along separated waterfront bikeways that are entirely car-free and on-road bike lanes where traffic is mostly light. There's moderate to heavy traffic along the on-road portion from the East River waterfront to the entry to the Queensboro Bridge. Stay especially alert here.

Things to see: East River Park, United Nations, Queensboro Bridge, Pulaski Bridge, East River State Park, Brooklyn Navy Yard, Building 92, Manhattan Bridge

Map: *New York City Bike Map*

Getting there: By public transportation: Take the F subway to the East Broadway stop. Bike west on East Broadway 1 block. Turn left onto Pike Street to reach the waterfront bikeway. GPS coordinates: N40 42.572' / W73 59.449'

Your starting point affords a unique perspective on Manhattan's southern-most bridges—an eye-level view of the Brooklyn Bridge's pillars and the Manhattan Bridge's underbelly—that neatly frame Downtown Brooklyn across the water. From here, head north along the waterfront esplanade, with warehouse depots obscuring your water views a short stretch before you turn to reach the East River Esplanade. Going north, you'll pass a string of ball fields, playgrounds, and sculpted gardens. Across the water you can spot Brooklyn's near-equivalent waterfront hangout, the East River State Park. (You can visit it later.) Continuing northward, you'll go through Stuyvesant Cove Park up ahead and slowly approach the Queensboro Bridge. When you reach the ferry docks, use the traffic signal on your left to traverse the road and go west on East 35th Street. At the end of the block, a bikeway along the west side of 1st Avenue then leads you past the United Nations toward the Queensboro Bridge, which you'll access on the west side of 1st Avenue at East 60th Street.

Bike Shops

Conrad's Bike Shop: 25 Tudor City Place; (212) 697-6966
Founded in the backroom of the owners' former drapery business, this shop provides custom bike fittings, hand-built wheels, vintage parts, and more.
Silk Road Cycles: 76 Franklin St.; (718) 389-2222
The friendly team at this Greenpoint bike shop offer full-service repairs and sell everything from parts to brand-name accessories (D'Emploi, Bern, Giro) and bikes (Raleigh, and more).

Going uphill toward the bridge's midpoint, spot the Roosevelt Island cable car on your left, but stick to the right side of the bikeway, staying out of the way of Manhattan-bound cyclists. After passing Roosevelt Island, the bridge then glides downhill to Queens. Slow down toward the end of the bridge to make a sharp left-hand U-turn at the end of the bikeway toward the waterfront. Vernon Boulevard then leads you south toward Long Island City, where cafes and diners line the way. The Pulaski Bridge then carries you across Newtown Creek, an East River estuary that separates Queens from Brooklyn here. Slow down as you approach the end of the bridge in Greenpoint as the bikeway spills directly onto the street.

Franklin Street then takes you through Greenpoint, past an amalgam of Eastern European eateries, secondhand stores, trendy boutiques, and hipster cafes. As Franklin Street becomes Kent Avenue, you're entering Williamsburg. To check out East River State Park on your right, dismount and walk your bike.

Biking north along the East River Park esplanade, with the Williamsburg Bridge in the distance.

(Biking is prohibited.) The site was a shipping dock in the nineteenth century, and certain remnants remain—the cobblestone road, the railroad tracks—making for a slightly rugged park experience. To proceed en route, remount your bike and continue south, heading underneath the Williamsburg Bridge. The terrain soon becomes more industrial here as you head toward the Brooklyn Navy Yard. A separated greenway, though, allows for a lovely car-free, uninterrupted ride southward.

Up ahead, stay alert for oncoming cyclists as you approach the Brooklyn-Queens Expressway. The bikeway narrows and veers right, with a cement partition on your left between you and the road. Flushing Avenue then takes you past Building 92, a visitor center and exhibit space that sheds light on the Brooklyn Navy Yard's development from past to present. Stop off for a visit or continue west to the Manhattan Bridge. Use the bike-pedestrian crossings (and signals) to access the bridge ramp, which loops around, going uphill and across the East River. Stick to the right along the bridge bikeway and slow down as you near its end. The bikeway veers sharply right and descends onto Canal Street, which brings you back to your starting point via Pike Street.

MILES AND DIRECTIONS

0.0 Bike north along the water.

0.7 Before entering the gate to East River Park, turn right and down to the water's edge. Follow the waterfront esplanade north.

2.8 Veer slightly left to continue along the bikeway, with the Water Club on your right. Then veer right to continue along the water.

3.5 Turn left onto East 35th Street.

3.6 Cross 1st Avenue and turn right, going north along 1st Avenue's bikeway.

4.7 Turn right onto East 54th Street, followed by a left onto Sutton Place.

5.1 Turn left onto East 59th Street, followed by a right onto 1st Avenue.

5.3 At East 60th Street, access the bikeway to your left to cross the Queensboro Bridge.

6.7 At the end of the bridge ramp, make a U-turn, following the greenway to your left (heading west).

7.0 Cross 21st Street and catch the greenway on the other side, next to the public housing development.

7.3 Turn left onto Vernon Boulevard.

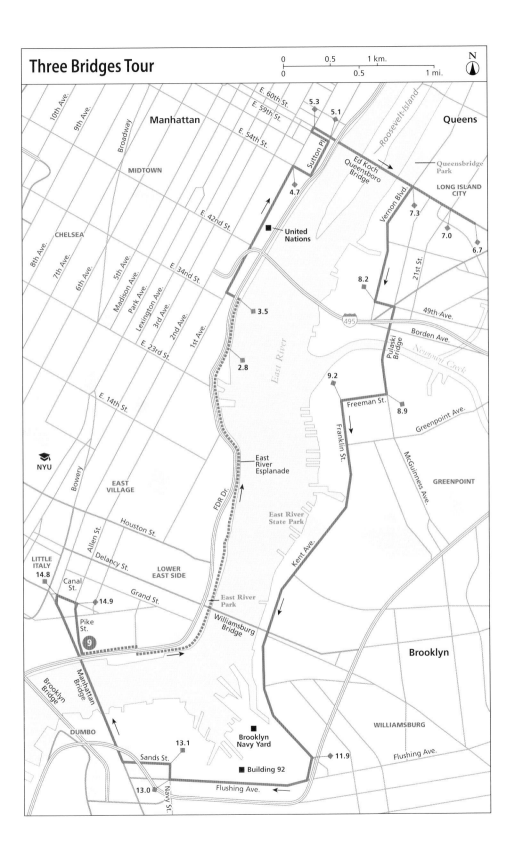

Three Bridges Tour

0   0.5   1 km.

0   0.5   1 mi.

N

Manhattan

10th Ave.

9th Ave.

Broadway

MIDTOWN

E. 60th St.

E. 59th St.

E. 54th St.

E. 42nd St.

CHELSEA

8th Ave.

7th Ave.

6th Ave.

5th Ave.

Madison Ave.

Park Ave.

Lexington Ave.

3rd Ave.

2nd Ave.

1st Ave.

E. 34th St.

E. 23rd St.

E. 14th St.

5.3

5.1

Sutton Pl.

4.7

United Nations

3.5

2.8

Queens

Roosevelt Island

Ed Koch Queensboro Bridge

Queensbridge Park

LONG ISLAND CITY

Vernon Blvd.

7.3

7.0

6.7

21st St.

8.2

49th Ave.

Borden Ave.

495

East River

Pulaski Bridge

Newtown Creek

9.2

Freeman St.

8.9

Greenpoint Ave.

Franklin St.

McGuinness Ave.

GREENPOINT

NYU

Bowery

EAST VILLAGE

Houston St.

Allen St.

Delancy St.

LITTLE ITALY

14.8

Canal St.

14.9

Grand St.

Pike St.

9

Brooklyn Bridge

Manhattan Bridge

DUMBO

FDR Dr.

East River Esplanade

East River State Park

LOWER EAST SIDE

East River Park

Williamsburg Bridge

Kent Ave.

Brooklyn

WILLIAMSBURG

Flushing Ave.

13.1

Sands St.

Navy St.

13.0

Brooklyn Navy Yard

Building 92

11.9

Flushing Ave.

TD Five Boro Bike Tour

Founded in 1977 by a New York City schoolteacher and called Five Boro Challenge at the time, the Five Boro Bike Tour began as a bicycle safety program. Eric Prager had been commissioned by the city's department of education to develop a program that would help young people acquire safe cycling practices. The program he designed included cycling clinics and repair workshops, and culminated in a city day trip around the five boroughs during which students could put their newly acquired skills into practice. The ride was unique in that most other organized recreational rides at the time led into the countryside, not the city. About 200 bike club members and 50 to 60 students participated in that first ride, which covered 50 miles and was free. There were rest stops, too, with hot dogs and soda at one.

Since then, the ride has expanded considerably, with 32,000 riders participating in a given year and 2,000 volunteers guaranteeing a smooth run. Other things have changed, too. The route is now 40 miles and entirely closed to traffic, with rest stops serving more nutritious snacks along the way. All registrants must now also pay a required charitable donation as entry fee. The route begins in Lower Manhattan, and then goes north to Central Park, historic Harlem, and the Bronx. From there, it goes southward along the FDR Drive before traversing the East River into Queens and then Brooklyn. It then goes along the BQE before crossing onto Staten Island via the Verrazano-Narrow Bridge otherwise inaccessible to cyclists.

The ride today is coproduced by the bike advocacy group Bike New York. Check their ride website for registration and other details (www.bikenewyork.org/ride/five-boro-bike-tour).

8.2 Turn left onto 49th Avenue and access the Pulaski Bridge at the end of the block.

8.9 Slow down as you approach the end of the bridge. The bikeway spills onto the road. At the end of the block, turn right onto Freeman Street.

9.2 Turn left onto Franklin Street. Franklin Street becomes Kent Avenue.

11.9 Follow the bikeway, veering right onto Flushing Avenue.

13.0 Turn right onto Navy Street.

13.1 Turn left onto Sands Street. Access the bikeway along the median.

13.4 To access the Manhattan Bridge bikeway, cross the road straight ahead at the traffic signal. Then use the traffic signal to cross the road to your left and access the bikeway to your left. It then loops to the right and uphill across the water.

14.8 Exit the bridge ramp, turning right onto Canal Street to go east.

14.9 Cross Allen Street to turn right onto the greenway along the median. Allen Street becomes Pike Street.

15.3 Arrive at your starting point.

RIDE INFORMATION

Local Events/Attractions
Bldg 92: A Navy Yard visitor center and exhibition space. 863 Flushing Ave., Brooklyn; (718) 907-5992; bldg92.org

East River Park: A narrow swath of city-owned park space with an amphitheater, bike paths, playgrounds, sports fields, gardens, and more alongside the East River in Manhattan. www.nycgovparks.org/parks/eastriverpark

East River State Park: A 7-acre state park of historical, environmental, and recreational import, opened in 2007. 90 Kent Ave., Brooklyn; nysparks.com/parks/155

Restrooms
Mile 1.8: There are restrooms in East River Park in the park building.

Mile 7.3: There are restrooms and water fountains in Queensbridge Park to your right when you reach Vernon Boulevard in Queens.

10

Governors Island

This tranquil ride on car-free Governors Island takes you past historic forts, nineteenth-century buildings, arts enclaves, and sprawling lawns that offer a welcome respite from the hectic nature of city life. A half-day on the island will carry you back to the nineteenth century, when most of the redbrick buildings here served as officer housing units. Bring food, water, and a picnic blanket, and enjoy some time away from urban life. It's a great ride for families, too.

Start: Soissons Dock, where ferries arrive from Manhattan

Length: 4.0-mile loop

Approximate riding time: 1.5 hours

Best bike: Road, hybrid, or mountain bike

Terrain and trail surface: The roads are paved except for a short stretch of cobblestones at the end of Barry Road.

Traffic and hazards: Governors Island is entirely car-free. Try to get here early in the day, when pedestrian and bike traffic is lightest.

Things to see: Castle Williams, Fort Jay, Parade Ground, Governors Island, Liggett Hall, Colonel's Row, Chapel of Saint Cornelius

Maps: *New York City Bike Map,* Governors Island Map: www.govisland .com/downloads/pdf/map.pdf

Getting there: By public transportation: From Manhattan, take the free ferry from the Battery Maritime Building at South and Whitehall Streets in Lower Manhattan. From Brooklyn, take the free ferry from Pier 6 in Brooklyn Bridge Park. Then, if coming from Brooklyn, once you reach the island, bike northwest along the water about 0.2 mile to get to the starting point. Take note that ferries operate during summer months only. GPS coordinates: N40 41.549' / W74 00.932'

THE RIDE

Governors Island is a 22-acre car-free national park site with sprawling lawns and historic forts that protected New York's harbor over two centuries ago. During summer months the island hosts performances, traditional crafts workshops like glass blowing, outdoor installations, and more. (The month I visited, a quirky miniature golf course served both as interactive art installation and recreational site.)

This route first leads you past major historical sites along internal park roads and then circumnavigates the island along its perimeter. From the ferry dock, go uphill to Andes Road, where Fort Jay sits on the grassy knoll straight ahead. Leave the fort behind you for now to turn right and bike toward Castle Williams along Andes Road. This red sandstone bastion was built in the early nineteenth century, but had ceased its defensive duties by the 1830s. It was later used as a military prison for almost seventy years and served as a community center with a photo lab, scouts headquarters, art studios, and more. Enter the castle through the main passageway to check out the exhibits or join one of the park rangers on a guided tour to the roof for sweeping views of the waters below.

To continue, exit the castle and turn left, going down to the water. Skirt the castle's outer wall to Colonel's Row via Clayton Road. The redbrick buildings that line this allée were built in the late nineteenth to early twentieth centuries to house Army officers and their families. Bike along the tree-lined boulevard, passing Liggett Hall on your right. It once served as a barracks and spans almost the entire width of the island.

At the end of Hay Road, veer left, hugging the southern tip of the Parade Ground, a 12-acre lawn where you'll find kite flyers, arts installations, and sunbathers, among others. Veering left around the green-and-red buoy in front of the small, white-wooded chapel, you'll come face-to-face with Saint Cornelius chapel. This 100-year-old gray stone chapel contains brilliant stained-glass windows. Check it out if you wish and then head north on Nolan Park, alongside a string of yellow buildings. They, too, housed officers and their families in their heyday. Make a U-turn at the end of the road to return to Saint Cornelius chapel, where you'll veer left to head to the waterfront once more and go north. Glance across the water to the Brooklyn Cruise Terminal, where Queen Mary 2 docks when she's in town.

Bike down a short, cobblestone slope toward the Brooklyn ferry landing before turning left to go uphill to Fort Jay once more, sitting at the island's highest point. This star-shaped fort was built in the late eighteenth century, shortly after the British surrendered the island in 1783 to the governor of New York. It was part of a larger-scale attempt to fortify all coastal areas. Enter the

A late-nineteenth-century building along Colonel's Row, originally constructed for Army officers and their families.

fort's main gate to reach the former commons area. Officers and their families lived in the terraced barracks that surround the commons. Explore at your leisure. Then continue en route to Soissons Dock.

The next leg of your journey carries you along the island's perimeter in one sweeping, waterfront loop. From Soissons Dock, bike west past the water taxi beach and down to the waterfront to your right. Heading southwest, you'll have head-on views of Ellis Island, the Statue of Liberty, and the Verrazano-Narrows Bridge. At the southwestern tip of the island, Picnic Point, with sprawling lawns, food stands, and benches, is a lovely spot for a break. When you're ready to continue, head north along the island's east edge, following the waterfront back to Soissons Dock.

MILES AND DIRECTIONS

0.0 Go straight up the hill and turn right onto Andes Road.

0.2 Enter Castle Williams through the archway. To explore or for a guided tour to the top, lock up your bike and do so on foot. To continue, exit the castle, turning left and heading to the water. Turn left at the water.

0.4 Turn left onto Clayton Road and bear left, hugging the exterior wall of Castle Williams.

0.6 Turn right onto Hay Road. Continue southeast onto Clayton Road when Hay Road ends.

Naming an Island

Before the Dutch arrived in the 1620s, the Lenape Indians seasonally used Governors Island as a site for fishing and collecting nuts. They are said to have called the island "Pagganck" (or "Island of Plentiful Nuts") for the copious oak, hickory, and chestnut trees that dot the terrain. Later, when a Dutch government representative purchased the island from the locals in the 1630s, it became known as "Nooten Eylandt" (or "Nut Island"). A few decades later, the British seized New Amsterdam and soon declared that the island ought to be given to "His Majesty's Royal Governors" for personal use. The island thus became known as "The Governor's Island." In time, both the "the" and apostrophe were dropped from the name.

Governors Island

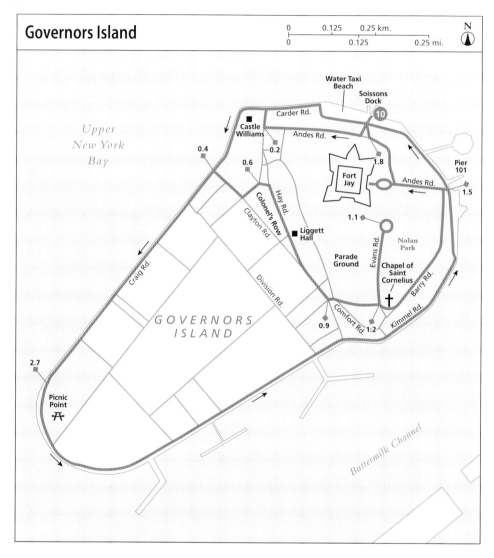

0.9 Veer left onto Comfort Road and continue to veer left onto Barry Road and Evans Road (hugging the southern end of the Parade Ground) to head north past the Chapel of Saint Cornelius.

1.1 When the road ends, make a U-turn to retrace your route along Evans Road toward the chapel.

1.2 Veer left, skirting the edge of the chapel along Evans Road, which becomes Barry Road as it veers farther left (heading northeast).

1.5 After crossing the cobblestones, turn left up Andes Road and enter Fort Jay in front of you. To continue, exit the fort and turn left, continuing north along Andes Road.

1.8 When you get back to the hill next to Soissons Dock, turn right, going downhill. At the bottom, turn left onto Carder Road. Follow Carder Road as it snakes right and left again around the Water Taxi Beach.

2.7 Picnic Point marks the island's southwestern point. Stop for a break if you wish. Then head north along the waterfront, along the island's southeast shore.

4.0 Arrive at your starting point.

RIDE INFORMATION

Local Event/Attraction

Governors Island National Monument is a former defense bastion that is now a national park site. The 22-acre island has 5 miles of car-free bikeways. www.govisland.com; www.nps.gov/gois

Restrooms

Start/end: Restrooms are located in the building that houses the ferry waiting room at Soissons Dock.

Roosevelt Island

Roosevelt Island is one of New York City's best-kept secrets when it comes to stress-free biking. The 147-acre island is circumscribed by a narrow shorefront pathway, shared by cyclists, joggers, and pedestrians. Water views and sweeping city skylines accompany you throughout this leisurely journey that gives a unique perspective on New York City. Southpoint and FDR Four Freedoms Park, at the south end of the 2-mile-long island, are great for exploring on foot and taking a break.

Start: Roosevelt Island Tram Station

Length: 5.3-mile loop

Approximate riding time: 1 hour

Best bike: Hybrid or mountain bike

Terrain and trail surface: The terrain is mostly flat. The route is paved throughout. Most of the route is a smooth-brick promenade.

Traffic and hazards: The first part of this route, circumventing Roosevelt Island via a waterfront esplanade, has no traffic. Yield to pedestrians along the way. The second part of the journey, leading "inland," runs along Main Street, a narrow road with moderate, slow-traveling traffic. (Skip this portion for an entirely car-free journey.)

Things to see: Roosevelt Island, Southpoint Park, Franklin D. Roosevelt Four Freedoms Park, Smallpox Hospital, The Lighthouse

Maps: *New York City Bike Map,* Roosevelt Island Operating Corporation Map: www.rioc.com/pdf/RI_Map.pdf

Getting there: By public transportation: Take the Tramway from East 59th Street and 2nd Avenue to Roosevelt Island. Or take the F subway to the Roosevelt Island station. Then bike south along Main Street 0.2 mile to the tram station. By car: Take the Queensboro Bridge to 21st Street. Go north on 21st Street. Turn left onto 36th Avenue. Continue across the Roosevelt Island Bridge. The Motorgate Garage is on your right on the other side of the bridge. Bike south on Main Street to reach the tram station. GPS coordinates: N40 45.467' / W73 57.268'

THE RIDE

From the tram station, a short stretch of on-road biking on West Road leads you to the access point for the island's waterfront bikeway, opposite the F subway station. Most of the esplanade is narrow and made of smooth bricks, so go slowly and yield to pedestrians along the way. Along the first part of your journey, which orbits the island, you'll be almost at water level most of the time, with the East River gushing close by. The second part then leads inland to explore the island's interior. Just 2 miles long and up to 800 feet wide, you'll cover almost the entire island on this ride.

Cycling north along the western waterfront brings you past a mellow riverfront cafe and gives you views of the Upper East Side shoreline. You'll come upon a boat prow dock that juts over the water and pass ball fields, open lawns, barbecue pits, and residents out for a stroll. You'll then skirt the edge of the Coler Campus, a hospital and rehabilitation center with a slightly desolate feel. In Manhattan, across the water, you'll spot the Upper East Side's Carl Schurz Park before arriving at Lighthouse Park, a handsomely groomed park with the 50-foot Lighthouse at the island's northernmost point. Sunbathers, Frisbee players, fishermen, and other leisurists make good use of the park. From here, glance northward across the water for views of Randall's Island, with the RFK Bridge crossing the east arm of the East River to Astoria, and the Randall's Island footbridge crossing the west arm to Manhattan. Looking east from here, you'll spot the sculptures on display at the Socrates Sculpture Park in Queens.

Continuing en route, you'll go south along the island's eastern waterfront. After passing the Coler Campus once more, turn right onto Main Street, if you wish, to check out one of the island's historical relics, the Octagon. Built in 1839, the domed, octagonal building was the early "Lunatic Asylum." It's now part of a condominium complex surrounded by public gardens and ball fields. Then, return to the eastern waterfront to continue south. You'll pass underneath Roosevelt Island Bridge, the only car-access to the island.

After passing underneath the Queensboro Bridge, you'll soon reach Southpoint Park at the island's southern tip. Dismount your bike to enter the park on foot. (Biking prohibited.) You'll find well-groomed gardens and the island's best-known relic, the ruins of the Smallpox Hospital, in the park. At

Looking north through Lighthouse Park, with Manhattan and Randall's Island across the water. The lighthouse was built mostly through inmate labor in 1872.

its very southern end sits FDR Four Freedoms Park, which pays tribute to the life and work of President Roosevelt. The 4-acre triangular park is framed by waterfront tree-allées on either side, pointing toward a spectacular city skyline in the far. Take a break on one of the waterfront benches before returning to the park entrance, remounting your bike, and going north along the western waterfront bikeway.

When the bikeway ends just south of the Queensboro Bridge, you'll descend onto the road and reach the tram station just ahead. You here have the option of ending your journey or taking Main Street northward to explore the island's interior. Main Street is a narrow two-lane road that often gets congested, so stay alert. As you head north, take note of the white-wooded colonial-style Blackwell House on your right. And just beyond, the historic Chapel of the Good Shepherd, a landmarked church, sits at the heart of a red-brick plaza. You'll then pass the Roosevelt Island Bridge once more. On Saturday, a sizable farmers' market serves the community here. Then, take the first road to the right (after passing the fire station) to return to your starting point along the eastern waterfront. Check out the Roosevelt Island Historical Society's booth on a knoll beside the tram station before heading home.

MILES AND DIRECTIONS

0.0 Go west to catch West Road northward.

0.2 Veer left to access the waterfront esplanade. Yield to pedestrians.

1.3 Circumvent the north end of Lighthouse Park to then go south along the east coast.

Welfare Island

Roosevelt Island was inhabited by Alongquin Indians until the Dutch purchased it in 1637, naming it "Varckens Eylandt" (or "Hog Island"). About three decades later, the British took over and soon bestowed the island to then-sheriff of New York Captain John Manning. When Manning died in 1686, his stepdaughter inherited the island and named it "Blackwell's Island" after her husband. (The Blackwells' son, James, lived in a charming colonial home still standing on Main Street today.) The Blackwells and their descendants owned and farmed the island until the City of New York purchased it in 1828 to serve as a place for hospitals, mental institutions, and prisons.

In 1921 the island was renamed Welfare Island, but as the twentieth century progressed, most of the "welfare" institutes on the island fell into disrepair and became obsolete. One significant relic remains standing, in ruins, at the southern tip of the island—the Smallpox Hospital. Built in the mid-nineteenth century, the institute facilitated a more rigorous quarantine of people suffering from smallpox. Even though a vaccine against smallpox was already in use at this time, the disease was still rampant, with Civil War soldiers and recently arrived immigrants among the most stricken. Today, the hospital's ruins form a picturesquely spooky Gothic tableau.

Another relic from that time stands at the island's northern tip, the Lighthouse. It is made mainly from stone that was quarried through convict labor from the island itself. Inmates from the nearby penitentiary also contributed most of the work for the construction of the 50-foot lighthouse. If you look closely, though, you'll spot a plaque that indicates a different story. "This is the work Was done by John McCarthy," begins the inscription. Local legend has it that one particularly paranoid inmate, John McCarthy, had been allowed to build a fort at the island's northern tip to stave off a much-feared (by him) British invasion. According to the legend, when plans for the lighthouse were put in place, Mr. McCarthy was paid off with fake money and he personally destroyed his fort and built the new lighthouse.

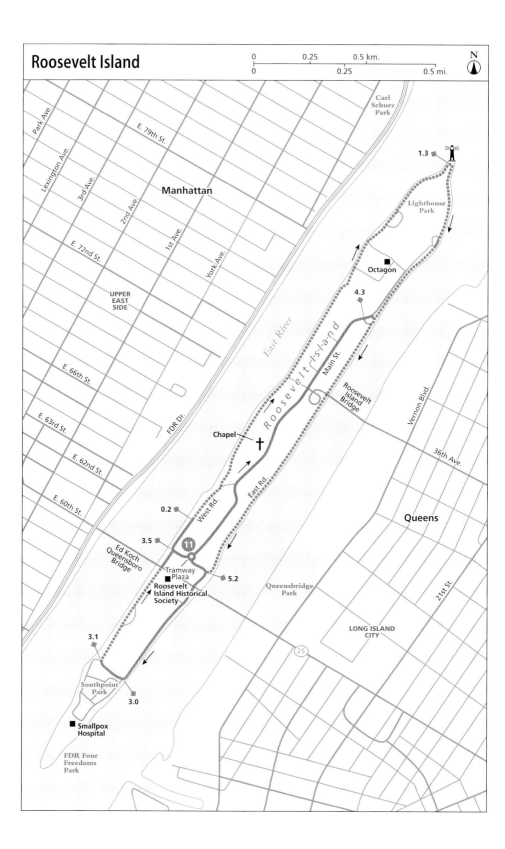

Roosevelt Island

N

0   0.25   0.5 km.
0   0.25   0.5 mi.

Carl
Schurz
Park

1.3

Lighthouse
Park

Manhattan

Park Ave.

Lexington Ave.

3rd Ave.

2nd Ave.

1st Ave.

York Ave.

E. 79th St.

E. 72nd St.

UPPER
EAST
SIDE

E. 66th St.

E. 63rd St.

E. 62nd St.

E. 60th St.

FDR Dr.

East River

R o o s e v e l t   I s l a n d

Octagon

4.3

Main St.

Roosevelt
Island
Bridge

Vernon Blvd.

36th Ave.

Queens

Chapel

West Rd.

East Rd.

0.2

3.5

5.2

Ed Koch
Queensboro
Bridge

Tramway
Plaza

Roosevelt
Island Historical
Society

Queensbridge
Park

21st St.

LONG ISLAND
CITY

25

3.1

Southpoint
Park

3.0

Smallpox
Hospital

FDR Four
Freedoms
Park

1.8 After passing the community garden on your right and the road forks, stay left to continue along the waterfront.

2.4 Stay left of the playground, continuing along the water.

3.0 Follow the pathway as it bends right.

3.1 The entrance to Southpoint Park is on your left. Dismount your bike to explore. Franklin D. Roosevelt Four Freedoms Park can be accessed from the southern end of Southpoint Park. To proceed, return to the entrance of Southpoint Park, and go north along the west waterfront pathway.

3.4 Descend onto the road when the bikeway ends just south of the Queensboro Bridge.

3.5 Turn right onto Tramway Plaza. Either end your journey here, or, to explore the island's interior, turn left onto Main Street up ahead.

4.3 Turn right onto East Road, followed by a right onto the waterfront pathway, going south along the eastern waterfront once more.

5.0 Stay left of the playground.

5.2 After the baseball diamonds, turn right. Dismount your bike and walk it east along Tramway Plaza (one-way).

5.3 Arrive at your starting point.

RIDE INFORMATION

Restrooms
Mile 1.5: There are restrooms at the northeast corner of Lighthouse Park.
Mile 3.1: There are restrooms in Southpoint Park.

Liberty State Park—A Waterfront Tour

This ride travels along riverfront promenades in Manhattan and New Jersey, offering splendid views of the water and the city skyline along the way. It leads to Liberty State Park, south of Jersey City, and returns to Manhattan via tranquil ferry ride. (There's also a return option via PATH train.) The journey can be adapted to suit distinct levels of cycling comfort. The long version of the route crosses the Hudson River from Manhattan via the George Washington Bridge and returns via ferry to the World Financial Center in Lower Manhattan. This option requires some on-road cycling in New Jersey where traffic is moderate to heavy at times, so considerable road-cycling comfort is required. The short version of the route is a leisurely jaunt that ambles almost exclusively along New Jersey's riverfront esplanade and greenways in Liberty State Park. Traffic is scarce to nonexistent on the short version of the route, making it accessible to less experienced cyclists, too.

Start: West Harlem Piers, on the Hudson River at West 125th Street (long option) / Hoboken Transit Terminal in New Jersey, at mile 15.4 in the directions (short option)

Length: 28.7-mile loop (long option) / 20.4 miles one-way (truncated long option, ending in Battery Park City in Lower Manhattan) / 5 miles one-way (short option, from Hoboken to Liberty State Park, ending in Lower Manhattan via ferry)

Approximate riding time: 4 hours (long option); 1.5 hours (short option)

Best bike: Road, hybrid, or mountain bike

Terrain and trail surface: The trail is smoothly paved along most of the route. The riverfront route along New Jersey's waterfront is made of smooth bricks. Part of the riverfront esplanade is a wooden boardwalk. The long version has one steep ascent to reach the George Washington Bridge in Manhattan along the bikeway. It then has one sweeping descent in New Jersey, leading south from the George Washington Bridge along Hudson Terrace and River Road. The short version is flat.

Traffic and hazards: The long version of this route leads along River Road and Port Imperial Boulevard in New Jersey, where traffic is moderate to heavy. Stay alert. Weekend mornings are the best time for finding lighter traffic. Both versions travel along New Jersey's riverfront esplanade, where bikes and pedestrians share the pathway. Go slowly and yield to pedestrians. Also, keep an eye out for Canada geese, who like to populate portions of the esplanade. To get from the riverfront to Liberty State Park, the ride travels along Grand Street, where traffic is light. Check the Liberty Landing Ferry schedule before taking this route to make sure the ferry is running.

Things to see: George Washington Bridge, New Jersey riverfront, Manhattan riverfront, Manhattan skyline, historic Jersey City, Liberty State Park

Maps: *New York City Bike Map,* Liberty State Park map accessible at www .libertystatepark.org

Getting there: By public transportation: Take the A, B, C, or D subway to the 125th Street subway station. Bike west along West 125th Street until you reach the waterfront (long option).

To start in Hoboken, take the PATH train to the Hoboken Transit Terminal. Exit the station to the south (short option). GPS coordinates: N40 49.209' / W73 57.583' (West Harlem Piers, long option); N40 44.127' / W74 01.652' (Hoboken Transit Terminal, short option)

THE RIDE

To commence your journey, head north from the West Harlem Piers through the open fields of Riverbank State Park, with the George Washington Bridge looming large up ahead. A sweeping riverfront journey carries you all the way to the foot of the bridge, where the Little Red Lighthouse sits on an outcropping in the bridge's shadows. From here, a steep uphill climb leads you across the Henry Hudson Parkway and through Washington Heights. You'll then access the George Washington Bridge bikeway from the south, along Cabrini

Bike Shop

Mani's Bicycle Shop: 8 Bennett Ave.; (212) 927-8501
A neighborhood bike shop just a few blocks away from the Manhattan entrance to the George Washington Bridge.

Boulevard. Use your lowest gear to access the narrow, two-way ramp (with hairpin turn). On the bridge itself, keep right and stay alert for oncoming and passing cyclists. Enjoy some of the best views in town from the bridge crossing—the Palisades, the city skyline, and the Hudson River. When you reach New Jersey, you'll be in Fort Lee, where you'll glide downhill, going south toward the entrance to Palisades Interstate Park. This is where your road route begins along River Road, so stay alert. Running parallel to the riverfront, River Road takes you from Fort Lee to Edgewater, where small homes with a waterfront vibe sit next to sprawling strip malls and high-rise condos, giving the area a patchwork feel. Before reaching the Edgewater golf range, turn left onto Archer Road for an optional riverfront side trip that offers respite from the constant hum of traffic along the main road. The riverfront path hugs the rear of the golf range and numerous shopping complexes. With tranquil benches and piers, the esplanade feels miles removed from the humdrum of business on the other side and offers pleasing views of Manhattan's Riverside Church across the river. When the esplanade ends, return to River Road via the parking lot of the City Place shopping area to continue south via the main route.

As you continue south, the steep cliffs of the Palisades tower overhead on your right and the river makes intermittent appearances on your left. When the road forks and River Road becomes Port Imperial Boulevard, traffic tends to increase, so remain alert. After 0.5 mile, turn left onto Riverwalk Place, which leads through a shopping complex to the riverfront. The lookout at the end of Riverwalk Place offers grand views of the George Washington Bridge in the north, the Manhattan skyline across the water, and downtown Jersey City in the south. The riverfront esplanade leads all the way south to Jersey City from here, jutting right and left to follow the contours of the land and passing numerous marinas and recreational spots along the way. (There's an empty lot and shopping complex or two en route, too.) To stay on the riverfront promenade, just hug the river as closely as possible whenever the pathway splits, and yield to pedestrians along the way, especially as you get farther south and foot traffic increases. Take note that the riverfront path was disrupted at a few short spots (about 0.3 mile total) when I last rode it. If this remains the case, you'll follow on-road segments for brief spurts, before returning to the esplanade as soon as possible.

Heading south, you'll soon come to the Port Imperial ferry terminal and then brush up against the backside of handsomely maintained, terraced duplex apartments. Although this is a public esplanade, it feels singularly private. Then, after passing ball fields on your right and veering along a forest of chord grass, the esplanade discontinues for a short stretch. Take the sidewalk to your left along Port Imperial Boulevard before resuming the promenade

Views of Midtown Manhattan from New Jersey at Riverwalk Place.

along Harbor Boulevard just south of here. After passing Lincoln Harbor, you'll circumnavigate Weehawken Cove. On the south side of the cove sits the Hudson Tea Building, a former Lipton tea warehouse that has been transformed into a residential complex. Farther south, after passing Hoboken's 14th Street ferry terminal, cycle around Maxwell Place Park, a ledge of land that pokes out into the Hudson. At Frank Sinatra Drive, the promenade is interrupted for a short stretch again, so take the road southward until you reach Sinatra Park. The park and drive are two of many Hoboken sites named for the famed singer and actor who was born and grew up in a Hoboken apartment not far from here.

Continuing south, a marked bike lane greets you on the esplanade, separating cyclists from walkers. Follow the bike lane past riverfront benches, outdoor cafés, and Pier A Park to reach the Hoboken Transit Terminal. The current transit terminal was built in 1907 and is today a national historic landmark. Dismount your bike, walk through the terminal, and emerge on the other side, where you can hop on your bike once more to continue south on the esplanade. (This is where the short version of this route begins.)

Just south of here at Newport, the esplanade leads inland along Pavonia Avenue and next to the Newport Financial Center, an area bustling with businesspeople and bedecked with sleek office high-rises. A wooden waterfront boardwalk then takes you south alongside more cafes with outdoor seating and riverfront benches. The boardwalk circumnavigates the Harborside Financial Center, a business complex that juts out into the water. On the south side of the complex, you'll reach Exchange Place, the core of Jersey City's financial center. Cycle past the pier and continue south toward the Paulus Hook historic district and 9/11 memorial at Grand Street. The benches along the way here are lovely spots to take a break and watch the river flow by before heading to Liberty State Park.

The last part of your New Jersey journey leads you away from the waterfront to reach Liberty State Park along Grand Street. Along the way, cycle past

Views of Midtown Manhattan from New Jersey near Lincoln Harbor.

a blend of long-standing, low-slung pubs and houses, and shiny new business high-rises. Enter Liberty State Park via the small bridge at the end of Jersey Avenue and explore the park at your leisure. Along with open fields, picnic spots, bikeways, and playgrounds, you'll find the former terminal of New Jersey's Central Railroad, built in 1889, still standing tall along the waterfront. The Statue of Liberty, Ellis Island, and downtown Manhattan all seem within arm's reach from the river promenade, and Jersey City's Colgate Clock decorates the waterscape to the north. Dating back to 1924, the clock marks the site of the former Colgate-Palmolive & Company.

When you've explored enough, catch the ferry at Liberty Landing to return to Manhattan. (Alternately, you could bypass the ferry and instead retrace your route back to the Hoboken Transit Terminal, where you can catch the PATH train back to Manhattan.) The ferry deposits you at the World Financial Center at Battery Park City. From here, either call it quits or return to your starting point via a straight shot north on the Hudson River Greenway.

MILES AND DIRECTIONS

0.0 Head north along the bikeway from the West Harlem Piers.

0.1 Turn right onto West 135th Street, followed by a quick left to continue along the bikeway, running parallel along the Henry Hudson Parkway overhead.

0.7 Follow the bikeway as it veers left and underneath the parkway to continue north along the water.

1.6 Veer right to follow the bikeway.

2.4 Go under the George Washington Bridge to go uphill.

2.5 Cross the wooden railway bridge, duck under the parkway overpass, and turn sharply right, going steeply uphill. The path then makes a sharp left and veers north again. It's steep.

2.8 Use the ramp to cross Henry Hudson Parkway. Go slowly so you can make a quick right upon exiting the ramp.

2.9 Turn left onto West 181st Street, going uphill.

3.1 Turn right onto Fort Washington Avenue.

3.3 Turn right onto West 177th Street.

3.4 Turn right onto Cabrini Boulevard.

3.5 At the end of Cabrini Boulevard, turn left onto the sidewalk to access the ramp for the George Washington Bridge on your left. The sidewalk and ramp are narrow, so go slowly, and the ramp makes a sharp

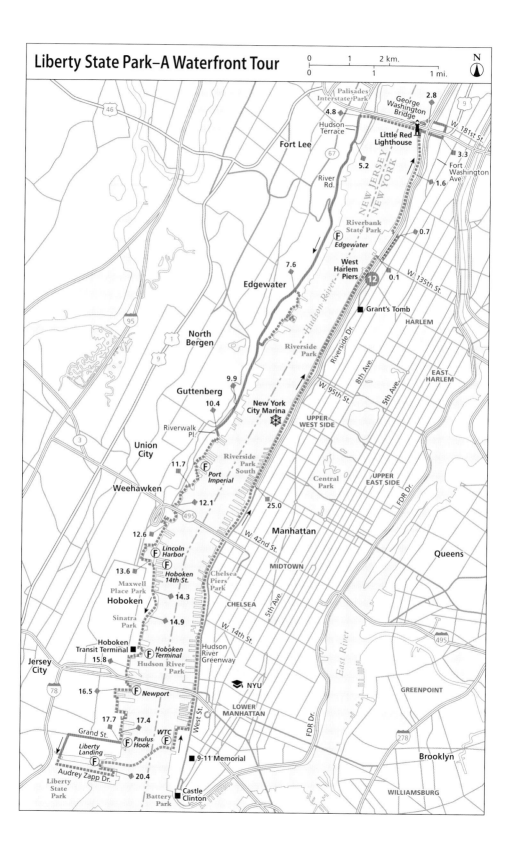

Liberty State Park–A Waterfront Tour

0   1   2 km.
0   1   1 mi.

N

Palisades Interstate Park

George Washington Bridge

2.8

4.8

Hudson Terrace

Little Red Lighthouse

W. 181st St.

Fort Lee

67

3.3

River Rd.

5.2

Fort Washington Ave.

1.6

NEW JERSEY
NEW YORK

0.7

Riverbank State Park

(F) Edgewater

West Harlem Piers

0.1   W. 135th St.

7.6

12

Edgewater

Grant's Tomb

HARLEM

Hudson River

EAST HARLEM

North Bergen

1

9

Riverside Park

Riverside Dr.

W. 95th St.

8th Ave.

5th Ave.

95

9.9

Guttenberg

10.4

New York City Marina

UPPER WEST SIDE

Riverwalk Pl.

Union City

3

11.7

(F) Port Imperial

Riverside Park South

Central Park

UPPER EAST SIDE

FDR Dr.

Weehawken

12.1

25.0

495

12.6

Manhattan

Queens

(F) Lincoln Harbor
(F)

W. 42nd St.

13.6

MIDTOWN

Hoboken 14th St.

Maxwell Place Park

Chelsea Piers Park

14.3

Hoboken

CHELSEA

5th Ave.

14.9

Sinatra Park

W. 14th St.

East River

495

Hoboken Transit Terminal

(F) Hoboken Terminal

Hudson River Greenway

15.8

Hudson River Park

Jersey City

78

16.5

(F) Newport

NYU

GREENPOINT

LOWER MANHATTAN

17.7   17.4

FDR Dr.

Grand St.

WTC (F)

278

(F) Paulus Hook

West St.

Liberty Landing

(F)

Brooklyn

Audrey Zapp Dr.

20.4

9-11 Memorial

Liberty State Park

Battery Park

Castle Clinton

WILLIAMSBURG

hairpin turn, which can be tricky to navigate. As you cross the bridge, stick to the right side of the bike pathway and slow down to circum-navigate the bridge pillars. It's nearly impossible to see oncoming cyclists.

4.8 Go through the gate at the end of the bridge. Then turn left onto the sidewalk on the east side of Hudson Terrace, going downhill along the bike route.

5.2 At the entrance to Palisades Interstate Park, stop to check for oncoming traffic. Then cross to the west side of Hudson Terrace/River Road to continue south along what becomes River Road.

7.6 For a short riverfront side trip, turn left onto Archer Road (option described below). Alternately, and following the subsequent main route description and mileage, continue straight.

9.9 When the road forks, stick to the left arm to continue straight. River Road becomes Port Imperial Boulevard.

10.4 Turn left onto Riverwalk Place.

10.6 At the end of the road, access the circular pavement plaza and take the riverfront promenade heading south to your right.

11.7 Cross Carlyle Court and continue along the riverfront on the other side. Residential buildings will be on your right.

12.1 Veer to the left of the playground and ball field, continuing along the water.

12.5 Turn left to continue along the riverfront route along the road a short stretch.

12.6 Turn left to head down to the water again along the bikeway along Harbor Boulevard.

13.6 Turn left along the waterfront route along 15th Street, to continue toward the water. Follow the route as it veers along the water along Frank Sinatra Drive.

14.1 Follow the waterfront route as it turns left and then right to circum-navigate Maxwell Place Park along the water.

14.3 There's a short interruption in the waterfront greenway, so you have to take the road. Turn left onto Frank Sinatra Drive.

14.6 Access the waterfront route on your left, along the east side of Frank Sinatra Drive.

14.7 Descend from the promenade once more to continue on Frank Sinatra Drive a short stretch.

14.9 Enter Sinatra Park on your left and retake the waterfront route.

15.0 Access the painted bike lane along the waterfront route.

15.4 When you hit the Hoboken Transit Terminal, dismount your bike and walk it through the transit terminal. This is where the short version of the route begins. Exit on the south side to retake the waterfront route, continuing south. Follow the path as it veers along the water's edge, snaking left and right along the contours of the land.

15.8 Follow the route along 14th Street/Park Lane South a short bit to make a quick left, following the waterfront route.

15.9 The waterfront route turns left to go down to the river. When I last took the route, the waterway was interrupted here a short stretch. If that's the case, continue straight to head south on River Road and veer down to the water as soon as you can.

16.3 After passing the Newport ferry terminal, follow the riverfront route to the right.

16.4 Follow the route as it goes inland along Pavonia Avenue 1 block.

16.5 Retake the Hudson riverfront route to your left. Continue south, following the contours of the land along the riverfront route.

17.4 Follow the waterfront route left as it circumnavigates the outcropping.

17.7 When you hit the 9/11 Memorial at Exchange Place, turn right onto Grand Street, heading west and away from the water.

18.6 Turn left onto Jersey Avenue to go south.

18.9 Follow the path across the small bridge.

19.1 Cross Audrey Zapp Drive to turn left onto the bikeway along the south side of the drive, heading toward the waterfront.

20.0 When you reach the waterfront, explore the park at your leisure. When you are ready to continue, go north along the waterfront and follow the bikeway as it turns left to continue west.

20.4 Take the Liberty Landing Ferry across the river to the World Financial Center.

20.4 Back in Manhattan, head north along the waterfront along the edge of Battery Park City.

20.7 Turn right to continue along the waterfront.

20.9 Turn left to take the Hudson River Greenway all the way back to your starting point at the West Harlem Piers.

25.0 Enter Riverside Park South and veer right to continue along the bike-way (not along the water's edge), running directly underneath the Henry Hudson Parkway.

27.0 Continue north along the Cherry Walk.

28.7 Arrive at your starting point at the West Harlem Piers.

Option Archer Road Riverfront

0.0 Turn left onto Archer Road.

0.1 At the end of the road, access the riverfront promenade on your right, hugging the edge of the water.

1.2 Exit the riverfront promenade by descending through the parking lot and taking the road called Promenade.

1.4 Just before hitting River Road at the end of the road, turn left to go through the City Place parking area. (Turning left onto River Road ahead isn't possible.) Veer left through the parking area in front of the hotel.

1.5 Turn right to exit the parking onto City Place.

1.6 Turn left to continue south along River Road. (Add 0.7 mile to your mileage from here southward.)

RIDE INFORMATION

Local Event/Attraction

Liberty State Park is a 1,200-acre oasis of green that is perfect for biking, boating, bird watching, picnicking, crabbing, fishing, and more. You can also join an eco-tour by kayak (pre-registration required), explore the historic railroad terminal of New Jersey's Central Railroad, learn about the site's ecology at the Liberty Science Center, or simply take in the singular views of the city skyline, Ellis Island, and Statue of Liberty across the Hudson.

Restrooms

Mile 2.3: There are restrooms in the park building just south of the George Washington Bridge in the park of the Little Red Lighthouse.

Mile 14.9: There are restrooms in the park building at Frank Sinatra Memorial Park.

Mile 19.8: There are restrooms in the park building at Liberty State Park.

Mile 23.0: There are restrooms on your left at Chelsea Piers at West 22nd Street in Manhattan.

13

A Great Escape—The Palisades

This great escape from New York City begins with a car-free voyage high above the Hudson River along the George Washington Bridge, where superb views extend far north and south. The ride continues in New Jersey on the other side, where a riverside road undulates high and low along the steep cliffs of the Palisades. You can rest at a riverfront picnic spot mid-journey before scaling the Palisades from bottom to top and returning to the George Washington Bridge via Bike Route 9.

Start: Columbia University Medical Center, at West 168th Street and Saint Nicholas Avenue

Length: 21.7-mile loop (partial)

Approximate riding time: 3.5 hours

Best bike: Road or mountain bike (small gears will serve you well)

Terrain and trail surface: The trail is paved throughout. The terrain is very hilly, especially along Henry Hudson Drive (aka River Road) in New Jersey. There are multiple ascents and descents of 100 feet or more and one major ascent of almost 500 feet from the Alpine picnic area to Bike Route 9. The return journey along Bike Route 9 is also hilly, but the hills are less steep.

Traffic and hazards: Crossing the George Washington Bridge, pedestrian and cycling traffic is heavy on weekends. They share a narrow, car-free pathway along the southern edge of the bridge. Go slowly, especially when circumnavigating the bridge pillars where oncoming cyclists are only visible at the last second. In New Jersey, the first half of the route travels along the nearly car-free Henry Hudson Drive where the few cars you do come upon will be traveling slowly. At all times, stay alert, though—there's a steep drop-off down to the river on your right. The second half of the route leads along a designated cycling route, Bike Route 9. Cyclists enjoy a wide shoulder along this road, which has moderate traffic. Comfort cycling alongside motor vehicles is required. (If sharing the road with cars is not for you, you can retrace your outbound journey and return southward via Henry Hudson Drive whence you came.)

Things to see: George Washington Bridge, River Road, Hudson River, Palisades Interstate Park, Bike Route 9

Maps: *New York City Bike Map,* Palisades Interstate Park map accessible for download at www.njpalisades.org/maps.html

Getting there: By public transportation: Take the A, C, or 1 subway to the 168th Street station. Your starting point is at the corner of West 168th Street and Saint Nicholas Avenue, at Columbia University Medical Center. By car: From Midtown take the West Side Highway (NY 9A) north. Take exit 15 onto Riverside Drive South. After about 0.3 mile, turn left onto West 165th Street. The Fort Washington Garage sits just ahead at Fort Washington Avenue, on the south side of the road. To begin your journey, bike north on Fort Washington Avenue 3 blocks, where you'll join the route description at mile 0.2 and continue north on Fort Washington Avenue. GPS coordinates: N40 50.451' / W73 56.363'

THE RIDE

On summer weekends, throngs of cyclists traverse the George Washington Bridge along one of the region's most popular cycling routes, Bike Route 9, and follow it northward up the Hudson Valley. To begin this route, hop on the George Washington Bridge bikeway from Cabrini Boulevard on the south side of the bridge. West 168th Street's southern sidewalk leads onto the bridge via a narrowly winding access ramp with hairpin turn. Use your lowest gear and go slowly as the two-way ramp is tight to navigate. The bridge itself, by contrast, provides an easy, car-free ride with some of the best views in town—the Palisades, the city skyline, and

Bike Shop

Strictly Bicycles: 2347 Hudson Ter., Fort Lee, NJ; (201) 944-7074
This bike shop is conveniently located along one of the region's most popular cycling routes. The shop is chock-full of brand-name bikes and merchandise. On weekends, it's swamped with cyclists stopping off on their journeys north (or south) along Bike Route 9. A small cafe counter has coffee and snacks.

Views south from the George Washington Bridge, with Manhattan on the left and New Jersey on the right.

the Hudson River. Here, too, stay alert for oncoming and passing cyclists. Keep right so they can pass with ease.

The bridge soon brings you to the cliff-top town of Fort Lee, New Jersey, on the other side. You'll here head from high- to low-point of the Palisades within about 0.5 mile. Go downhill along the east sidewalk (and bike route) along Hudson Terrace to enter the gates to Palisades Interstate Park about midway down the hill. Just 0.5 mile wide, the park extends northward about 12 miles, covering 2,500 acres of riverfront cliffs and uplands. Hiking trails crisscross the terrain, and boat basins, picnic spots, and playgrounds dot the park. From the park's entrance gate, Henry Hudson Drive, also known as River Road, takes you down toward the water and north underneath the underbelly of the George Washington Bridge.

The ensuing 8 miles lead you northward via countless hills through the rugged woodlands at the foot of the Palisades. Be prepared for a hilly ride, with several rapid ascents (and descents). From the river shore, the Palisades rise almost 600 feet on your left, forming a sound barrier between you and everyday life above. Enjoy the nearly car-free ride—while keeping an eye on the drop-off to your right—and allow bird song, cricket chirr, and other sounds of nature to take over. You'll pass several lookout points along your journey northward before eventually reaching a riverfront rest area at Alpine. (Be sure to bring your own provisions.) Take a riverside break by the boat basin or picnic grove to refuel.

When you're ready to continue, you have two options. You could exit the picnic area from whence you came and retrace the hilly, tranquil riverfront route all the way back to the George Washington Bridge. Alternately (and if following the subsequent route description), exit the picnic area along the path you entered upon, but then make a hairpin turn to the right at the first fork in the road toward Route 9W. A steep uphill climb of almost 500 feet over the next 1 mile brings you past a Palisades park headquarters on your right. When the road forks up ahead, veer left toward the Palisades Interstate Parkway. Slow down and check for oncoming traffic before crossing the off-ramp from the parkway. Then duck underneath the parkway to catch Route 9W—or Bike Route 9—heading south on the other side.

Biking along Bike Route 9, a designated state cycling route, is a singular experience. The route's broad shoulder makes for an exhilarating cruise along rolling hills that provide occasional glimpses of the river below. Despite this being a Bike Route, however, remain alert. You're sharing the road with motorists. On your journey southward, you're bound to encounter scores of spandex-sporting cyclists—especially on fair-weather weekends. Then, as you head back into Fort Lee near the George Washington Bridge, the town's bike shop, Strictly Bicycles, sits on your right. It's a popular stop-off spot for interstate cyclists looking for a tune-up for bike or self (they have power bars and snacks galore). Check out their offerings if you wish and then return to Manhattan via the George Washington Bridge.

MILES AND DIRECTIONS

0.0 Make your way via pedestrian traffic signals to the north side of West 168th Street. Then bike west along West 168th Street.

0.2 Turn right onto Fort Washington Avenue.

0.7 Turn left onto West 177th Street, followed by a right onto Cabrini Boulevard.

0.8 At the end of Cabrini Boulevard, turn left onto the sidewalk to access the ramp for the George Washington Bridge. The sidewalk and ramp are narrow, so use caution. Once on the bridge, stick to the right side of the bikeway, so oncoming and faster-traveling cyclists can pass on your left. Then, slow down before circumnavigating the bridge pillars, which obscure oncoming cyclists until the last second.

2.1 Go through the gate at the end of the bridge. Then turn left onto the sidewalk on the east side of Hudson Terrace, going downhill along the bike route.

2.5 Turn left through the gate into Palisades Interstate Park. Follow the road as it veers to the left to head north.

3.5 When the road splits, the Ross Dock picnic area is accessible to your right. Keep left to continue en route.

5.0 When the road splits, the Engelwood picnic area and boat basin are accessible to your right. Keep left to continue en route.

5.3 Continue straight toward the Alpine picnic area.

9.7 Veer downhill to the right to reach the Alpine picnic area and boat basin.

10.1 Arrive at the Alpine picnic area. Take a break by the water. To continue en route, retrace the preceding 0.4 mile of your journey to the junction with Henry Hudson Drive. (You here have the option of retracing your entire riverfront route back to the George Washington Bridge. The ensuing route description, however, leads you back to the bridge via Bike Route 9, or Route 9W, which runs along the crest of the Palisades.)

10.5 Make a sharp right turn to go uphill toward Route 9W. The next mile is a steady uphill climb.

11.5 The headquarters of the Palisades Interstate Park is on your right. To continue en route, continue north past the headquarters and then veer left when the road forks. When you hit the off-ramp of the Palisades Interstate Parkway come to a complete stop to check for oncoming traffic. Then duck underneath the parkway to turn left on the other side, to catch Route 9W heading south.

18.0 Look behind you before merging left to turn left onto East Palisades Avenue. Alternately, if merging left makes you nervous, cross East Palisades Avenue. Then stop and swivel left to use the traffic signal to cross the road and head east on East Palisades Avenue.

18.2 Turn right onto Hudson Terrace.

19.0 The bike shop Strictly Bicycles is on your right.

19.6 After passing underneath the George Washington Bridge, stop. Wait for a clearing in the north-southbound traffic and cross to the east side of Hudson Terrace to access the bridge bikeway. Alternately, if crossing Hudson Terrace without a traffic signal makes you nervous, continue to the end of the block, where you can use a traffic signal to cross safely to the other side and then head north along the road's east sidewalk to access the bridge bikeway.

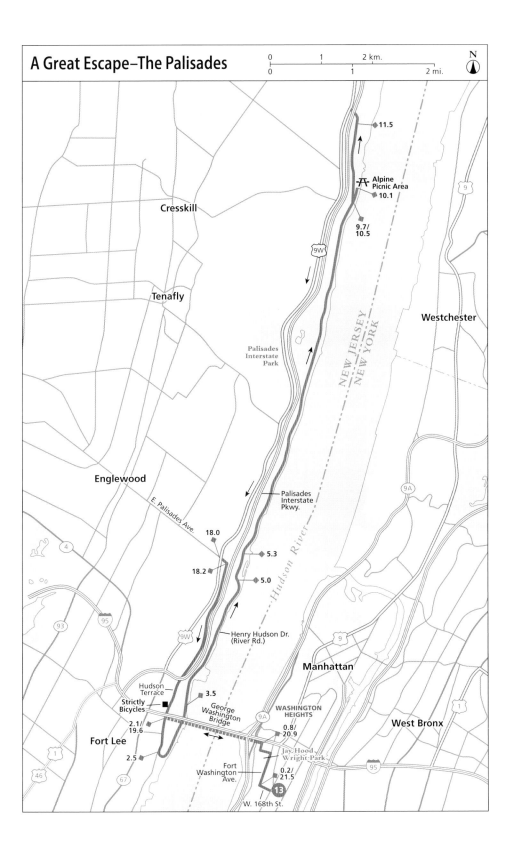

A Great Escape–The Palisades

0   1   2 km.
0   1   2 mi.

N

Cresskill

Tenafly

Englewood

E. Palisades Ave.

Palisades
Interstate
Park

Palisades
Interstate
Pkwy.

NEW JERSEY
NEW YORK

Westchester

9W

9A

Hudson River

Henry Hudson Dr.
(River Rd.)

9W

11.5

Alpine
Picnic Area
10.1

9.7/
10.5

18.0

5.3

18.2

5.0

Hudson
Terrace

Strictly
Bicycles

3.5

George
Washington
Bridge

WASHINGTON
HEIGHTS

9A

0.8/
20.9

Manhattan

West Bronx

2.1/
19.6

Fort Lee

2.5

Fort
Washington
Ave.

Jay Hood
Wright Park

0.2/
21.5

13

W. 168th St.

4

93

95

9W

9

9A

9

95

1

1

46

67

New York State Bike Route 9 and the Palisades

New York State Bike Route 9 is one of few signed bike routes in the Hudson Valley. Along signed bike routes, cyclists and motorists share the road, with signs along the way alerting drivers to cyclists. The routes mostly follow state highways with broad shoulders of at least 4 feet, as is true for Bike Route 9.

Bike Route 9 begins in New York City and travels across the George Washington Bridge to Fort Lee, New Jersey. It then heads north, following the rolling hills of Route 9W through northern New Jersey. The road's broad shoulder runs along the edge of the Palisades, offering views of the Hudson River and New York's shoreline across the water in certain spots along the way. At some points, the Palisades rise more than 600 feet from the waters below, forming a dramatic vertical wall. Early-sixteenth-century explorers are said to have named the cliffs for their resemblance to the forts local Native Americans built using vertical logs, with the word "Palisades" stemming from the Latin word "palus," meaning "stake." In the late nineteenth century, the terrain along the Palisades was being threatened by stone quarries. This brought about the creation of an interstate New York–New Jersey park commission, dedicated to protecting the cliffs. Now, since 1984, the Palisades have been a protected National Natural Landmark. (For more information, visit www.njpalisades.org.)

Farther north, Bike Route 9 reenters New York State and continues north for about 340 miles through Bear Mountain, Poughkeepsie, Hudson, and Albany, culminating near Montreal.

20.9 Slow down to loop to the right along the bike ramp and descend from the bridge. Then turn right along the sidewalk at the end of the ramp. Continue straight off the sidewalk onto West 178th Street.

21.0 Turn right onto Fort Washington Avenue.

21.5 Turn left onto West 168th Street.

21.7 Arrive at your starting point.

RIDE INFORMATION

Restrooms

Mile 0.6/21.1: There are restrooms in the park building in Jay Hood Wright Park on the west side of Fort Washington Avenue at West 175th Street.

Mile 10.1: There are restrooms in the park building at the Alpine picnic area.

Mile 19.0: There are restrooms at the bike shop Strictly Bicycles.

Brooklyn

Views of Manhattan and New Jersey from the 68th Street Pier next to Owl's Head Park (Ride 15).

Measured in terms of new miles of bike lanes, Brooklyn is the bike-friendliest of the five boroughs, receiving 35 percent of all new bike lanes in the city since 2007. As a result, an increasingly diverse cycling community that reaches far beyond the daredevil is thriving in Brooklyn. Dutch style bikers, fixed-gear cyclists, rugged road racers, one-speed cruisers, high-end touring riders—you'll find them all populating the streets alongside one another as you explore distinct Brooklyn communities, glide along miles of waterfront greenways, get to know some of the borough's cultural icons, and visit neighborhoods with deep historical roots.

The Ocean Parkway bikeway stands testament to the borough's more than one-hundred-year commitment to cycling culture. Red Hook builds upon the city's maritime moorings. Central Brooklyn showcases some of the borough's most celebrated Victorian architecture. Coney Island and Sheepshead Bay exude a relaxing beachside vibe. Brooklyn Heights, Cobble Hill, Park Slope, and Fort Greene are marked by some of the nation's most significant literary icons. Whatever your interests, Brooklyn has something to offer.

Bridging Two Boroughs—From Downtown Brooklyn to Downtown Manhattan

This route traverses the East River via its two southernmost bridges and visits the downtown areas of the two boroughs they connect—Manhattan and Brooklyn. You'll pass Brooklyn's Fulton Ferry Landing, one of the borough's most historic spots, where ferries to Manhattan launched in 1642. You'll then cross the East River via its oldest bridge, cycle down some of Manhattan's oldest alleés in downtown Manhattan, and return to downtown Brooklyn via the Manhattan Bridge.

Start: The fountain in front of Brooklyn Borough Hall, at Columbus Park

Length: 13.0-mile loop (11.6-mile loop if you bypass Trinity Church and the 9/11 Memorial)

Approximate riding time: 2 hours

Best bike: Hybrid, road, or mountain bike

Terrain and trail surface: The route is paved throughout except for 4 blocks of cobblestones in South Street Seaport area. The Brooklyn Bridge bikeway is partially made of smooth wooden planks, as is the East River Bikeway at the South Street Seaport. The terrain is mostly flat with slight inclines across both bridges. There's also one steep downhill jaunt from Brooklyn Heights to Fulton Ferry Landing. It then goes gently uphill to Cadman Plaza.

Traffic and hazards: Most of this route leads along on-road bike lanes in downtown Brooklyn or narrowly snaking roads in downtown Manhattan. Although it's a city route with moderate traffic, cars travel slowly. Stay alert as you exit the Brooklyn Bridge in Manhattan and head north. You'll cycle alongside cars exiting the bridge. Along a short optional stretch southward along Broadway and northward along Trinity Place in Manhattan, traffic is heavy. Skip this section if you want to avoid heavy traffic. The route requires city cycling comfort. Keep an eye on parked cars throughout the journey to avoid getting doored.

Things to see: Brooklyn Borough Hall, Cadman Plaza, Brooklyn Heights Promenade, Fulton Ferry Landing, Brooklyn Bridge, Trinity Church, 9/11 Memorial, City Hall Park, South Street Seaport, Stone Street, Manhattan Bridge

Map: *New York City Bike Map*

Getting there: By public transportation: Take the 2, 3, 4, 5, R, or N subway to the Brooklyn Borough Hall station. Columbus Park is on Court Street at Remsen and Montague Streets. GPS coordinates: GPS N40 41.602' / W73 59.433'

THE RIDE

Standing majestically at the south end of Columbus Park, Brooklyn Borough Hall is the borough's oldest public building and has formed the heart of its civic center ever since its completion in 1848. Leave the civic center behind you, heading west through Brooklyn Heights toward the East River. At the end of Montague Street, the neighborhood's main drag, you can access the famed Brooklyn Heights Promenade. It offers some of the best-known views of Manhattan's skyline. To explore, dismount and walk your bike on the promenade. (Biking prohibited.) To continue, head north along Pierrepont Place, which leads to a steep descent toward Fulton Ferry Landing, offering water views

Bike Shops

Adeline Adeline: 147 Reade St., Manhattan; (212) 227-1150
This bike boutique founded by the former graphic designer Julie Hirschfield focuses on style, aesthetics, and function. Fashionable bikes and accessories resemble those found on the roads of Copenhagen, bringing everyday European cycling culture to the New World.
Brooklyn Heights Bike Shoppe: 278 Atlantic Ave., Brooklyn; (718) 625-9633
A full-service neighborhood bike shop on the border of downtown Brooklyn with a more than three-decade-long history. It's a great place to find anachronistic bike parts.
Gotham Bike Shop: 112 W. Broadway, Manhattan; (212) 732-2453
Between Duane and Reade Streets, this full-service bike shop has a big selection of all bike types, high-tech accessories, and clothing, including triathlon gear.

Views from the Brooklyn Bridge bikeway, heading toward Manhattan with the Empire State Building in the distance.

along the way. At the foot of the hill, dismount your bike to explore the landing (biking prohibited) and check out historic Brooklyn scenes depicted along the pier deck. Then return to Old Fulton Street to continue en route.

Slip under the Brooklyn Bridge along Washington Street to reach Cadman Plaza, an expansive park space lined with civic buildings all the way southward to Borough Hall. Pass the state and federal court buildings along the edge of the park, and the Brooklyn War Memorial, a granite-and-limestone structure with two 24-foot-tall victory figures, at its center. Tillary Street then soon brings you downhill to access the Brooklyn Bridge bikeway. Heed the pedestrian traffic signal to access the bikeway.

As you cross the bridge, keep to the right of the painted line (the left side is for pedestrians) and stay alert for pedestrians who might wander across the divider. Be prepared to stop. Take in the views of the Manhattan Bridge and Midtown Manhattan on one side, downtown Manhattan and the Statue of Liberty on the other. Slow down as you approach the end of the bridge. You'll veer right to descend from the bridge at the pedestrian crosswalk. Descend with the pedestrian signal to then head north into Manhattan's civic center along Centre Street, passing Foley Square and numerous colonnaded court buildings.

Having reached the north end of the civic center at White Street, you'll return southward. This soon brings you to the African Burial Ground memorial off Reade Street. Here, for about 100 years beginning in the 1690s, free and enslaved Africans were buried. Continuing south, you'll then reach the west side of City Hall Park, where you have two route options. You can continue south to follow the main route past three defining lower Manhattan landmarks—Saint Paul's Chapel (Manhattan's oldest public building), Trinity Church, and the 9/11 Memorial. It then returns to this spot via Trinity Place. This route has heavy traffic, though. So, to bypass this traffic, turn left through City Hall Park, yielding to pedestrians and skip ahead in the miles.

Either way, after traversing City Hall Park, you'll leave Manhattan's civic center behind for good and enter downtown Manhattan's mazelike historic streets. In the South Street Seaport area at the end of Fulton Street, cobbled roads are lined with restored nineteenth-century buildings that now house clothing stores, bars, and cafes. Bike toward the waterfront, where you'll access the wood-planked East River Bikeway to go south. The seaport's pier deck just ahead, with a pair of restored historic ships moored offshore, is a lovely spot for a waterside break.

To proceed en route, continue south toward the Whitehall Ferry Terminal before heading inland onto Manhattan's oldest streets at Hanover Square. Take note of Stone Street on your left, which dates back to the mid-seventeenth century and feels as though frozen in time. Old-fashioned street lanterns line the pedestrian-only cobblestone road, framed by historic homes and dozens of cafes and bars with outdoor seating. You'll snake northward along William Street from here, and soon pass the 1840s-era former Merchant's Exchange at 55 Wall Street. The diminutive Maiden Lane then returns you to William Street for a last jaunt along narrow Manhattan streets.

Gold Street then brings you to wider roads once more before you'll retake the waterfront route again, this time heading north into Two Bridges, a neighborhood roughly delineated by the Brooklyn and Manhattan Bridges. Access the Manhattan Bridge from Canal Street, where you'll use the traffic signal at Forsyth Street to pick up the bridge bikeway. Stick to the right to avoid Manhattan-bound cyclists as you cross the bridge and check out the Williamsburg and Queensboro Bridges in the distance. As you approach the end of the bridge, slow down. The bikeway loops 360 degrees to the left and deposits you on Jay Street. Use the pedestrian signal to cross Jay Street and turn left, heading toward downtown Brooklyn.

When you spot the Marriott hotel on your right and Starbucks on your left, turn left onto Metrotech Commons, a car-free promenade that leads through downtown Brooklyn's business center. At the end of the commons, you'll enter downtown Brooklyn's main commercial drag on Fulton Street. Farther east you can see Brooklyn's emblematic clock tower. Completed in 1929 as part of the Williamsburgh Savings Bank, it now houses luxury condos. Pass the New York Transit Museum along Schermerhorn Street on your left and then return to Brooklyn Borough Hall.

MILES AND DIRECTIONS

0.0 Descend onto Montague Street, heading west from Columbus Park.

0.5 To access Brooklyn Heights Promenade, dismount your bike and walk onto the promenade. (Biking prohibited.) To proceed en route, bike north on Pierrepont Place, hugging the edge of the playground up ahead to continue onto Columbia Heights.

1.0 Turn left onto Old Fulton Street. Dismount your bike at Fulton Ferry Landing to explore the pier deck. To continue, go uphill (southeast) on Old Fulton Street.

1.2 Turn left onto Front Street.

1.4 Turn right onto Washington Street.

1.8 Turn left onto Tillary Street, using the bikeway along the north side of the road.

1.9 At the bottom of Tillary Street, use the traffic signal to cross the motorist exit road to the Brooklyn Bridge and access the bikeway.

3.4 Slow down and veer right at the end of the Brooklyn Bridge to descend onto the road at the pedestrian crosswalk. (Use the traffic signal to descend with the pedestrians.) Head north on Centre Street.

3.8 Turn left onto White Street, followed by a left onto Lafayette Street.

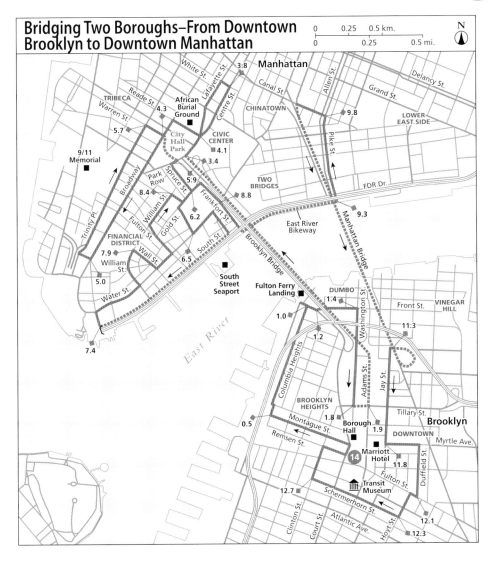

4.1 Turn right onto Reade Street. The African Burial Ground memorial is accessible via a quick right onto Elk Street. The memorial is on your left at Duane Street. Walk your bike back to Reade Street to continue en route.

4.3 At City Hall Park, south of Chambers Street, you have two options. Continue straight, following the main route or, to bypass heavy

Citi Bike NYC: Bike Sharing New York City

In May 2013, New York City launched its first bike share program, the country's largest, with 600 solar-powered docking stations providing access to nearly 6,000 bikes in select city neighborhoods. At the program's inception, all of the stations were located south of Central Park in Manhattan and in designated sections of Brooklyn, with stations particularly ubiquitous in downtown Manhattan. (When the program launched, plans were in place to expand into other parts of the boroughs, too, though.)

There are various ways to use the Citi Bike program. You can purchase an annual membership online ($95), which gives you unlimited access to 45-minute trips throughout the year. Overtime fees are charged for longer rides. Alternately, you can purchase a 24-hour or 7-day pass ($9.95 and $25, respectively) at the touch-screen kiosks of bike docking stations. These passes give you unlimited access to 30-minute rides within the timeframe you purchased, with overtime fees for longer rides.

Citi Bikes are three-speed bikes with step-thru frames that are suitable for a wide range of heights (with adjustable seats). All bikes are also equipped with bell, front- and back-lights, fenders, and a bike rack. The bike sharing program is particularly useful for short rides, but not intended for multihour trips. For longer rides, it is recommended to rent from bike shops (most of which have rentals) or rental companies like Bike and Roll. For more information, up-to-date data on Citi Bike prices, and docking station locations, go to their website (citibikenyc.com).

traffic, turn left through City Hall Park, yielding to pedestrians, and skip to mile 5.9 below. Continue south to follow the main route.

5.0   Turn right onto Morris Street, followed by a right onto Trinity Place.

5.7   Turn right onto Warren Street. After crossing Broadway, enter City Hall Park.

5.9   Exit City Hall Park with a right onto Park Row. Then turn left at the first traffic signal to catch Spruce Street.

6.2   Turn right onto Gold Street, followed by a left onto Fulton Street. Enter the South Street Seaport area at the end of Fulton Street.

6.5   Turn left onto Front Street, followed by a right onto Peck Slip. Cross South Street (underneath FDR Drive) to catch the bikeway next to the water's edge. Turn right to head south along the bikeway.

7.4 When the waterside bikeway hits Whitehall Ferry Terminal, access the bikeway along the south side of Whitehall Street. At the end of Whitehall Street, use the traffic signal to cross to the north side of the street and go east up Water Street.

7.6 At Hanover Square/Old Slip, turn left onto Hanover Square. Historic Stone Street leads to your left just ahead. To continue, follow Hanover Square and veer right onto William Street.

7.9 Turn right onto Wall Street, followed by a left onto Water Street.

8.1 Turn left onto Maiden Lane, followed by a right onto William Street.

8.4 Turn right onto Ann Street, followed by a left onto Gold Street, and a right onto Frankfort Street.

8.8 Cross Pearl Street and access Dover Street on the other side. At the end of Dover Street, cross South Street at the pedestrian crosswalk to access the bikeway by the water's edge, turning left to go north.

9.3 Turn left onto Pike Slip. Use the separated bikeway along the median.

9.8 Turn left onto Canal Street. After crossing Forsyth Street, use the traffic signal to access the Manhattan Bridge bikeway on your left.

11.3 Cross Jay Street and turn left to go south on Jay Street, slightly uphill.

11.8 At Myrtle Avenue at the Marriott hotel, turn left onto Metrotech Commons (next to Starbucks). Bike down the alleé along the right side of Starbucks.

11.9 At the end of the mall at Oratory Place, turn right onto Duffield Street.

12.1 Turn right onto Fulton Street, followed by a quick left onto Hoyt Street.

12.3 Turn right onto Schermerhorn Street.

12.7 Turn right onto Clinton Street.

12.9 Turn right onto Remsen Street.

13.0 Arrive at your starting point.

RIDE INFORMATION

Restrooms

Mile 1.6: There's a comfort station and there are water fountains in Cadman Plaza Park.

Mile 7.3: There are public restrooms and water fountains in the Whitehall Ferry Terminal.

15

Harbor Views

This tour gives you unique perspectives of the city's harbor life—first from afar and then from up close. You'll cycle through the southwest Brooklyn communities of Sunset Park and Bay Ridge to visit two tucked-away neighborhood parks on hills—Owl's Head Park and Sunset Park—each offering unobstructed views of the harbor below. Then bike along 9 miles (out and back) of waterfront greenway, flanking those same New York waters. A shorter route option skips the on-road portion of the ride and begins by the water at Owl's Head Park, making it a great ride for car-averse bikers.

Start: The southwestern exit to Prospect Park at Park Circle (main route)/ Owl's Head Park (short option)

Length: 19.3 miles out and back (main route)/ 9.9 miles out and back (short option)

Approximate riding time: 2.5 hours/1 hour

Best bike: Hybrid, road, or mountain bike

Terrain and trail surface: The trail is paved throughout. To reach the overlooks in Sunset and Owl's Head Parks, you'll walk your bike uphill. (Biking prohibited on park-internal pathways.)

Traffic and hazards: This route leads along on-road bike lanes from Prospect Park to Owl's Head Park along roads with moderate traffic. The shorefront portion (and short option) of the route is entirely car-free.

Things to see: Sunset Park, Owl's Head Park, 69th Street Pier, Verrazano-Narrows Bridge, Green-Wood Cemetery, New York Harbor

Maps: *New York City Bike Map*

Getting there: By public transportation: Take the F or G subway to the Fort Hamilton Parkway stop. Exit the station and go north half a block on Prospect Avenue. Turn right onto Greenwood Avenue and go 3 blocks (about 500 feet). Turn right onto Prospect Park Southwest. Park Circle lies just ahead. GPS coordinates: N40 39.093' / W73 58.309'

THE RIDE

Sunset Park and Owl's Head Park are two out-of-the-way parks that both offer far-reaching views of New York's harbor life and Manhattan's jagged skyline. Bike lanes connect them both to Prospect Park, making them great to reach by bike. From Prospect Park, catch the bike lane along Fort Hamilton Parkway, heading southwest. You'll skirt the edge of Green-Wood Cemetery before turning south toward Sunset Park, known for its striking sunset views. From the park's highest point, you can view New York's waterways below, the city skyline, and Statue of Liberty in the distance, as well as surrounding Brooklyn neighborhoods and Staten Island across the water. To enter the park, dismount and walk your bike up one of the paths to the park's highest point. (Biking prohibited.)

Bike Shop

Arnold's Bicycles: 4220 8th Ave.; (718) 435-8558
An old-fashioned neighborhood bike store with a decades-long history, at 43rd Street.

To resume your journey, continue southwest along 7th Avenue, past restaurants, delis, churches, and stores that show touches of Hispanic and Asian influences. South of 65th Street, you're approaching Bay Ridge and Brooklyn's Chinatown. Stay alert here as the journey takes on several quick turns. Next, you'll reach Owl's Head Park, where more views beckon. (The short option starts here.) At the end of 68th Street, catch the bikeway to your right that runs along the park's perimeter. You can then enter the park along Colonial Road on your right. Dismount and walk your bike to the top of the hill to reach Owl's Head overlook (biking prohibited), where you'll find a terrace with benches overlooking the bay.

To continue, journey down to the waterfront by ducking under the parkway overpass at Shore Road. The pier just ahead gives you a ground-level view of the Manhattan and New Jersey skylines northward across the bay and Staten Island due west. From here, a nearly 5-mile shorefront greenway takes you toward the Verrazano-Narrows Bridge and Coney Island. Stick to the marked bikeway along the east side of the greenway; the west side is reserved for walkers, joggers, and skaters. Approaching the bridge, you can spot Fort Wadsworth on Staten Island across the bay. This military bastion helped protect the city for almost two centuries starting in the late eighteenth century.

The greenway ends next to the parking lot of a large shopping mall at Bay Parkway. Turn left to pass the tennis center and then left again to catch the greenway back along Shore Parkway toward the Verrazano-Narrows Bridge (retracing your route). Bike all the way back to the pier at 68th Street, then

Biking underneath the Verrazano-Narrows Bridge along the Shore Parkway Greenway.

turn right under the parkway, and left onto Shore Road to catch Owl's Head Park's greenway once more. After exiting the park at Colonial Road, continue along the bike lane all the way back to your starting point at Prospect Park.

MILES AND DIRECTIONS

0.0 Go counterclockwise around the traffic circle along the bike lane. Cross Prospect Park Southwest and Ocean Parkway before turning right onto the greenway that runs along the right side of Fort Hamilton Parkway. The parkway will be on your left.

0.5 Turn left onto McDonald Avenue, followed by a quick right onto Caton Avenue.

0.6 Turn left onto Dahill Road.

0.7 Turn right onto 12th Avenue.

1.1 Turn right onto 36th Street.

1.2 Turn left onto Fort Hamilton Parkway, followed by a right onto 37th Street, skirting the cemetery.

1.6 Turn left onto 9th Avenue.

1.8 Turn right onto 41st Street.

Harbor Views

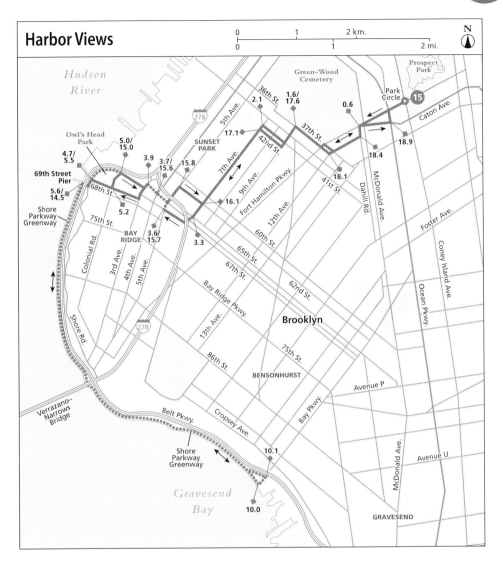

2.1 Turn left onto 7th Avenue.

3.3 Cross 65th Street to veer to the right side of the triangular island.

3.4 Turn right onto 67th Street. The bikeway runs alongside the green space with basketball courts on your left.

3.6 Turn right onto 5th Avenue, followed by a quick left onto 66th Street, continuing along the bike route.

15

Legends of a Name: Owl's Head Park
Few New York City parks have inspired as many namesake legends
as Owl's Head Park. One such legend claims that the terrain at one
time resembled an owl's head. Another states that owls used to call
this area home. Some say there used to be a hotel that sported the
same name on 69th Avenue, or that the entranceway to a nearby
estate was framed by a set of stone owls. The truth, thus far, remains
unknown.

3.7   When the road splits, stick to right and follow the bike route as it
mounts the sidewalk (pedestrian mall). Cross 4th Avenue and continue along the bikeway on the other side.

3.9   Turn left onto 3rd Avenue

4.1   Turn right onto 68th Street.

4.7   Turn right into Owl's Head Park at the end of 68th Street. Circle the
park's perimeter along the greenway.

5.0   Turn right onto Colonial Road.

5.1   To enter the park, dismount and walk your bike. (The short route
begins here.) To reach the overlook, veer right to go uphill along the
path. Descend on the other side and return to Colonial Road, where
you'll turn right.

5.2   Turn right onto 68th Street.

5.5   Cross Shore Road to catch the separated bikeway that veers left.

5.6   Turn right, going under the parkway. Check out the pier. Then head
south on the bikeway toward the Verrazano-Narrows Bridge.

10.0   At the end of the greenway, turn left past the tennis center on Bay
Parkway.

10.1   Turn left onto the bikeway along Shore Parkway, returning west
toward the Verrazano-Narrows Bridge.

14.5   Turn right underneath the overpass, followed by a quick left onto
Shore Road. Cross 68th Street to catch the Owl's Head Park greenway
once more.

15.0   Exit the park, cross Colonial Road, and continue north along Wake-
man Place. (This is where the short version ends.)

15.3 Turn left onto 3rd Avenue, followed by a quick right onto the green-way that mounts the sidewalk (pedestrian mall).

15.6 Follow the greenway as it descends the sidewalk, crossing the street, and mounting the sidewalk on the other side. Continue north with the basketball courts on your right.

15.7 Turn left onto 5th Avenue.

15.8 Turn right onto 62nd Street.

16.1 Turn left onto 7th Avenue.

17.1 Turn right onto 42nd Street.

17.4 Turn left onto 9th Avenue.

17.6 Turn right onto 37th Street.

18.1 Turn left onto 12th Avenue.

18.4 Turn left onto Dahill Road.

18.5 Turn right onto Caton Avenue.

18.9 After crossing the overpass, cross Ocean Parkway. Then swivel left to cross to the north side of Caton Avenue, where you'll catch the greenway on the sidewalk along Ocean Parkway, going north.

19.2 Follow the greenway counterclockwise around Park Circle until you reach Prospect Park.

19.3 Arrive at your starting point.

RIDE INFORMATION

Restrooms

Start/end: There are restrooms at the Tennis House on Parkside Avenue. Go clockwise around the traffic circle and exit to your left onto Parkside Avenue. Go 440 feet and the Tennis House will be on your right.

Mile 4.7/14.5: The park building in Owl's Head Park has restrooms.

Floyd Bennett Field

This route leads you from Brooklyn College via Marine Park to historic Floyd Bennett Field, the city's first municipal airport. Today, the decommissioned airport serves as helicopter base and an array of other purposes—model airplane gliding, nature excursions, and bike racing, to name a few. The wide-open runways and winds from Jamaica Bay make for an exhilarating cycling experience. The ride is adaptable to distinct levels of cycling comfort, with an alternate starting point at Floyd Bennett Field itself, bypassing the road portion of this route.

Start: Brooklyn College, on Bedford Avenue at Campus Avenue / Floyd Bennett Field Ryan Visitor Center, at mile 5.5 in the directions (short option)

Length: 16.4-mile loop (main route) 4.5-mile loop (short option, Floyd Bennett Field only)

Approximate riding time: 2.5 hours (main route) 1 hour (short option)

Best bike: Hybrid, road, or mountain bike

Terrain and trail surface: The trail is paved throughout except, potentially, for a short stretch of greenway at Plumb Beach. In 2009, Hurricane Ida destroyed this bit, and, upon last biking it in 2013, it still hadn't been fixed. If this remains the case, dismount and push your bike through the sand here. The terrain is flat.

Traffic and hazards: The first stretch of the ride leads along on-road bike lanes on city streets with light to moderate traffic. Some city cycling comfort required. Along the Flatbush Avenue bikeway, stay alert for cracked and uneven pavement, as well as crossroads. Come to a complete stop to check for traffic before crossing. The short option is essentially car-free.

Things to see: Brooklyn College, Marine Park Salt Marsh, Floyd Bennett Field, Sheepshead Bay

Maps: *New York City Bike Map,* Floyd Bennett Field Bicycle Map, National Parks Service: www.nps.gov

Getting there: By public transportation: Take the 2 or 5 subway to the Flatbush Avenue/Brooklyn College stop. Go west 1 block on Hillel Place. Turn right onto Campus Road, followed by a left to stay on Campus Road. Turn left onto Bedford Avenue. The college entrance is on your left. By car: Take I-278 W/Brooklyn-Queens Expressway. Exit onto Hamilton Avenue toward Battery Tunnel. Go 1.1 miles. Turn left onto 17th Street. Go 0.3 mile. Turn left onto NY 27 E. Follow NY 27 E onto Prospect Expressway and Ocean Parkway. Go 2.7 miles. Turn left onto Foster Avenue for 1.1 miles. Turn right onto Bedford Avenue. Brooklyn College is just down the block. Turn right onto Campus Avenue and look for parking.

To start at Floyd Bennett Field: Take I-278 W/Belt Parkway to exit 11S for Flatbush Avenue S toward the Rockaways. Follow Flatbush Avenue south to the 4th traffic light (last light before the bridge). Turn left to enter the park. GPS coordinates: N40 37.872' / W73 57.142' (Brooklyn College, main route); N40 35.286' / W73 53.826' (Floyd Bennett Field, short option)

THE RIDE

Brooklyn College is a picturesque starting point for this journey. With a neo-Georgian campus established in 1930, it was recently ranked the nation's "Most Beautiful Campus" by the Princeton Review. From here, Bedford Avenue leads you south through the residential Midwood section of Brooklyn, where one-family homes sit on tree-lined roads. This soon brings you to Marine Park, with 530 acres of marshland, lawns, playing fields, and more. You'll circumnavigate the park along a greenway, heading southeast alongside ball fields on your left. For sweeping views

> ### Bike Shop
> **Ride Bikes Pro Gear:** 4176 Bedford Ave.; (347) 492-6200
> Edward, the no-nonsense owner of this neighborhood bike shop, says he does "a little bit of everything." Known for impeccable tune-ups, he has a loyal clientele.

of the Marine Park Salt Marsh, enter the park's nature center, sitting on the south side of Avenue U, and go to the back terrace. Your sightline reaches across the mellow marshlands all the way south to the Marine Parkway-Gil Hodges Memorial Bridge and Rockaway Peninsula.

To continue en route, follow the narrow, paved trail along the edge of the salt marsh eastward. Hug the edge of the marshland, zigzagging right and left, until you reach Flatbush Avenue. Catch the Flatbush Avenue greenway along its west border, going southeastward alongside the Marine Park Golf Course on your right and Mill Basin, an arm of greater Jamaica Bay, on the left side of Flatbush Avenue. Stay alert for cracked pavement, protrusions, and crossroads as you head south. Come to a complete stop before crossing any of the crossroads. When the greenway switches to the east side of Flatbush Avenue, use the pedestrian signal to cross the road. Then continue southward, with the marina on the opposite side of the road. You'll cycle along the west edge of Floyd Bennett Field, brushing up against cord grass and a series of playing fields. This soon brings you to the Ryan Visitor Center, sitting in the

Floyd Bennett Field

Floyd Bennett Field opened as New York City's first municipal airport in 1931 and was named after Floyd Bennett, the pilot who in 1926 was the first person to fly over the North Pole. Within two years, the airport became the country's second busiest. It boasted exceptionally long runways for the time and thus soon began attracting innovative aviators like Wiley Post and Howard Hughes who were out to break records for speed and distance. Wiley Post took off from and landed at Floyd Bennett Field for his record-breaking around-the-world flight in 1933. He circled the globe in just under eight days, thus breaking his own previous record. When he landed at Floyd Bennett Field, thousands of spectators cheered him on. A replica of Wiley's aircraft is on view in Hangar B.

But Floyd Bennett Field's leading role as a commercial airport was short-lived. It closed in 1939, soon after what is now LaGuardia Airport opened. Two years later, the US Navy purchased the airfield, turning it into the country's most-used military airport during World War II.

Much of what you see at Floyd Bennett Field today resembles its 1930s existence. What is now the Ryan Visitor Center used to be the main passenger terminal. After many years of disrepair, the redbrick neo-Georgian building was recently restored to look like it did during its prime. Even the wall panels along the ceiling, depicting steam engines, gliders, sailboats, and other forms of transportation, have been made to look like they did in 1939.

The vastness of the airfield's runways are as appealing to a city cyclist today as they were to pioneering aviators almost a century ago.

The Ryan Visitor Center at Floyd Bennett Field, housed in the 1930s-era airport terminal.

airfield's restored 1930s-era airport terminal. Stop off, if you wish, to check out an interactive display that brings the country's aviation history to life. Then continue southward to enter Floyd Bennett Field via Floyd Bennett Drive (also known as Aviation Road) at the ranger station.

Floyd Bennett Field now offers miles of sweeping runways to cycle along. This route leads through the northern portion of the airfield where you'll pass Hangar B, an aircraft storage spot that now houses restored historic aircrafts. Stop off if you wish. Then, continuing along the runways, the route passes Jamaica Bay's campsite, which gives access to the surrounding waters. At the north end of the runway, Mill Basin Inlet is the starting point of a network of walkable nature trails that afford up-close views of the bay's ecology. From here, you'll go south past a model airplane field and soon head toward the airfield's western edge, next to the Aviator Sports Center and back to the Ryan Visitor Center. Exit the airfield through the parking area to return to the Flatbush greenway.

Heading north along Flatbush Avenue, you'll retrace your route a short spurt and traverse to the west side of Flatbush at the pedestrian crossing once more. When the greenway forks just thereafter, hug the marshland on your left to bend westward. The route here is framed by the Belt Parkway on one side and languid grasslands on the other. Stay alert as you cross the bridge up ahead and the bikeway narrows. On your right you can catch views of Marine Park marshlands once more, while on your left, views reach across Dead Horse Bay to the Rockaways. Fishing and recreational boats often dot the bay. Descending the bridge then brings you to Plumb Beach, where a section of

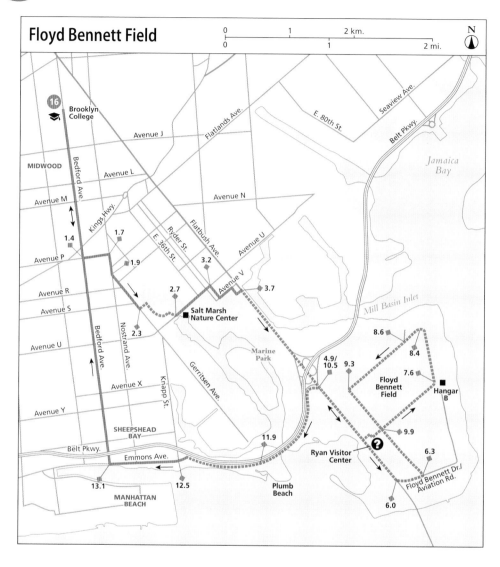

Floyd Bennett Field

MIDWOOD

Brooklyn College

Avenue J

Flatlands Ave.

E. 80th St.

Seaview Ave.

Belt Pkwy.

Jamaica Bay

Avenue L

Avenue M

Bedford Ave.

Kings Hwy.

1.4

1.7

Avenue N

Avenue P

Ryder St.

E. 36th St.

Flatbush Ave.

1.9

3.2

Avenue U

Avenue V

Avenue R

2.7

3.7

Avenue S

Salt Marsh Nature Center

Mill Basin Inlet

8.6

8.4

Bedford Ave.

Nostrand Ave.

2.3

Avenue U

Marine Park

4.9/ 10.5

9.3

7.6

Gerritsen Ave.

Floyd Bennett Field

Hangar B

Avenue X

Knapp St.

Avenue Y

9.9

SHEEPSHEAD BAY

11.9

Ryan Visitor Center

6.3

Belt Pkwy.

Emmons Ave.

13.1

12.5

Plumb Beach

Floyd Bennett Dr./ Aviation Rd.

MANHATTAN BEACH

6.0

bikeway was destroyed in 2009 by Hurricane Ida. Walk your bike through the sand up ahead, continuing westward, until you reach the paved portion of the route once more. Just beyond, the Comfort Inn marks the end of the greenway. Emmons Avenue then leads you through Sheepshead Bay, where yachts are moored offshore and sidewalk cafes, cruise charters, and street vendors line the way, creating a strikingly Mediterranean vibe. Take a bay-side break and then return to Brooklyn College via Bedford Avenue.

0.0   Bike south on Bedford Avenue's on-road bike lane.

1.4   Turn left onto Avenue P.

1.7   Turn right onto Nostrand Avenue.

1.9   Veer left onto Gerritsen Avenue.

2.3   Turn left onto Avenue S and enter Marine Park straight ahead. Turn right onto the bikeway that circles the sports fields.

2.7   Exit the bikeway into the parking lot to your right. Veer right to bike through parking lot towards Avenue U and the water.

2.8   Cross Avenue U to get to the Salt Marsh Nature Center straight ahead.

2.9   To visit the nature center, lock up your bike and explore. To continue en route, follow the narrow, paved trail along the edge of the salt marsh eastward toward Flatbush Avenue.

3.2   After passing the handball courts and playground on your right descend onto Avenue U at East 38th Street to head northeast for 1 block along Avenue U.

3.3   Turn right onto Ryder Street.

3.4   Turn left onto Avenue V.

3.5   Turn right onto Hendrickson Street (no sign).

3.6   Make a quick left, hugging the edge of the marshland.

3.7   Turn right at Flatbush Avenue onto the greenway (on the sidewalk). Stay alert for uneven terrain and cracked pavement. Come to a complete stop before crossing any of the four access roads.

4.9   Use the pedestrian crossing (press the button) to traverse to the east side of Flatbush Avenue. On the other side, turn right to catch the greenway, continuing south.

5.5   (The short route begins here.) The Ryan Visitor Center is on your left. Lock your bike to explore, if you wish. Then continue southward.

6.0   At the traffic light traverse Floyd Bennett Drive (Aviation Road) to turn left along the road toward the ranger station.

6.3   After passing the ranger station, turn left toward the historic part of the field.

6.9   Turn right toward Hangar B.

7.6 Hangar B is in front of you to your right. Lock your bike to explore, if you wish. Then follow the runway northward, with the campsite on your right.

8.4 At Mill Basin Inlet, turn left to go south toward the model airplane field.

8.6 After passing the model airplane field on your left, veer right at the runway crossroads to go southwest.

9.3 Follow the runway as it turns left toward the recreation complex and visitor center.

9.9 Veer right to go through the visitor center parking area and exit Floyd Bennett Field onto the Flatbush Avenue greenway, going north.

10.5 Use the pedestrian crosswalk to cross to the west side of Flatbush. Then turn right (continuing north) and veer quickly left when the path splits to leave Flatbush Avenue behind.

11.9 At Plumb Beach, the bikeway was destroyed in 2009. If this remains the case, descend the bikeway into the parking lot and bike to its northwestern corner. Dismount your bike and push it through the sand, continuing westward about 0.1 mile, where the paved portion picks up again.

12.5 Turn right at the end of the greenway and cross to the north side of Emmons Avenue. Turn left to bike west along Emmons Avenue.

13.1 Turn right onto Bedford Avenue.

16.4 Arrive at your starting point.

RIDE INFORMATION

Local Event/Attraction
Floyd Bennett Field was the city's first municipal airport and now offers miles of former runways to bike along, nature trails to explore Jamaica Bay's wildlife, and exhibits that shed light on the city's aviation history. www.nps.gov/gate/historyculture/floyd-bennett-field.htm

Restrooms
Mile 2.8: Restrooms are in the Salt Marsh Nature Center.
Mile 5.5/10.0: There are restrooms at the Ryan Visitor Center of Floyd Bennett Field.

Brooklyn's Maritime Moorings

This route leads through Brooklyn Bridge Park to the waterfront neighborhood of Red Hook, surrounded by water on three sides. Bustling with longshoremen and dockworkers from the 1850s to 1950s, the neighborhood today maintains a relaxed, maritime vibe. This leisurely ride affords waterfront views, leads along cobblestone roads, brushes past homes and businesses with seaside decor, and abuts Civil War–era warehouses-turned-artist-galleries. It then offers ample opportunity to enjoy the sculpted piers and parks of Brooklyn Bridge Park.

Start: Fulton Ferry Landing, next to the Brooklyn Ice Cream Factory

Length: 7.5-mile loop

Approximate riding time: 1.5 hours

Best bike: Hybrid or mountain bike

Terrain and trail surface: The Brooklyn Bridge Park Greenway is mostly made of brushed gravel. The streets in Red Hook are mostly paved, except Van Dyke and Beard Streets, which are cobbled. The terrain is flat.

Traffic and hazards: Much of this ride travels along a car-free greenway. The on-road portions run along bike lanes on roads with light traffic. The cobblestone streets can be tricky, though not impossible, to navigate with a road bike with slim tires. Wider tires will serve you well. Along Clinton Street, stay alert as you cross Hamilton Avenue underneath the BQE. The bikeway switches from the right to left side of the road.

Things to see: Fulton Ferry Landing, Brooklyn Bridge Park, Valentino Pier, Red Hook, Brooklyn Waterfront Artists Coalition, Waterfront Museum, Empire Fulton Ferry State Park

Maps: *New York City Bike Map,* Brooklyn Bridge Park Interactive Map: brooklynbridgepark.org; Southwest Brooklyn Industrial Development Corp. Red Hook Visitor's Guide: sbidc.org

Getting there: By public transportation: Take the F subway to the York Street stop. Go west on York Street 0.3 mile. Turn left onto Front Street for 0.1 mile. Turn right onto Old Fulton Street. Fulton Ferry Landing is just ahead. Alternately, take the A or C subway to the High Street station. Exit onto Cadman Plaza. Bike north (downhill) along Old Fulton Street to Fulton Ferry Landing. GPS coordinates: N40 42.180' / W73 59.669'

THE RIDE

Having served as a ferry landing site as early as 1642, Fulton Ferry Landing has a centuries-long history. Today, a former fireboat building on the landing houses the popular Brooklyn Ice Cream Factory, and an offshore barge hosts chamber-music concerts. It's also a main gateway to Brooklyn Bridge Park. To begin your journey, catch the Brooklyn Bridge Park Greenway southward, keeping to the left side of the greenway. (The right side is for pedestrians.) This leads alongside the open lawns and sculpted gardens of Pier 1 on your right, with occasional views of the East River just beyond. You'll pass Squibb Park Bridge, a floating pedestrian ramp to Brooklyn Heights and then head past Pier 2, 3, and 4, still under development when last I biked it. Pier 5's Picnic Peninsula and sports fields greet you farther south, as does Pier 6, where the greenway leads alongside beach volleyball courts and the Governors Island ferry launch pad. Hug the edge of the playgrounds on your left to round the bend and exit Brooklyn Bridge Park.

The Columbia Street bikeway up ahead then brings you past an amalgam of old and new establishments—from antiques shops to trendy ethnic restaurants to dimly lit dive bars. On your right, industrial cargo containers line the way, and the city skyline and Lady Liberty are visible in the distance. Imlay Street then takes you past warehouses and artist workshops and the Brooklyn

> ### Bike Shops
>
> **Dog Day Cyclery:** 115 Van Brunt St.; (347) 799-2739
> This small neighborhood bike shop provides full-service repairs, tune-ups, and sells a select selection of bike accessories.
> **Recycle-A-Bicycle:** 35 Pearl St. (between Plymouth Street and John Street); (718) 858-2972
> This Dumbo bike shop is dedicated to sustainable cycling practices. It refurbishes donated bikes (which are for sale) and educates community members through cycling events and classes— youth programs, adult education, and volunteer opportunities abound.

Cruise Terminal. Up ahead, Van Brunt Street, the neighborhood's main drag, is lined with spots that evoke the neighborhood's maritime past—Bait and Tackle, Hope and Anchor, Dry Dock Wine and Spirits. At the end of cobbled Van Dyke Street, you'll reach Valentino Park, where a pier affords unique views of Governors Island, the Statue of Liberty, and the New Jersey shore. The stately redbrick warehouses that abut the park served the shipping industry here in the nineteenth century.

Continuing onward to Pier 41, you'll find Civil War–era warehouses that today house an array of merchants—from Steve's Famous Key Lime Pies (try one—they're famous for a reason) to a glassworks shop. For a visit to the Waterfront Museum, housed on a barge from 1914, lock your bike and head down the narrow Red Hook Waterfront Garden pathway. Then, continuing en route along cobbled Van Dyke and Beard Streets, you'll reach another idiosyncratic waterfront spot at the end of Van Brunt Street. The Brooklyn Waterfront Artists Coalition occupies 25,000 square feet of artist galleries in the Civil War–era warehouses on your left, and a waterfront esplanade to the right leads past an old trolley car to a waterfront cafe (operated by Fairway Market) and sculpted gardens. It's a lovely spot for a break. Dismount and walk your bike to explore. (Biking prohibited.)

To proceed, head eastward toward the hulking Ikea store and turn right onto Erie Basin Park esplanade just before getting there. Bike along this waterfront path, snaking past a water taxi stop, waterside lounge chairs, manicured gardens, and sculpted green spots. You'll then follow the bike route onto Columbia Street, leading toward the Red Hook playing fields on your right. The spot attracts New Yorkers from near and far on summer weekends with an array of street food vendors—El Salvadoran, Columbian, Guatemalan, and more (try some).

Continuing en route, you'll go north on Clinton Street. Use caution as you pass underneath the BQE, where the bike lane swings to the left side of the road. This soon brings you back to the Brooklyn Bridge Greenway, which you'll follow all the way back to Fulton Ferry Landing. Before ending your journey, head north to check out Empire Fulton Ferry Park, just north of the Brooklyn Bridge. In the park you'll find open lawns, waterfront picnic spots, and Jane's Carousel, a historic carousel from 1922 that now lives in a Jean Nouvel–designed glass pavilion. Return to your starting point from here.

MILES AND DIRECTIONS

0.0 Bike south along the Brooklyn Bridge Park Greenway.

0.7 Hug the edge of the playground on your left to follow the greenway as it turns left just ahead.

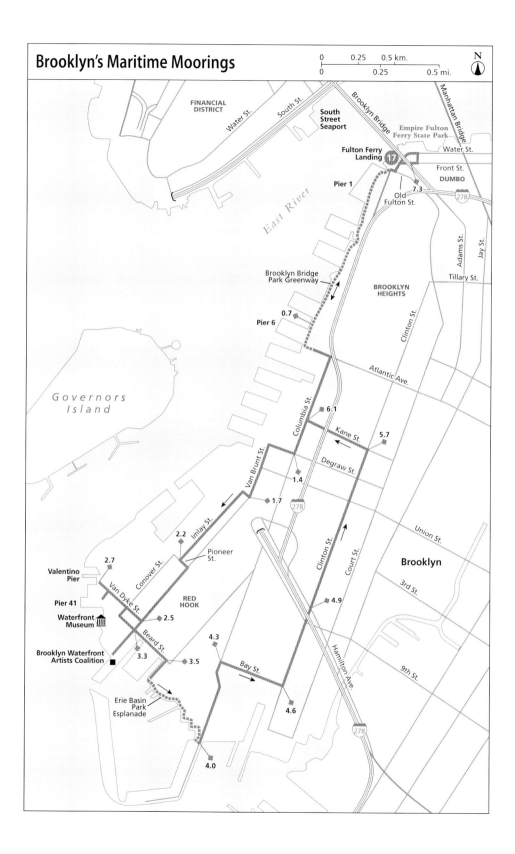

Brooklyn's Maritime Moorings

0   0.25   0.5 km.

0   0.25   0.5 mi.

N

FINANCIAL
DISTRICT

Water St.

South St.

South
Street
Seaport

Brooklyn Bridge

Empire Fulton
Ferry State Park

Manhattan Bridge

Water St.

Fulton Ferry
Landing

17

Front St.

DUMBO

Pier 1

Old
Fulton St.

7.3

278

East River

Adams St.

Jay St.

Tillary St.

Brooklyn Bridge
Park Greenway

BROOKLYN
HEIGHTS

Clinton St.

Pier 6

0.7

Governors
Island

Atlantic Ave.

Columbia St.

6.1

Kane St.

5.7

Van Brunt St.

1.4

Degraw St.

1.7

278

Union St.

Imlay St.

2.2

Pioneer
St.

Clinton St.

Court St.

Brooklyn

3rd St.

2.7

Valentino
Pier

Conover St.

RED
HOOK

4.9

Pier 41

Van Dyke St.

Waterfront
Museum

2.5

Brooklyn Waterfront
Artists Coalition

3.3

Beard St.

3.5

4.3

Bay St.

Hamilton Ave.

9th St.

Erie Basin
Park
Esplanade

4.6

278

4.0

1.4   At Degraw Street, turn right to continue on the bikeway.

1.5   Turn left onto Van Brunt Street.

1.7   Turn right onto Summit Street.

1.8   Turn left onto Imlay Street.

2.2   Turn left onto Pioneer Street, followed by a right onto Van Brunt Street.

2.5   Turn right onto Van Dyke Street.

2.7   Enter Valentino Park to your right and walk your bike onto the pier for bay views. (Biking prohibited.) To continue, exit the park onto Van Dyke Street and return eastward.

2.8   Turn right to access Pier 41 (follow the signs to Steve's Authentic Key Lime Pie). Explore the pier esplanade to the left of Steve's or lock up your bike to visit the Waterfront Museum, via the Waterfront Garden pathway. To continue en route, return to Van Dyke Street, turning right to go east. Make a quick right onto Conover Street.

2.9   Turn left onto Beard Street.

3.0   Turn right onto Van Brunt Street. Enter the pier area straight ahead. Dismount your bike to explore. (Biking prohibited.) To continue, go north on Van Brunt Street.

3.3   Turn right onto Beard Street.

3.5   Turn right before Ikea to access the Erie Basin Park esplanade. Follow the esplanade as it veers left and behind Ikea along the water.

4.0   Exit Erie Basin Park and turn left onto Columbia Street (unmarked).

4.3   Turn right onto Bay Street.

4.6   Turn left onto Clinton Street.

4.9   Cross Hamilton Avenue (underneath the expressway) to continue along Clinton Street. It veers left and immediately right. Use caution and look behind you before following the bike lane from the right to left side of the road.

5.7   Turn left onto Kane Street.

6.1   Cross Columbia Street to mount the bikeway (sidewalk) on the western side of the street. Turn right, heading north along bikeway. Follow the bikeway back to Brooklyn Bridge Park.

7.2   Arriving back at Fulton Ferry Landing, veer right to follow the bikeway onto Old Fulton Street.

7.3 Turn left onto Front Street, followed by a quick left onto Old Dock Street. Enter Empire Fulton Ferry Park. Dismount your bike and explore on foot. To continue, exit the park via Old Dock Street for a quick right onto Water Street.

7.5 Arrive at your starting point.

RIDE INFORMATION

Local Events/Attractions

Brooklyn Waterfront Artists Coalition: 25,000 square feet of artist space in a Civil War–era warehouse. 499 Van Brunt St.; (718) 596-2506; bwac.org

Steve's Authentic Key Lime Pie: One of Red Hook's culinary claims to fame comes in single-serving size or regular pie size. 204 Van Dyke St.; steves authentic.com

Waterfront Museum: Located on a century-old barge, the museum hosts exhibits that help highlight the city's maritime history. 290 Conover St.; (718) 624-4719, ext. 11; www.waterfrontmuseum.org

Restrooms

Start/end: Restrooms are located in the park building next to the start of the Brooklyn Bridge Park Greenway.

Mile 3.1: There are restrooms at Fairway Market at the end of Van Brunt Street.

Literary Lives of Brooklyn

This route runs through iconic Brooklyn historic districts, framed by tree-lined roads and stately brownstones, making it a pleasing ride even if you don't marvel at the (past) presence of the writerly crowd. In Brooklyn Heights, the route passes the former brownstone homes of many a mid-twentieth-century writer. The route then continues into the neighboring communities and historic districts of Cobble Hill, Carroll Gardens, and Park Slope, where Italianate brownstones and tranquil streets now attract innumerable contemporary writers. (For in-depth information on the writers' homes you'll pass along this ride, check out Evan Hughes's informative book, Literary Brooklyn, *which inspired much of this route and can be found at www.literarybrooklyn.com.)*

Start: The fountain in front of Brooklyn Borough Hall, in Columbus Park

Length: 12.8-mile loop (5.7-mile loop, short option, bypassing Carroll Gardens and Park Slope)

Approximate riding time: 2 hours (1 hour, short option)

Best bike: Hybrid or mountain bike

Terrain and trail surface: The trail is paved throughout except for approximately 0.3 mile on Front and York Streets, which are cobbled. There's one steep descent from Columbia Heights to Fulton Ferry Landing and a subtle ascent back to Brooklyn Heights. Then there's one gentle, steady ascent through Park Slope toward Prospect Park. From there it's downhill back to Brooklyn Heights. Otherwise the route is flat.

Traffic and hazards: The route runs mainly along residential streets with light traffic and roads with bike lanes. Streets are mostly narrow, so cars you encounter should be traveling slowly. Old Fulton Street has moderate traffic, but a bike lane along the border gives cyclists ample space. The trek into Carroll Gardens and Park Slope leads mainly along relatively narrow roads. Stay alert of parked cars to avoid getting doored. When you approach Prospect Park at the top of 14th Street, use caution when crossing Prospect Park West (use the traffic signal) as traffic on Prospect Park West travels fast. Also, look both ways before accessing the Prospect Park West bikeway—cyclists ride in both directions. Lastly, Grand Army Plaza is a busy intersection. Follow the bikeway to circumvent the plaza clockwise, using the traffic signals.

Things to see: Brooklyn Heights Promenade, Brooklyn Historical Society, Brooklyn Inn, Plymouth Church, Fulton Ferry Landing, literary landmarks

Maps: *New York City Bike Map,* Literary Brooklyn Map: www .literarybrooklyn.com

Getting there: By public transportation: Take the 2, 3, 4, 5, R, or N subway to the Brooklyn Borough Hall station. GPS coordinates: GPS N40 41.602' / W73 59.433'

THE RIDE

Brooklyn has long lured literary leaders to its shores. It started in the mid-1800s when the poet and journalist Walt Whitman took permanent root in the borough. It then continued into the twentieth century with writers such as Truman Capote, Norman Mailer, and Thomas Wolfe settling here. It persists today with contemporary authors like Paula Fox, Colson Whitehead, Nicole Krauss, and Paul Auster calling it home.

The first community you'll explore is Brooklyn Heights. To do so, head west along Montague Street, the neighborhood's main drag, with boutiques, cafes, and restaurants lining the way. Bike past the playwright Arthur Miller's former dwelling at number 62 before turning left onto Montague Terrace,

Bike Shops

718 Cyclery: 254 3rd Ave.; (347) 457-5760
This bike shop helps you put your own bike together from scratch with parts and components that are truly you.
9th Street Cycles: 375 9th St.; (718) 768-2453
A Felt dealer that will satisfy any of your tune-up, sales, rental, and repair needs just 3 blocks from Prospect Park.
On the Move: 400 7th Ave.; (718) 768-4998
A full-service bike shop that carries a wide range of bike brands (Giant, Raleigh, Haro, and more), and parts and accessories for every taste (BMX, touring, commuting, racing, and more).

a tranquil, tree-lined street parallel to the neighborhood's famed Brooklyn Heights Promenade. Check out the former brownstone home of the poet W. H. Auden at number 1. He lived here after arriving in the United States from Britain in 1939. Just a few houses south, at number 5, the novelist Thomas Wolfe lived a few years before that, in 1933.

Up ahead, Montague Terrace dead-ends at Remsen Street, where you'll have sweeping views of the East River below on your right. Norman Mailer, author of *The Naked and the Dead,* lived at this corner at 20 Remsen St. in the mid-twentieth century. Just a few blocks down, one of his idols—Henry Miller—lived about two decades earlier. Miller, who authored *Tropic of Cancer,* lived at number 91 with his wife June Smith (Mansfield) in the mid-1920s.

Heading north on Hicks Street, you'll then cycle past Plymouth Church, a national historic landmark that has stood here since 1847. The church's first preacher was Henry Ward Beecher, brother of Harriet Beecher Stowe (author of *Uncle Tom's Cabin*). An outspoken opponent of slavery, Beecher's sermons attracted such large crowds from Manhattan (before bridges existed) that the Brooklyn-Manhattan ferry at the time was dubbed Beecher's Ferry.

Continuing on, slither along the narrow alleé of Middagh Street, evoking times gone by with its low-slung brick buildings. At Willow Street, glance down at the Brooklyn-Queens Expressway with the Brooklyn Bridge in the distance. This is where, starting in 1940, the famed literary hot spot February House stood (at number 7 at the time). It housed an ever-changing crowd of literati—Carson McCullers; Richard Wright; Klaus, Thomas, and Erika Mann; and Paul and Jane Bowles among them. The building was razed for the development of the BQE circa 1945.

Tranquil Willow Street then takes you past Truman Capote's former home at number 70. He lived in this yellow-hued building in 1956, shortly before his best-selling novella, *Breakfast at Tiffany's,* came out. While living here, Capote spotted a *New York Times* news blurb about a murdered Kansas family, which famously gave rise to his nonfiction novel, *In Cold Blood.* A few houses south, at number 77, the poet Hart Crane lived while working on his famed long poem, *The Bridge.* Just beyond this, at number 155, Arthur Miller resided (during Capote's time, but their lives barely intersected).

To explore the Brooklyn Heights Promenade at the end of Pierrepont Street, dismount your bike and access the promenade on foot. (Biking is prohibited.) The promenade's sweeping East River and Manhattan views entice New Yorkers and tourists alike.

To continue en route, head north on Columbia Heights. More than any other Brooklyn Heights road, Columbia Heights has attracted innumerable writers over the years, presumably for its grand East River views. Norman Mailer lived at 142 starting in the 1960s; Hart Crane lived just beyond at 130

Looking north from Fulton Ferry Landing, with the Manhattan and Brooklyn Bridges in the background. This was the launch site of the earliest Brooklyn-Manhattan ferry service in 1642.

and 110 after leaving his Willow Street residence in 1929; and Thomas Wolfe resided at 111 and 101, shortly after Hart Crane was here.

Leaving Brooklyn Heights behind, a steep downhill slope takes you to Fulton Ferry Landing, the landing site of the earliest Brooklyn-Manhattan ferry in 1642. To reach the landing, turn left at the foot of the hill and walk your bike (biking prohibited) onto the ferry landing for up-close views of the East River and down-under views of the Brooklyn Bridge. The railing that circumscribes the wood-planked ferry landing is inscribed with Whitman's poem "Crossing Brooklyn Ferry." You can now catch the New York water taxi and enjoy old-fashioned ice cream at the ice cream factory here.

To continue, return to Old Fulton Street and Front Street (where Whitman lived at 120) to head underneath the Brooklyn and Manhattan Bridges for a brief stint along Dumbo's historic cobblestone roads. Today, Dumbo (short for Down Under the Manhattan Bridge Overpass) is an amalgam of former warehouses, artist spaces, tech start-ups, organic eateries, and modish hangouts, making for an eclectic vibe. You'll then return to Brooklyn Heights from here via Old Fulton Street.

The next jaunt heads south from Brooklyn Heights toward neighboring Cobble Hill, Carroll Gardens, and Park Slope. After crossing Atlantic Avenue, keep your eyes peeled for a narrow lane lined with former carriage houses on your left, Verandah Place. The novelist Thomas Wolfe lived here at number 40 in 1931. (You here have the option of bypassing Carroll Gardens and Park Slope, and returning to Brooklyn Borough Hall via Clinton Street. To do so, skip ahead in the route description.) Continuing south on Henry Street brings you into the Cobble Hill historic district, where time-honored brownstones sit on tree-lined streets. Tompkins Place, a short road of row houses, many dating from the nineteenth century, is especially picturesque. The writer Paul Auster lived on this block for some time at number 18.

After crossing Degraw Street, you'll then enter Carroll Gardens, an Italian neighborhood that still boasts innumerable family-owned shops. Turn left onto Carroll Street (Auster lived on this block at number 153 for some time, too) and then hug the edge of Carroll Park, a small but lively neighborhood park with playgrounds, ball courts, and benches—a nice spot for a break.

Continuing en route, after crossing Smith and Hoyt Streets, Carroll Street dips downhill and across the Gowanus Canal along a blue-framed, wooden-planked drawbridge dating to 1889. On the other side, cycle uphill through upscale Park Slope toward Prospect Park. Majestic brownstones, top-rated restaurants, bars, and boutiques frame the road as you head south through the neighborhood's historic district. The writer Pete Hamill has lived at numerous spots at the southern end of the neighborhood. You'll first pass 378 7th Avenue, then 435 13th Street, and lastly 471 14th Street, just a block from Prospect Park. You'll then continue uphill toward Prospect Park and come to a complete stop before crossing Prospect Park West. Use the traffic signal to safely cross this heavily trafficked road and look both ways, checking for cyclists, before accessing the bikeway on the other side to go north along Prospect Park.

At the north end of the park, when you hit Grand Army Plaza, follow the bikeway along the southwestern edge of the plaza until you reach Lincoln Place. Go downhill through Park Slope from here and continue east through Boerum Hill along Bergen Street. (The writers Jonathan Lethem and Paula Fox, among others, have lived on adjacent Dean Street.) Check out the historic Brooklyn Inn, a bar at Hoyt and Bergen Streets that is a longtime favorite among the literati. Then continue along Bergen Street to return to Cobble Hill next to Cobble Hill Park (and Verandah Place). Stop off in the park if you wish before returning to Brooklyn Borough Hall.

MILES AND DIRECTIONS

0.0 Descend from the west side of the plaza at Brooklyn Borough Hall to go west on Montague Street.

0.5 Turn left onto Montague Terrace, followed by a left onto Remsen Street.

0.7 Turn right onto Henry Street, followed by a right onto Joralemon Street.

0.8 Turn right onto Hicks Street.

1.3 Turn left onto Middagh Street, followed by a left onto Willow Street.

1.7 Turn right onto Pierrepont Street. To access the Brooklyn Heights Promenade, dismount your bike at the end of the block to explore on foot. (Biking prohibited.) To continue, go north on Columbia Heights.

2.3 Turn left onto Old Fulton Street. Dismount your bike to access Fulton Ferry Landing. (Biking prohibited.) To continue, return to Old Fulton Street to go southeastward.

2.5 Turn left onto Front Street.

3.1 When Front Street ends, turn right onto Hudson Avenue, followed by a quick right onto York Street.

3.8 Turn left onto Front Street, followed by a left onto Old Fulton Street.

4.0 Turn right onto Henry Street.

4.9 Verandah Place is on your left. To bypass Carroll Gardens and Park Slope, turn left onto Verandah Place, walking your bike alongside Cobble Hill Park to Clinton Street and skip to mile 12.1. Otherwise continue south on Henry Street.

5.2 Turn left onto Degraw Street.

5.3 Turn left onto Tompkins Place, followed by a left onto Kane Street.

5.6 Turn left back onto Henry Street.

6.0 Turn left onto Carroll Street.

6.3 When you hit Smith Street, Carroll Street continues slightly to your right. To continue along Carroll Street, cross Smith Street. Dismount and walk your bike a quarter of a block along the sidewalk to your right to then mount your bike at Carroll Street, turning left to continue on Carroll Street.

6.4 At Hoyt Street, Carroll Street continues slightly to your left. Cross Hoyt Street, walk your bike a quarter of a block to your left to then remount your bike to continue on Carroll Street.

7.3 Turn right onto 6th Avenue.

7.9 Turn left onto 10th Street, followed by a right onto 7th Avenue.

8.2 Turn left onto 14th Street.

8.3 Turn left onto 8th Avenue, followed by a left onto 13th Street.

8.5 Turn left onto 7th Avenue, followed by a left onto 14th Street again.

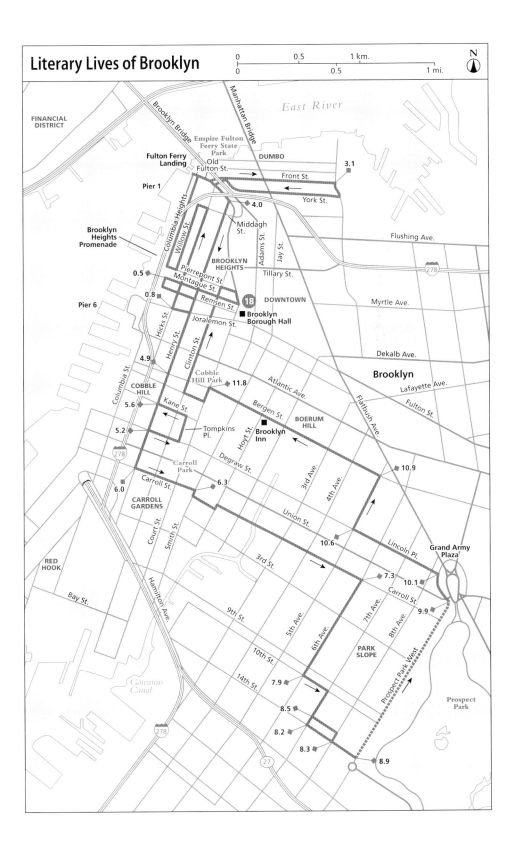

Literary Lives of Brooklyn

N

East River

FINANCIAL DISTRICT

Brooklyn Bridge

Manhattan Bridge

Empire Fulton Ferry State Park

Fulton Ferry Landing

DUMBO

Old Fulton St.

3.1

Pier 1

Front St.

York St.

4.0

Columbia Heights

Willow St.

Middagh St.

Adams St.

Jay St.

Flushing Ave.

Brooklyn Heights Promenade

BROOKLYN HEIGHTS

278

0.5

Pierrepont St.

Montague St.

Tillary St.

0.8

Pier 6

Remsen St.

18

DOWNTOWN

Myrtle Ave.

Hicks St.

Henry St.

Joralemon St.

Brooklyn Borough Hall

Dekalb Ave.

Columbia St.

Clinton St.

4.9

Cobble Hill Park

11.8

Atlantic Ave.

Brooklyn

Lafayette Ave.

COBBLE HILL

5.6

Kane St.

Bergen St.

BOERUM HILL

Flatbush Ave.

Fulton St.

5.2

Tompkins Pl.

Hoyt St.

Brooklyn Inn

278

Carroll Park

Degraw St.

3rd Ave.

4th Ave.

10.9

6.0

Carroll St.

6.3

CARROLL GARDENS

Union St.

10.6

Lincoln Pl.

Grand Army Plaza

RED HOOK

Court St.

Smith St.

3rd St.

Bay St.

Hamilton Ave.

9th St.

5th St.

6th Ave.

7.3

10.1

Carroll St.

9.9

10th St.

7th Ave.

8th Ave.

Prospect Park West

Gowanus Canal

14th St.

7.9

PARK SLOPE

Prospect Park

8.5

8.2

278

8.3

8.9

27

0   0.5   1 km.

0   0.5   1 mi.

8.9 Use the traffic signal to cross Prospect Park West. Look both ways before accessing the separated bikeway that hugs the edge of the park. Turn left along the bikeway to head north along the park.

9.9 When you hit Grand Army Plaza, turn left to continue along the bikeway, crossing Prospect Park West. (Grand Army Plaza will be on your right.) Follow the bikeway as it swerves right, crossing Plaza Street West and then taking the bikeway as it turns left again to continue north along Plaza Street West. (Grand Army Plaza will still be on your right.)

10.1 Turn left onto Lincoln Place.

10.6 Turn right onto 5th Avenue.

10.9 Turn left onto Bergen Street.

11.8 Turn left onto Court Street, followed by a right onto Warren Street.

12.0 Turn right onto Clinton Street.

12.1 Cobble Hill Park is on your left. (This is your pick-up point if you bypassed Park Slope.) Continue north on Clinton Street.

12.6 Turn right onto Pierrepont Street.

12.7 Turn right onto Cadman Plaza.

12.8 Arrive at your starting point.

RIDE INFORMATION

Local Events/Attractions

Brooklyn Heights Promenade: A go-to spot for leisurely ambles and extraordinary views. Popular among tourists and locals alike. www.nyharborparks .org/visit/brhe.html

Brooklyn Historical Society: In a landmark Brooklyn Heights building, a cultural center that connects past to present. 128 Pierrepont St.; (718) 222-4111; www.brooklynhistory.org

Brooklyn Inn: A legendary Brooklyn watering hole. 148 Hoyt St.; (718) 522-2525

Plymouth Church: Established in 1846 with Henry Ward Beecher as its first preacher; popular among the likes of Walt Whitman. 75 Hicks St.; (718) 624-4743; www.plymouthchurch.org

Restrooms

Mile 2.4: There are restrooms at Fulton Ferry Landing.
Mile 9.3: There are restrooms at Harmony Playground in Prospect Park, at 9th Street.

Williamsburg and Greenpoint

This ride journeys through the two northwest Brooklyn neighborhoods of Williamsburg and Greenpoint, where an array of cultures vie for space. You'll bike through the heart of Williamsburg, where hipster culture reigns supreme, and traverse the Williamsburg Bridge for a bird's-eye view of the neighborhood. You'll then cycle southward through the Hasidic enclave of South Williamsburg before heading into Greenpoint farther north. Also known as Little Poland, the community's Eastern European roots are evident on almost every block. Grab some local delicacies as you bike through the neighborhood's historic district and relax at the end of the ride in McCarren Park.

Start: The southwest edge of McCarren Park at Driggs Avenue, next to the domed cathedral

Length: 16.3-mile loop

Approximate riding time: 2.5 hours

Best bike: Hybrid, road, or mountain bike

Terrain and trail surface: The trail is paved throughout and mostly flat. The bridge ramp has a slight incline.

Traffic and hazards: This ride leads mainly along neighborhood streets with on-road bike lanes, where traffic is light. Willoughby, Throop, and Manhattan Avenues have more moderate traffic, but bike lanes afford cyclists ample space.

Things to see: McCarren Park, Brooklyn Brewery, Williamsburg Bridge, Williamsburg Art and Historical Center, Newtown Creek, East River State Park

Map: New York City Bike Map

Getting there: By public transportation: Take the L subway to the Bedford Avenue stop. Exit the station onto North 7th Street and bike east on 7th 1.5 blocks. Turn left onto Roebling Street. After crossing

North 11th Street, veer left onto Union Avenue, followed by another quick left onto North 12th Street along the edge of the park. Your starting point at the cathedral is just ahead. GPS coordinates: N40 43.190' / W73 57.208'

THE RIDE

This ride begins next to the striking domed Russian Orthodox Cathedral at the edge of McCarren Park. Built in 1922, the cathedral's Byzantine-revival architecture—the only example of its kind in the city—forms a striking presence in this neighborhood of hipster cafes, bars, boutiques, and galleries. To begin your journey, bike south along Driggs Avenue. This soon brings you toward one of Williamsburg's emblematic art galleries, Pierogi, on North 9th Street. The two-decades-old gallery sits on a block festooned with vintage clothing, used-book, and antiques stores. To proceed en route, continue south on Driggs Avenue.

You'll continue past vintage clothing stores, antiques sellers, and a Williamsburg mainstay on Metropolitan Avenue, the City Reliquary, which houses a quirky collection of New York City paraphernalia from past to present—subway tokens, bits of buildings, dentures, and more. Sitting on a block packed with delis and cafes, it's easy to miss the museum's narrow storefront. Continuing onward, Fillmore Place leads through Williamsburg's 1-block historic district, where mid-nineteenth-century row houses frame the road, dating from when Williamsburg was still a country village.

Bike Shops

Affinity Cycles: 616 Grand St.; (718) 384-5181
A bike manufacturer in East Williamsburg that specializes in pioneering track and road frame designs, just a block west of Manhattan Avenue at Leonard Avenue.
Landmark Bicycles: 376 Bedford Ave.; (347) 799-2116
Located in the heart of Williamsburg on its main commercial drag.
Spokes and Strings: 140 Havemeyer St.; (718) 599-2409
A full-service bike shop just a few blocks east of the Williamsburg Bridge bike ramp, this shop specializes in bikes and gear that suit city cycling.
Time's Up!: 99 S. 6th St.; (212) 802-8222
A bike shop and more under the Williamsburg Bridge. Operated by the environmental group Times Up!, the folks here offer regular free classes and workshops on cycling and bike maintenance.

Just off Driggs Avenue at South 5th Street up ahead, you'll then access the Williamsburg Bridge bikeway. As you cross the East River, keep to the north side of the path to avoid oncoming bikers, skaters, and skateboarders, and enjoy the views of Williamsburg below and Midtown Manhattan across the water. (The very southern side of the pathway is for pedestrians.) The bridge descends you to Manhattan's Lower East Side, where large-scale public housing complexes reach skyward toward the bridge. At the end of the bridge, slow down to make a U-turn and retrace your route back to Brooklyn, again staying on the right side of the bikeway (pedestrians will be on your right).

The next part of your journey leads north along Bedford Avenue, Williamsburg's main drag, where an ever-changing selection of cafes, boutiques, yoga studios, and the like line the way. There's no bike lane here and the two-way road is narrow and busy, so stay alert. North 6th Street then takes you away from the brew of cafe culture and back onto more open roads. Just south of the Williamsburg Bridge, on Broadway, sits another community stronghold, the Williamsburg Art and Historical Center. It was one of the first arts centers

Bikes in Williamsburg just off Bedford Avenue.

that opened south of the bridge when this part of the neighborhood was still considered dangerous by most. Today, Williamsburg north and south of the bridge are still two strikingly distinct enclaves, with hipster lifestyles giving way to Hasidic cultures south of the bridge.

From the southern edge of the neighborhood, Throop Avenue then slowly carries you north again, through more diverse residential communities, past public housing projects on Manhattan Avenue, and back toward the trendier parts of Williamsburg. You'll skirt the edge of McCarren Park, lined with luxury condos, to then head toward the waterfront. Along the way, pass the Brooklyn Brewery on North 11th Street, where local beer has been brewed for a quarter century. You'll then reach the waterfront next to the Northside Piers, an enclave of mint condos with marvelous East River views. East River State Park sits just north of here off Kent Avenue. To explore the park, dismount your bike and walk it into the park. (Biking prohibited.)

Proceeding en route, you'll soon reach Greenpoint's Little Poland. Newtown Creek, at the north of the neighborhood, separates Greenpoint from Queens. You can explore the creek's natural habitat on a 0.5-mile (round-trip) nature walk that starts at the tip of Paidge Avenue if you wish. Greenpoint Avenue then takes you into the heart of the neighborhood's historic district, which takes in about 4 blocks between Manhattan and Franklin Avenues. As you near the end of your journey, pick up some rustic bread or pastries at any of the Polish bakeries that line the way on Leonard Street and return to your starting point at McCarren Park, a perfect spot to devour your provisions.

MILES AND DIRECTIONS

0.0 From the southwestern edge of McCarren Park at the Russian Orthodox Cathedral, bike southwest along Driggs Avenue.

0.2 Turn right onto North 8th Street.

0.3 Turn right onto Bedford Avenue.

0.4 Turn right onto North 9th Street. The art gallery Pierogi sits on your left. To continue, turn right onto Driggs Avenue again, continuing southwest.

0.6 Turn left onto North 5th Street.

0.8 Turn right onto Havemeyer Street, followed by a quick right onto Metropolitan Avenue. The City Reliquary is across the street.

0.9 Turn left onto Roebling Street, followed by a right onto Fillmore Place through the historic district.

1.1 Turn left onto Driggs Avenue.

1.3 Turn left onto South 5th Street, followed by a right onto the bikeway onto the Williamsburg Bridge. Bike across the bridge, sticking to the right side of the bikeway (eastbound bike traffic is on the left).

2.8 Make a U-turn and retrace your route across the bridge.

4.3 Descend the bikeway to the left and turn left onto South 4th Street just ahead, following the bike lane.

4.4 Turn right onto Bedford Avenue.

4.8 Turn left onto North 6th Street.

5.0 Turn left onto the on-road bike lane on Wythe Avenue.

5.7 To visit the Williamsburg Art and Historical Center, turn left onto Broadway.

5.9 The center is on the north side of Broadway. To continue, bike west on South 6th Street.

6.1 Turn left onto Wythe Avenue.

7.5 Turn left onto Willoughby Avenue, following the on-road bike lane.

8.3 Turn left onto Throop Avenue.

8.7 Turn right onto Whipple Street, followed by a quick left onto Broadway and an immediate right onto the bike lane on Manhattan Avenue. Just ahead, the bike lane switches to the left side of the road.

10.1 Turn left onto Bayard Street.

10.4 Turn right onto Union Avenue, followed by a left onto North 12th Street.

10.8 Turn left onto Wythe Avenue.

11.2 Turn right onto North 4th Street.

11.3 Follow the road as it veers right and then left to the Northside Piers.

11.4 Walk your bike once you reach the pier area to explore the piers and the park space. (Biking is prohibited.) Exit the park at the northeastern edge.

11.5 Remount your bike to head northeast (unmarked street) and then veer right onto North 7th Street.

11.6 Turn left onto Kent Avenue onto the on-road bike lane. East River State Park is just ahead on your left.

12.0 The bike lane switches to the other side of the road. Cross at the traffic signal and then continue on the bike lane on what becomes Franklin Street.

12.1 Turn left onto Calyer Street.

Williamsburg and Greenpoint

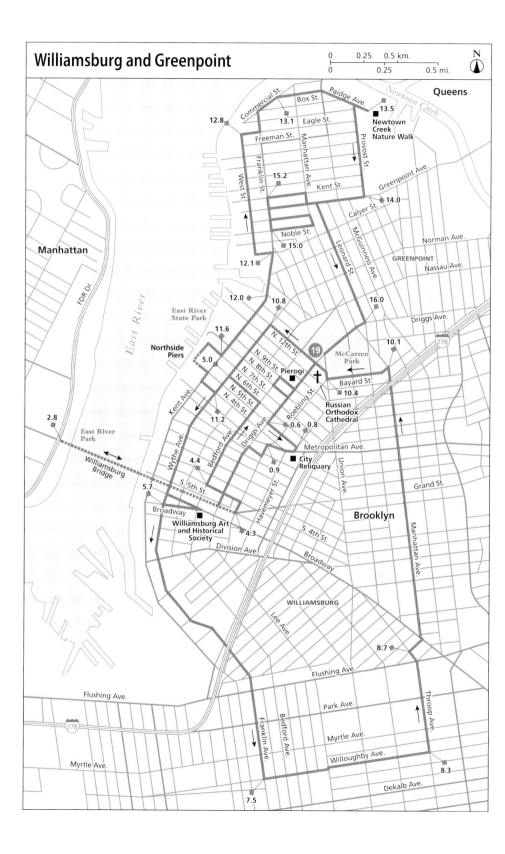

N

| 0 | 0.25 | 0.5 km. |

| 0 | 0.25 | 0.5 mi. |

Queens

Newtown Creek

Commercial St.
Box St.
Paidge Ave.
12.8
13.1   Eagle St.
13.5
Newtown Creek Nature Walk
Freeman St.
Franklin St.
West St.
Manhattan Ave.
Provost St.
15.2
Kent St.
Greenpoint Ave.
14.0
Noble St.
12.1
15.0
Calyer St.
Leonard St.
McGuinness Ave.
Norman Ave.
GREENPOINT
Nassau Ave.

Manhattan

12.0
10.8
16.0
Driggs Ave.
278

East River
East River State Park
11.6
N. 12th St.
19
McCarren Park
10.1
Northside Piers
5.0
N. 9th St.
N. 8th St.
N. 7th St.
N. 6th St.
N. 5th St.
N. 4th St.
Pierogi
Bayard St.
10.4
Russian Orthodox Cathedral
11.2
Kent Ave.
Roebling St.
Driggs Ave.
0.6   0.8

2.8

East River Park
Williamsburg Bridge
Wythe Ave.
Bedford Ave.
Driggs Ave.
Havemeyer St.
Metropolitan Ave.
Union Ave.
City Reliquary
0.9
Grand St.
4.4
5.7
S. 5th St.
Broadway
Brooklyn
Williamsburg Art and Historical Society
4.3
S. 4th St.
Manhattan Ave.
Division Ave.
Broadway
WILLIAMSBURG
Lee Ave.
8.7
Flushing Ave.
Flushing Ave.
278
Franklin Ave.
Bedford Ave.
Park Ave.
Throop Ave.
Myrtle Ave.
Myrtle Ave.
Willoughby Ave.
8.3
7.5
Dekalb Ave.

12.2 Turn right onto West Street.

12.8 Turn right onto Eagle Street, followed by a left onto Franklin Street.

12.9 Veer right following the road onto Commercial Street.

13.1 Turn right onto Box Street. Box Street veers slightly right and becomes Paidge Avenue.

13.5 To visit the nature walk at the end of Paidge Avenue, lock up your bike and enter. To continue, backtrack along Paige Avenue.

13.6 Turn left onto Provost Street.

14.0 Turn right onto Greenpoint Avenue, leading you into the historic district.

14.5 Turn left onto Franklin Street, followed by a left onto Milton Street.

14.7 Turn right onto Manhattan Avenue, followed by a right onto Noble Street.

15.0 Turn right onto Franklin Street.

15.2 Turn right onto Kent Street.

15.4 Turn right onto Manhattan Avenue, followed by a left onto Green-point Avenue.

15.5 Turn quickly right onto Leonard Street.

16.0 Turn right onto Driggs Avenue.

16.3 Arrive at your starting point.

RIDE INFORMATION

Local Events/Attractions

Brooklyn Brewery: A craft brewery since 1988, where you can enjoy tastings and tours. 79 N. 11th St.; (718) 486-7422; brooklynbrewery.com

City Reliquary: A community museum that exhibits quirky New York City paraphernalia. 370 Metropolitan Ave.; (718) 782-4842; www.cityreliquary.org

Newtown Creek Nature Walk: A 0.5-mile walk gives you a close-up look of an area where nature meets industry. At the end of Paidge Avenue; www.nyc .gov or www.nyc.gov/html/dep/html/environmental_education/newtown.shtml

Pierogi: One of innumerable art galleries in Williamsburg worth visiting. 77 N. 9th St.; (718) 599-2144; www.pierogi200.com

Williamsburg Art and Historic Center: An early South Williamsburg exhibition space. 135 Broadway; (718) 486-7372; www.wahcenter.net

Restrooms

Start/end: There are restrooms in the park building at McCarren Park.

Following a Fort Greene Forefather

This route leads from Fort Greene Park through the historic neighborhood of Fort Greene, known for being more diverse than most New York communities. One of Fort Greene's most celebrated cultural icons, the author Richard Wright, was an early harbinger of this trend. Following in his footsteps, you'll cycle past elegant brownstones into the historic parts of the neighboring communities of Clinton Hill, Crown Heights, and Bedford-Stuyvesant before returning to Fort Greene Park, where Wright's bench at the park's summit forms an ideal spot for a post-ride picnic.

Start: The northeast corner of Fort Greene Park, at Myrtle Avenue and Washington Park

Length: 7.5-mile loop

Approximate riding time: 1 hour

Best bike: Hybrid, road, or mountain bike

Terrain and trail surface: The trail is paved throughout and the terrain is mostly flat. It goes slightly downhill from Fort Greene Park toward the Brooklyn Academy of Music at the beginning of the ride. It goes slightly uphill to the park toward the end of the ride.

Traffic and hazards: This route leads mainly along on-road bike lanes with light to moderate traffic. Lafayette Avenue, through historic Fort Greene, has the heaviest traffic, so stay especially alert on this stretch. Road-side bike signage helps alert drivers of cyclists.

Things to see: Fort Greene, Fort Greene Park, Richard Wright Landmarks, Clinton Hill, Crown Heights, Bedford-Stuyvesant

Maps: *New York City Bike Map,* Literary Brooklyn Map: www.literary brooklyn.com

Getting there: By public transportation: Take the B, Q, or R subway to the DeKalb Avenue stop. Head north on Flatbush Avenue. After about

250 feet, veer right onto Fleet Place / Fleet Street. After 0.2 mile turn right onto Myrtle Avenue and bike to the northeast corner of Fort Greene Park along Myrtle Avenue 0.3 mile. GPS coordinates: N40 41.581' / W73 58.446'

THE RIDE

Fort Greene is associated with innumerable literary giants—Walt Whitman, Marianne Moore, and Henry Miller, to name a few. But the writer most closely linked to this Brooklyn neighborhood may well be Richard Wright, a seminal figure of African-American literature and the author of the groundbreaking novel *Native Son*. Wright's literary works are often credited with having reshaped race relations in the United States. Since Wright's time, Fort Greene has attracted a host of other icons of black culture—the saxophonist Branford Marsalis, film director Spike Lee, author Colson Whitehead, and the singer-songwriter Erykah Badu, among others.

The first Wright residence of your journey sits on Carlton Avenue, a tranquil street of brownstones, where Wright lived in 1938 in the back room of the apartment of his Chicago friends Jane and Herbert Newton. A plaque on the wall commemorates the spot. To continue, return to Fort Greene Park, hugging its eastern and southern edges. Historic brownstones along the way house a growing number of chic ground-floor cafes and boutiques. At the foot of the park, you'll head toward the Brooklyn Academy of Music, the United States's oldest performing arts center. Founded in 1861, it opened at its current location in 1908 and has been a Brooklyn mainstay ever since.

Bike Shops

Fulton Bikes: 1580 Fulton St.; (718) 778-2887
Fulton Bikes: 997 Fulton St.; (718) 638-2453
A full-service bike shop with locations in Bedford-Stuyvesant and Clinton Hill. They have a large selection of brand-name bikes and a range of closeout deals. They also offer weekly classes and group rides.
Red Lantern Bicycles: 345 Myrtle Ave.; (347) 889-5338
Just a block from Fort Greene Park, you can do more than fix your bike at this hipster-casual bike shop where they do overhauls, restorations, and custom builds. Get your own fix—from coffee to beer. Or take one of their scheduled classes.

After crossing Fulton Street, Lafayette Avenue then takes you back into historic Fort Greene, where stately brownstones frame the way once more. On your right, you'll pass the Lafayette Avenue Presbyterian Church, a progressive church with a 150-year history. Founded by abolitionists and known for its multiracial and multicultural congregation, the church's interior features a large-scale mural depicting local street life. Just a few blocks onward, you'll pass the imposing Brooklyn Masonic Temple. On Saturday during summer months, you'll find a popular Brooklyn flea market in the lot across the road—the Brooklyn Flea.

Richard Wright and Fort Greene

Wright wrote much of *Native Son* while living at 175 Carlton Ave. with his Chicago friends Jane and Herbert Newton in 1938. During this time, Wright reportedly rose around 6 a.m. every day, entered Fort Greene Park at Willoughby Avenue, climbed to the hilltop at the center of the park, and sat on a bench overlooking Brooklyn brownstones and the Navy Yard below, pen and notebook in hand. (Today, a bench at the top of the hill celebrates the author.) He then returned to the Newtons' apartment and shared breakfast and debate with Jane Newton before withdrawing to his room, where he would write for a few more hours. His afternoons were spent at the Brooklyn Public Library or visiting friends in Manhattan.

But Wright's life at 175 Carlton was short-lived. Before the end of 1938 the Newtons (and Wright with them) were forced to move because their landlord became ill. They all lived for a short while at 552 Gates Ave. in Bedford-Stuyvesant in a cramped apartment on a commercial street. Shortly thereafter, they all moved to 101 Lefferts Place in Clinton Hill.

The Newtons were Fort Greene harbingers of their own kind—Jane was white and Herbert was black, making them an interracial couple when interracial marriage was still illegal in most states. Today, Fort Greene is known for its exceptionally multiracial, multiethnic, and multicultural constitution. But the Newtons and, once Wright married the Jewish Ellen Poplar in 1941, the Wrights, too, were not always welcome in the area. The Newtons' landlord at 101 Lefferts asked them to move out because their racial mixing unsettled him. They moved to 343 Grand Ave. and were joined by Wright and his wife in 1941 for a short while before the Wrights found a four-bedroom apartment in Crown Heights at 11 Revere Place for themselves. Before long, though, the two newlyweds returned to Clinton Hill at 89 Lefferts Place.

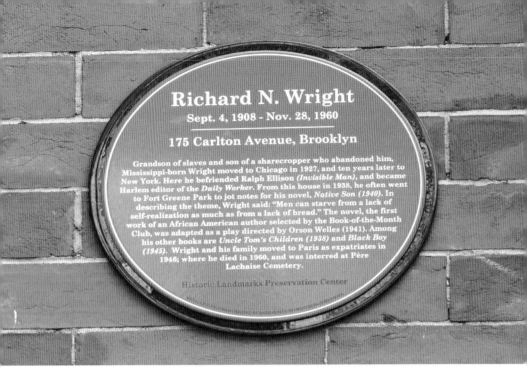

Richard Wright lived and wrote much of *Native Son* here.

Leaving Fort Greene behind, you'll then enter Clinton Hill, a neighborhood that looks strikingly similar to Fort Greene. On Clifton Place, you'll pass the former home of Truman Capote, author of *Breakfast at Tiffany's* and *In Cold Blood*. He lived here in the mid-1940s, not long after Wright was in the neighborhood (from about 1938 to 1941). Just a few blocks south, you'll pass Wright's former home on Grand Avenue, where he and his wife, Ellen (Poplar), lived for a short while with the Newtons.

Continuing onward, you'll exit Clinton Hill's historic district, heading toward Crown Heights along Lefferts Place. Wright lived here, too, with his friends the Newtons at 101 and with his wife at 89. It was here that he finished his influential memoir *Black Boy*. Lefferts Place then journeys underneath the elevated shuttle train and heads south toward the Crown Heights historic district. Stay especially alert as you cross Atlantic Avenue, where traffic is heavy. You'll then reach the historic district along Dean Street, another residential, tree-lined street of brownstones. And Wright lived here, too, on Revere Place.

The last part of your journey takes you across Atlantic Avenue once more to head north into Bedford-Stuyvesant, Fort Greene's increasingly gentrified eastern neighbor. Wright lived on Gates Avenue here, again with the Newtons, in a cramped apartment on what was then a busy commercial strip. From here a sweeping journey westward leads back to historic Fort Greene along the on-road bike lane on DeKalb Avenue. After passing Pratt Institute, a

Walt Whitman's Fort Greene Park

Were it not for the poet and journalist Walt Whitman, Fort Greene Park might not exist. A site of forts during the Revolutionary War, community members began to frequent the spot as a place of leisure shortly after the War of 1812. Thereafter, in the mid-1840s, while working as a newspaper editor for the *Brooklyn Daily Eagle,* Walt Whitman began writing and publishing strong appeals for the creation of a pleasant recreational spot where "on hot summer evenings, and Sundays" city residents "can spend a few grateful hours in the enjoyment of wholesome rest and fresh air." Through his newspaper editorials Whitman gathered popular support for the park project and, in 1847, the city approved its development as a public park (Brooklyn's first). Designed by the same duo of landscape artists who fashioned Prospect Park, Frederick Law Olmsted and Calvert Vaux, the park was initially called Washington Park but became known as Fort Greene Park in 1897.

private art school with a leafy campus, your route will be lined with gracious brownstones once more until you reach Fort Greene Park.

Stop off at a deli—or Red Lantern Bicycles—on Myrtle Avenue just east of the park to pick up provisions for a park picnic at the end of your ride. When you reach the park, dismount your bike, climb to the top of the park's central hill, in the footsteps of Richard Wright, sit on his bench, and contemplate your environs.

MILES AND DIRECTIONS

0.0 Go south along Washington Park.

0.1 Turn left onto Willoughby Avenue, followed by a left onto Carlton Avenue. Wright lived at number 175.

0.3 Turn left onto Myrtle Avenue, followed by a left back onto Washington Park, hugging the east edge of Fort Greene Park.

0.6 Turn right onto DeKalb Avenue. The bike lane is on the left side of the road.

0.9 Turn left onto Ashland Place.

Following a Fort Greene Forefather

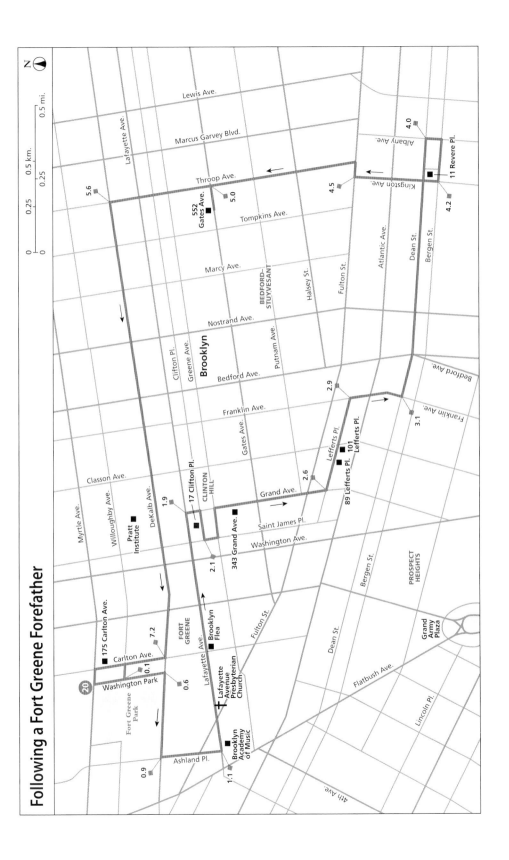

N

0   0.25   0.5 km.

0   0.25   0.5 mi.

Lewis Ave.

Marcus Garvey Blvd.

Lafayette Ave.

Throop Ave.

5.6

552 Gates Ave.

5.0

Tompkins Ave.

Marcy Ave.

Albany Ave.

4.0

11 Revere Pl.

Kingston Ave.

4.2

4.5

Dean St.

Bergen St.

Atlantic Ave.

Fulton St.

Halsey St.

Putnam Ave.

BEDFORD-STUYVESANT

Nostrand Ave.

Bedford Ave.

Brooklyn

Clifton Pl.

Greene Ave.

17 Clifton Pl.

CLINTON HILL

Gates Ave.

Franklin Ave.

2.9

Bedford Ave.

3.1

Franklin Ave.

Lefferts Pl.

101 Lefferts Pl.

89 Lefferts Pl.

2.6

Grand Ave.

343 Grand Ave.

Saint James Pl.

Washington Ave.

2.1

1.9

DeKalb Ave.

Classon Ave.

Willoughby Ave.

Pratt Institute

Myrtle Ave.

175 Carlton Ave.

7.2

Carlton Ave.

0.1

0.6

Washington Park

20

Fort Greene Park

FORT GREENE

Brooklyn Flea

Lafayette Ave.

Lafayette Avenue Presbyterian Church

Fulton St.

Bergen St.

PROSPECT HEIGHTS

Dean St.

Grand Army Plaza

Flatbush Ave.

Lincoln Pl.

Brooklyn Academy of Music

Ashland Pl.

0.9

1.1

4th Ave.

1.1 Turn left onto Lafayette, where the bike lane is on the right side of the road. Up ahead at Fulton Street, the bike lane switches back to the left side of the road.

1.9 Turn right onto Grand Avenue, followed by a right onto Clifton Place. Truman Capote lived at number 17.

2.1 Turn left onto Saint James Place, followed by a left onto Greene Avenue, and a right back onto Grand Avenue, continuing south. Wright lived at number 343.

2.6 Turn left onto Lefferts Place. Wright lived at numbers 101 and 89.

2.9 Turn right onto Franklin Avenue.

3.1 Turn left onto Dean Street.

4.0 Turn left onto Albany Avenue, followed by a left onto Bergen Street. Wright lived at 11 Revere Place up ahead on your right. Continue west along Bergen Street.

4.2 Turn right onto Kingston Avenue.

4.5 Turn right onto Fulton Street, followed by a quick left onto Throop Avenue.

5.0 Turn left onto Gates Avenue.

5.1 Wright lived at 552 Gates Ave. Make a U-turn and return to Throop Avenue.

5.2 Turn left onto Throop Avenue.

5.6 Turn left onto DeKalb Avenue.

7.2 Turn right onto Carlton Avenue.

7.4 Turn left onto Myrtle Avenue.

7.5 Arrive at your starting point.

RIDE INFORMATION

Local Event/Attraction
Fort Greene Park: Brooklyn's first public park. www.nycgovparks.org/parks/FortGreenePark

Restrooms
Start/finish: There are restrooms in the park building in Fort Greene Park.

21

Victorian Brooklyn

From the Brooklyn Museum, this route travels along a grand, tree-lined greenway on Eastern Parkway, designed in the nineteenth century as the nation's first parkway. You'll traverse three historic districts with elaborate Victorian homes, and pass two colonial houses, touching upon Brooklyn spots with one, two, or even three centuries of history, and giving you a feel of what parts of the borough were like in times gone by.

Start: The fountain in front of the Brooklyn Museum

Length: 12.4-mile loop

Approximate riding time: 2 hours

Best bike: Hybrid, road, or mountain bike

Terrain and trail surface: The trail is paved throughout. It goes slightly downhill along Eastern Parkway and Buffalo Avenue. At the end of the route it goes uphill 0.5 mile along Bedford Avenue.

Traffic and hazards: The Eastern Parkway Greenway is car-free but crosses several streets with moderate traffic. Heed the traffic signals. Some of the roads with on-road bike lanes have moderate traffic, notably Clarendon Road, Avenue I, and Bedford Avenue. Most of the roads without bike lanes run through residential neighborhoods with only light traffic, but a few connector stretches have heavy traffic—Church Avenue, most notably. City cycling comfort is required.

Things to see: Eastern Parkway, Wyckoff Farmhouse Museum, Historic Fiske Terrace and Midwood Park, Historic Ditmas Park, Historic Prospect Park South, Lefferts Historic House Museum

Map: *New York City Bike Map*

Getting there: By public transportation: Take the 2 or 3 subway to the Eastern Parkway/Brooklyn Museum stop. The fountain is in front of the museum on the left. By car: Take the Brooklyn Bridge to the first left exit at Tillary Street. Turn right onto Flatbush Avenue and continue straight 1.5 miles to Grand Army Plaza. Follow the traffic circle two thirds around. Turn right after the Brooklyn Public Library onto Eastern Parkway. The museum parking lot is on your right at Washington Avenue. GPS coordinates: N40 40.296' / W73 57.775'

THE RIDE

From the Brooklyn Museum, go east along Eastern Parkway's greenway, which runs along the parkway's southern flank. Conceived of by the landscape architects Frederick Law Olmsted and Calvert Vaux in 1866, the parkway was part of their larger scheme to construct a parkway system connecting parks throughout the area, thus bringing the country to the city. Four rows of trees extend eastward along the 2-mile boulevard that served for "pleasure riding" in its early days. Today, the left side of the greenway is for cyclists and the right side is for walkers, but the border is vague, so stay alert and be prepared to stop for pedestrians.

Toward the end of the parkway, you'll turn right onto Buffalo Avenue, hugging the edge of Lincoln Terrace Park to go downhill and southward toward central Brooklyn. A short stretch of on-road biking on Ditmas Boulevard soon brings you to New York City's oldest standing structure, the Wyckoff Farmhouse Museum, built circa 1652. You can visit the homestead's interior by guided tour only, but the homestead's yard is accessible all day long. To reach the spot, use the pedestrian crosswalk to cross to the south side of Clarendon Road.

To proceed en route, you'll return to the north side of Clarendon Road to continue westward toward Brooklyn College. Stay especially alert on Albany Avenue, where there's no bike lane. You'll then hug the northwestern edge of Brooklyn College's campus along Campus Road and cross one heavily trafficked intersection at Ocean Avenue. Stay alert.

On the other side, you'll suddenly find yourself riding along the tranquil streets of Victorian Fiske Terrace and Midwood Park. In stark contrast to the hustle along Ocean Avenue, one-family homes here have expansive lawns, spacious verandas, and lofty turrets, giving the neighborhood a far-flung feel. Historic Ditmas Park, just north of Newkirk Avenue, brings you past similarly striking homes and tree-covered malls. North of Beverley Road you'll then enter historic Prospect Park South, where Victorian homes continue to line the way.

Church Avenue up ahead then returns you to big-city hubbub, with cars, buses, and bikers vying for space. Stay alert here and watch for parked car

A home along Albemarle Road in historic Prospect Park South, known for its Victorian buildings.

doors. A calmer stretch of the journey begins just ahead at Bedford Avenue, where a bike lane takes you north. Then, for another venture into the past, you'll turn left onto Empire Boulevard to reach the Lefferts Historic House in Prospect Park. Built by a Dutch family in the late eighteenth century when the neighborhood was still a farming village, this historic house museum sheds light on Brooklyn's development from pre-Colonial times to today. To enter the house, dismount and lock your bike. The spots surrounding the house also make for pleasant rest spots before you return to Bedford Avenue and your starting point at Eastern Parkway.

MILES AND DIRECTIONS

0.0 Cross Washington Avenue at the eastern edge of the Brooklyn Museum to access the greenway on Eastern Parkway's southern flank.

2.0 Turn right onto Buffalo Avenue's on-road bike lane.

2.1 Veer left onto Rockaway Parkway.

3.5 Turn right onto Ditmas Boulevard.

4.2 Veer right onto Clarendon Road. The Wyckoff Farmhouse Museum is on your left at East 59th Street. Cross to the south side of Clarendon

Victorian Brooklyn

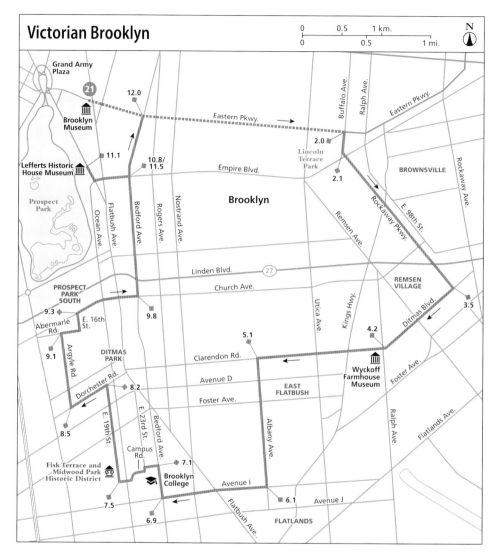

Road to enter the compound and explore. To head onward, continue west on Clarendon Road.

5.1 Turn left onto Albany Avenue.

6.1 Turn right onto Avenue I.

6.9 Turn right onto Bedford Avenue.

7.1 Turn left onto Campus Road.

7.2 Turn left onto East 23rd Street, followed by a quick right back onto Campus Road, hugging the edge of Brooklyn College.

7.4 Turn right onto Avenue H.

7.5 Turn right onto East 19th Street.

8.2 Turn left onto Dorchester Road.

8.5 Turn right onto Argyle Road.

9.1 Turn right onto Albemarle Road, followed by a left onto East 16th Street.

9.3 Turn right onto Church Avenue.

9.8 Turn left onto Bedford Avenue.

10.8 Turn left onto Empire Boulevard.

11.0 Cross to the west side of Flatbush Avenue reach Prospect Park to your right. Walk your bike along the sidewalk to your right a few steps to enter the park there on your left.

11.1 The Lefferts Historic House is on your right just beyond the park entrance. Lock up your bike and explore. To continue en route, return to Flatbush Avenue.

11.2 Use the pedestrian crosswalk to reach the east side of Flatbush Avenue and catch Empire Boulevard eastward.

11.5 Turn left onto Bedford Avenue.

12.0 Turn left onto the Eastern Parkway Greenway.

12.4 Arrive at your starting point.

RIDE INFORMATION

Local Events/Attractions

Brooklyn Museum: The museum's permanent collections include everything from ancient Egyptian art to contemporary works. 200 Eastern Pkwy.; (718) 638-5000; www.brooklynmuseum.org

Lefferts Historic House Museum: An eighteenth-century homestead that sheds light on what Brooklyn was like as a farming village. (718) 789-2822; www.prospectpark.org/lefferts

Wyckoff Farmhouse Museum: Built circa 1652, this is the city's oldest standing structure. Guided tours give insight into the lives of Brooklyn's early farming communities. 5816 Clarendon Rd.; (718) 629-5400; www.wyckoff association.org

Prospect Park

Prospect Park serves New York City's most populated borough with almost 600 acres of rolling meadows, dense woodlands, steep ravines, historic buildings, waterways, and more. This route orbits the park along its car-free outer drive and then cuts through the interior along its central drive. Cycle past ball fields, around a 60-acre lake, and stop off at the Brooklyn Botanic Gardens or park zoo if you wish. At the end of your journey, replenish with a picnic and rest on the Long Meadow or by the boathouse. This is an excellent ride for families and all cyclists looking for a respite from urban life.

Start: Grand Army Plaza, at the north entrance to Prospect Park

Length: 5.6-mile loop

Approximate riding time: 1.5 hours

Best bike: Hybrid, road, or mountain bike

Terrain and trail surface: The trail is paved throughout. It goes slightly downhill as you head south toward the lake along the park's western edge. There's a short uphill climb as you return toward Grand Army Plaza along the park's eastern edge.

Traffic and hazards: This route is entirely car-free during most hours. Check the park's website for up-to-date information on car-free hours (www.prospectpark.org). Cyclists must ride counterclockwise around the park, but stay alert for the occasional biker going in the wrong direction. The inner (or left-hand) edge of the drive is reserved for runners and rollerbladers. Slow cyclists hug the right edge of this runners' route. Fast cyclists use the outer (right-hand) side of the road. Don't swerve back and forth across the drive without looking behind you for oncoming traffic.

Things to see: Grand Army Plaza, Prospect Park, Bandshell, Concert Grove, Drummer's Grove, Audubon Center, Prospect Lake, Long Meadow, The Ravine, Prospect Park Zoo, Prospect Park Carousel, Brooklyn Botanic Gardens

Maps: *New York City Bike Map,* Prospect Park Map available for download at www.prospectpark.org/visit/plan/map

Getting there: By public transportation: Take the 2 or 3 subway to the Grand Army Plaza subway station. Cross to the south end of Grand Army Plaza, where you can enter Prospect Park via its main entrance. By car: From Manhattan take the Manhattan Bridge into Brooklyn and proceed along Flatbush Avenue at the end of the bridge. Stay on Flatbush Avenue until you reach Grand Army Plaza. Cross Grand Army Plaza to exit to the right onto Prospect Park West. Try to park along the park's edge along Prospect Park West. GPS coordinates: N40 40.337' / W73 58.187'

THE RIDE

Grand Army Plaza, your starting point for this journey, was designed by the leading nineteenth-century landscape architects Frederick Law Olmsted and Calvert Vaux. They intended the plaza to serve as buffer between the bustling streets of Brooklyn and the serenity of Prospect Park. At the plaza's center stands the grand Soldiers and Sailors Memorial Arch, erected around 1890 to memorialize fallen Civil War Union soldiers. Olmsted and Vaux also designed Prospect Park itself. They conceived of it in 1866, just one decade after they'd implemented plans for Central Park.

Enter Prospect Park from the southern end of Grand Army Plaza to go counterclockwise around the park on West Drive. If you're going at a leisurely pace, take the innermost cyclists' lane

Bike Shops

Dixon's Bicycle Shop: 792 Union St.; (718) 636-0067
This full-service bike shop in Park Slope, 2 blocks from Prospect Park, has been a family-owned and -operated institution for more than forty years. Get repairs, tune-ups, parts, and rent or buy bikes.
Juice Pedaler: 154 Prospect Park SW; (718) 871-7500
Juice Pedaler combines cafe culture with biking needs and sits on the border to Prospect Park. They have a limited selection of bikes and accessories for sale, do repairs, tune-ups, and have bikes for rent. The fresh juice and coffee selections are extensive.

as you circumnavigate the park. If going at a quicker tempo, take the outermost lane. Stretching southward on your left is the 90-acre Long Meadow. Calvert and Vaux designed this rolling meadow with soft edges and trees

Looking eastward across Prospect Park's Long Meadow ball fields.

scattered along the borders to resemble a natural environment as closely as possible. On fair-weather weekends, Brooklynites flock to the meadow from near and far for picnics, soccer, cricket, kite flying, and more.

After passing the 3rd Street entrance, the park's picnic house, with picnic tables and barbecue stations, is accessible on your left. Just beyond, on your right, sits the Bandshell, a popular site for concerts and performances during the summer. Follow West Drive as it bends left, hugging the edge of the Long Meadow ball fields. From here, the drive heads downhill toward the park's 60-acre lake, the outlet of an intricate network of waterfalls, pools, and streams that makes its way through the park.

At the southern edge of the lake, West Drive becomes East Drive and begins to head north again along the park's eastern edge. Leaving the lakeshore behind you, you'll come upon the Drummer's Grove on your right. The circular grove surrounded by wood benches has attracted drummers from across the borough for impromptu drum sessions on Sunday afternoons for more than three decades. On summer Sundays, innumerable food and craft sellers set up along the road, too, further enticing passersby to stop, listen, and watch.

Continuing onward, you'll pass the Concert Grove with its Ornate Oriental Pavilion on your left. It was built in the late nineteenth century to host open-air concerts. When you spot the Audubon Center on your left up ahead,

An Unlikely Duo—
Frederick Law Olmsted and Calvert Vaux

In the mid-nineteenth century, at a time when the nation was becoming increasingly urbanized, Frederick Law Olmsted and Calvert Vaux helped pioneer a national movement advocating public parks. The two men were at the helm of the nation's first landscape architecture firm and were intricately involved in the creation of innumerable public parks throughout New York City. Some of the park spaces they laid out include Brooklyn's Ocean and Eastern Parkways, Fort Greene Park, and Prospect Park. In Manhattan, they envisioned Central Park and Riverside Park, and in Queens, they had a hand in Forest Park. Although today the two men are often spoken of in a single breath—and usually in connection with their best-known creation, Central Park—their paths to fame were strikingly distinct.

Olmsted (1822–1903) was the son of a prosperous Connecticut family. He spent much of his youth on a farm and received little formal schooling. As a young man, he worked a series of odd jobs—farmer, news reporter, and clerk, among others—and became appointed superintendent of a planned park at the center of New York City in the 1850s through private connections. Calvert Vaux (1824–1895), by contrast, grew up in London, undertook a formal apprenticeship with a British architectural firm as a young man, and moved to New York in 1850 explicitly to work with some of the early advocates for public parks in New York City. The two men's paths crossed around 1857, when the board of New York City park commissioners launched a competition to design a central park. Vaux's former collaborator, Andrew Jackson Downing, had recently died, so Vaux and Olmsted joined as a team and designed their winning Central Park plan.

Soon thereafter a movement for a similarly expansive public park began in Brooklyn. Olmsted and Vaux submitted their winning proposal for Brooklyn's major park in 1866. One of their aims, greatly influenced by Olmsted's childhood on a farm, was to provide the borough's poor with a tranquil, rural escape in the middle of the city. Additionally, they designed the park's features—from the Long Meadow, to the Ravine, to the woodlands, to the water system—to mirror natural environments as closely as possible. Prospect Park was to become a more "natural" park than Central Park.

veer right, off East Drive, toward the Prospect Park Zoo, the Carousel, and the park exit from where you can access the Brooklyn Botanic Gardens. To reach the Botanic Gardens from the park's exit, dismount your bike and walk it about 100 feet along the sidewalk to your right. Then cross the road (Flatbush Avenue) at the pedestrian crosswalk and lock up your bike at the entrance to the Brooklyn Botanic Gardens on the other side. Explore the gardens at your leisure and then return to the park. Alternately, stop off at the Zoo or the Carousel on your left before you reach the park's exit. Then return to East Drive when you're ready.

A brief spurt northward on East Drive next to the Audubon Center soon brings you to a fork in the road. You'll here veer left off East Drive to take the park's Center Drive westward. The rugged ravine that rises high on your right formed the heart of Olmsted and Vaux's grand park design. On your left, the Nethermead, a rolling meadowland, is surrounded by woodland, hills, and water on all sides, giving it a tucked away feel and usually making it less crowded than the Long Meadow farther north. After passing Lookout Hill on your left, veer left to reconnect with West Drive for a short jaunt before making a sharp left-hand turn just as you reach the lake again. This will put you on Wellhouse Drive, which cuts back northeastward through the park, with the lake on your right. Cross one of the park's innumerable waterways—the Lullwater of Prospect Lake—on the quaint Terrace Bridge before emerging on East Drive once more. Up ahead you can access the Audubon Center and Boathouse via a narrow footpath on your left. Biking is prohibited on the path, so walk your bike. The center contains an environmental education center with child-friendly exhibits, a cafe, and charming views of Lullwater Bridge.

To continue, return to East Drive, which climbs uphill toward Grand Army Plaza. As you reach the top of the hill, you'll emerge next to a clearing on your right, Nellie's Lawn. Legend has it that the clearing is named for a young girl who would read books under an elm here for hours in the nineteenth century. When she died at a young age, her friends memorialized her by hanging a sign with her name on a tree. Relax on Nellie's Lawn or the Long Meadow on your left and then return to Grand Army Plaza.

MILES AND DIRECTIONS

0.0 Enter Prospect Park along the main drive to veer right and head south along West Drive.

1.0 Follow West Drive as it veers left, hugging the ball fields.

1.9 Follow the drive as it rounds the southern tip of Prospect Lake and becomes East Drive and heads northward.

2.7 To visit the Prospect Park Zoo, the Carousel, or the Brooklyn Botanic Gardens, veer right.

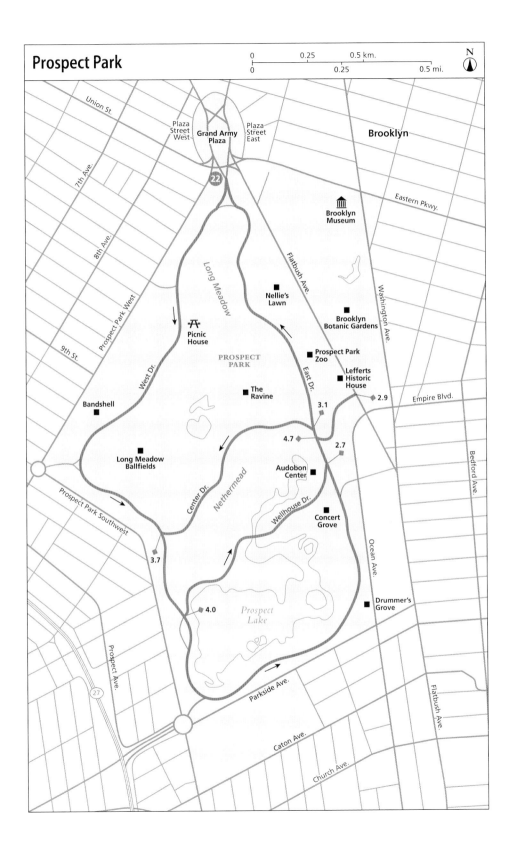

Prospect Park

0   0.25   0.5 km.

0   0.25   0.5 mi.

N

Union St.

Plaza Street West

Grand Army Plaza

Plaza Street East

Brooklyn

7th Ave.

8th Ave.

Eastern Pkwy.

Brooklyn Museum

9th St.

Prospect Park West

Long Meadow

Flatbush Ave.

Nellie's Lawn

Brooklyn Botanic Gardens

Washington Ave.

West Dr.

Picnic House

PROSPECT PARK

Prospect Park Zoo

East Dr.

Lefferts Historic House

The Ravine

3.1

2.9

Empire Blvd.

Bandshell

4.7

2.7

Bedford Ave.

Long Meadow Ballfields

Center Dr.

Nethermead

Audobon Center

Prospect Park Southwest

Wellhouse Dr.

Concert Grove

3.7

Ocean Ave.

4.0

Prospect Lake

Drummer's Grove

Prospect Ave.

27

Parkside Ave.

Flatbush Ave.

Caton Ave.

Church Ave.

2.9 Dismount your bike to enter the Zoo and Carousel area on your left. To reach the Brooklyn Botanic Gardens, continue a few dozen feet onward to the park exit. Dismount and walk your bike along the sidewalk to your right and then cross Flatbush Avenue to get to the entrance of the botanical garden. To continue, retrace your route to East Drive.

3.0 Turn right onto East Drive.

3.1 Turn left onto Center Drive, heading west and then southwest through the park.

3.7 Veer left to re-access West Drive, heading south.

4.0 Make a sharp left onto Wellhouse Drive to head northeastward with the lake on your right.

4.6 Continue onto East Drive, going north.

4.7 The footpath to the Audubon Center and boathouse is on your left. Dismount and walk your bike down the path if you wish to explore. Then return to East Drive, continuing north.

5.6 Arrive at your starting point at Grand Army Plaza.

RIDE INFORMATION

Local Event/Attraction

Prospect Park: Brooklyn's preeminent park space—almost 600 acres of rolling meadows, dense woodlands, steep ravines, historic buildings, waterways, and more, designed by the famed landscape architects Frederick Law Olmsted and Calvert Vaux. www.prospectpark.org

Restrooms

Mile 0.5: There are restrooms and water fountains at the picnic house.
Mile 2.6: There are restrooms in the park building on your right.
Mile 4.7: There are restrooms at the Audubon Center.

Cultures and Coasts—Historic Ocean Parkway to Coney Island

This ride journeys along the nation's oldest bike path, leading you from the greens of Prospect Park to the blues of the Atlantic Ocean at Coney Island. The protected greenway passes through the diverse neighborhoods of Kensington, Midwood, and Gravesend, where you're as likely to see a hijab as a tichel. The beach boardwalk then leads you past Coney Island's century-old rides and Brighton Beach's Little Odessa.

Start: The southwestern exit/entrance to Prospect Park at Park Circle

Length: 18.7-mile loop (partial)

Approximate riding time: 2.5 hours

Best bike: Hybrid, road, or mountain bike

Terrain and trail surface: The trail is paved throughout except for the boardwalk along Coney Island peninsula. The 3.3-mile boardwalk is made of wooden planks. The terrain is flat.

Traffic and hazards: The Ocean Parkway Greenway crosses multiple heavily trafficked intersections. Stay alert, especially for vehicles turning right. Although traffic lights govern these crossings, southbound traffic turning right has the go at the same time as you (when you are going straight)—drivers are often oblivious to cyclists to their right. The same is true for northbound traffic turning left. Along Ocean Parkway Greenway, also stay alert for pedestrians. Although a metal rail separates the pedestrian path from the bike path, people often cross the divide, so be prepared to stop. Slow down toward the southern end of this bike path (especially south of Avenue T) where tree roots protrude through the pavement. The on-road stretch along Neptune Avenue has moderate traffic. Although you'll be on an on-road bike lane, stay especially alert on this stretch.

Things to see: Ocean Parkway Greenway, Wonder Wheel, Cyclone, Nathan's Famous, Brooklyn Cyclones, Coney Island, New York Aquarium, Brighton Beach, Manhattan Beach Park, Coney Island Museum

Map: *New York City Bike Map*

Getting there: By public transportation: Take the F or G subway to the Fort Hamilton Parkway stop. Exit the station and go north half a block on Prospect Avenue. Turn right onto Greenwood Avenue and go 3 blocks (about 500 feet). Turn right onto Prospect Park Southwest. Park Circle lies just ahead. GPS coordinates: N40 39.093' / W73 58.301'

THE RIDE

Ocean Parkway carries historic weight when it comes to cycling culture in this country. Stretching 5 miles from the tranquil greens of Prospect Park to the excitement of Coney Island, Ocean Parkway boasts the country's first bike path, inaugurated in 1894. The parkway itself was designed years earlier, in 1866, by the acclaimed landscape architects Frederick Law Olmsted and Calvert Vaux (who were also responsible for Brooklyn's own Prospect Park). They intended the Parkway to resemble grand European boulevards and designated different "lanes" for different types of travel. The central lanes were for horse carriages out for leisurely drives. These lanes were flanked by tree-lined pedestrian promenades, which were in turn framed by service roads for local traffic.

Bike Shop

Roy's Sheepshead Cycle: 2679 Coney Island Ave.; (718) 648-1440
Roy's has been around since 1931, becoming a Brooklyn biking institution with a large selection of brand-name bikes and a large staff for repairs, tune-ups, sales, and advice.

In 1894, after concerted efforts by cyclists and sports buffs, the western pedestrian promenade was split into two adjoining lanes to give bikers their own 5-mile pathway linking park to beach. The speed limit for cyclists was initially set at 12 miles per hour to prevent the most enthusiastic bikers from wreaking havoc en route. On inauguration day, 10,000 cyclists, along with bike police, took to what was then a crushed limestone path to celebrate this newfound reprieve from the long-standing equestrian hazards on the corridor. (Horse carriages and horse droppings had until then reportedly been cause for cyclist complaint.)

Today equestrianism is no longer a serious obstacle. You might come across a small group of horses—and riders—from nearby Kensington Stables as you navigate around Park Circle, but the remainder of your trip should be equine-free. Follow the bikeway counterclockwise around Park Circle, crossing the Fort Hamilton Parkway access roads, and then turning right, following the bikeway along the northern edge of Ocean Parkway. The bikeway then mounts the sidewalk to continue south. You'll cross Church Avenue up ahead to then swivel right and cross Ocean Parkway, catching the greenway along the southbound median on the other side, where you'll go south. Keep to the left of the hip-high divider.

On the journey southward, you'll cycle through a wide array of cultures— Orthodox Jewish families out for a stroll; Eastern European men engrossed in backgammon; Pakistani women chatting under the trees. The buildings en route are just as varied—synagogues, single-family houses, pre-war brick apartment buildings, yeshivas, luxury high-rises, and more. You'll first cycle through Kensington, where pre-war brick apartment buildings are the norm. South of Avenue I you'll then enter Midwood, a predominantly Jewish, and increasingly Orthodox, neighborhood. Washington Cemetery, Brooklyn's largest Jewish graveyard, extends westward up ahead just south of Avenue J. Then, after crossing Kings Highway, you'll enter Gravesend, one of the original six towns of Brooklyn. Stay alert especially south of Avenue T, where tree roots protrude the pavement in spots.

After crossing Shore Parkway and Coney Island Creek, you're greeted by an unmistakable beach-town vibe. The creek once separated Coney Island—a true island at the time—completely from the mainland, but landfills have since made it a peninsula. At its southern end the greenway then descends

Kings Highway
In August of 1776, during the Revolutionary War, British troops marched to battle— the Battle of Brooklyn—along Kings Highway, eventually leading to the retreat of the Continental Army at Brooklyn Heights.

you onto Surf Avenue, which leads westward toward Coney Island's amusement parks where the iconic Wonder Wheel and Cyclone roller coaster stand tall up ahead. Just opposite the Stillwell Avenue subway terminal sits another Coney Island landmark: Nathan's Famous, New York's most acclaimed hot dog eatery. Then, after passing the Brooklyn Cyclones' minor league baseball stadium up ahead, turn left onto West 21st Street to reach the boardwalk.

As you access the boardwalk, take note that boardwalk cycling is permitted from 5 to 10 a.m. only. Then, heading west along the boardwalk, you'll pass several large-scale public housing projects before reaching the gated community of Sea Gate at its western end. You'll here make a U-turn to return

The New York Aquarium mural, along the Coney Island boardwalk.

eastward along the boardwalk. Check out the fishing pier on your left, where you can mingle with weatherworn fisherpersons and gaze out to cargo ships that dot the horizon. You'll pass Coney's amusement parks, with countless beachfront food stalls, arcades, and souvenir shops lining the way. In summer, it can get rambunctious, but it's a great place to satisfy a childhood craving for Italian ice or caramel corn. For a more tranquil beach-side experience, continue eastward, past the vibrant sea-themed mural along the New York Aquarium, to Brighton Beach, where the crowds are less crazed. Often called "Little Odessa" for the many residents from the Ukranian town of that name, you'll find signs of their culture throughout the neighborhood. Take a quick detour down Brighton 2nd Street to Brighton Beach Boulevard, where you can stock up on fresh fruit and savory piroshky at one of innumerable food stalls. Then return to the boardwalk for a break on one of the beachside benches.

To proceed en route, continue your journey eastward until you reach the end of the boardwalk. Here, a short on-road stretch brings you to Manhattan Beach Park, originally built as an exclusive resort for wealthy beach lovers. To explore, dismount and walk your bike. (Biking prohibited.) Glancing seaward from the park's shore, you can spot Breezy Point, the western tip of Queens, on Rockaway Peninsula. Also visible in the distance is the Marine Parkway-Gil Hodges Memorial Bridge, a vertical lift bridge that opened in 1937 to provide easy access from Brooklyn to the Rockaways.

Best Bike Rides New York City

Continuing en route, you'll cycle along Coney Island peninsula's northern shore at Sheepshead Bay, where ship masts clang gently offshore. Then, stay especially alert going westward along Neptune Avenue. The road gets quite busy at times, and cars pay cyclists little heed. When you reach Ocean Parkway, you'll retrace your route northward to your starting point.

MILES AND DIRECTIONS

0.0   Go counterclockwise around Park Circle along the bike path.

0.1   After crossing Fort Hamilton Parkway, turn right, following the bikeway onto Ocean Parkway. After about 250 feet, mount the sidewalk to your right to continue along the bikeway.

Historic Coney Island

When the earliest incarnation of Coney's present-day amusement park opened its doors in 1903, it lit up the night sky with 250,000 electric lights. Today, two amusement parks amuse the crowds side by side: Deno's Wonder Wheel Amusement and Kiddie Park and Luna Park NYC, each with its own landmarked ride.

Deno's amusement park is home to the nearly century-old Wonder Wheel, which started running in 1920. The wheel was purchased by Constantinos Dionysios Vourderis (Denos) in the 1980s. Denos had emigrated from Greece to the United States at age 14 and had an eclectic life in the United States—he joined the army, worked as a cook, sold from pushcarts, and ran a restaurant. The one constant in Denos's life was Coney Island, where he'd frequently visit with his family, enjoying the revelry and revelers. He often, so the saying goes, promised his wife that one day he'd give her the Wonder Wheel, a gigantic wedding ring she'd never lose. When the wheel's former owners put the wheel up for sale in 1983, they sold it to Denos Vourderis not because he made the highest bid, but because they knew he could be trusted to maintain the wheel's glamour. Together with his sons, Denos built what is now Deno's Wonder Wheel Amusement and Kiddie Park. The Wonder Wheel became an official New York City landmark in 1989.

Luna Park, just next door, is home to the Cyclone roller coaster, which made its debut in 1927. Since then, it's become the world's most copied roller coaster with seven reproductions rolling through Europe, Japan, and the United States. The Cyclone became an official New York City landmark in 1988.

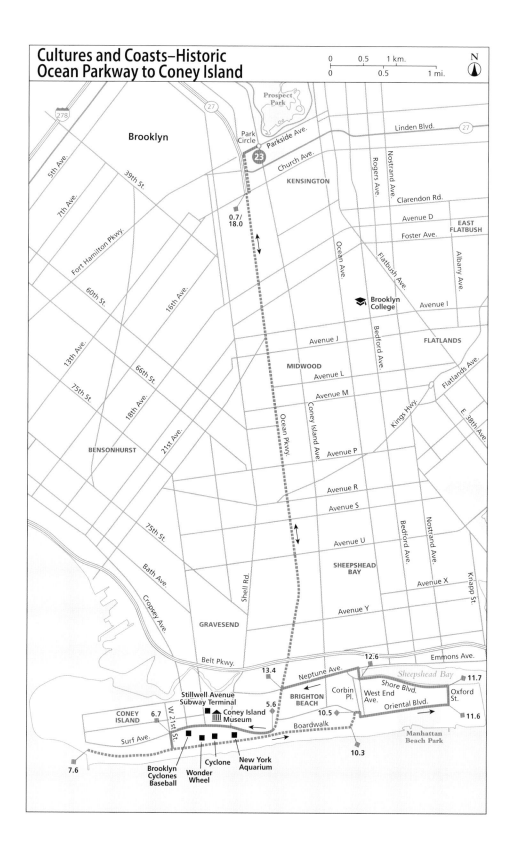

Cultures and Coasts–Historic
Ocean Parkway to Coney Island

| 0 | 0.5 | 1 km. |
| 0 | 0.5 | 1 mi. |

N

278

Prospect Park

27

Park Circle

Parkside Ave.

Brooklyn

Linden Blvd.

27

23

Church Ave.

KENSINGTON

5th Ave.

7th Ave.

39th St.

Rogers Ave.

Nostrand Ave.

Clarendon Rd.

0.7/
18.0

Avenue D

EAST
FLATBUSH

Foster Ave.

Fort Hamilton Pkwy.

60th St.

16th Ave.

Ocean Ave.

Flatbush Ave.

Albany Ave.

Brooklyn
College

Avenue I

13th Ave.

66th St.

Avenue J

Bedford Ave.

FLATLANDS

MIDWOOD

Avenue L

Flatlands Ave.

75th St.

18th Ave.

21st Ave.

Avenue M

Kings Hwy.

E. 38th Ave.

Ocean Pkwy.

Coney Island Ave.

Avenue P

BENSONHURST

Avenue R

Avenue S

Avenue U

Bedford Ave.

Nostrand Ave.

75th St.

Shell Rd.

SHEEPSHEAD
BAY

Avenue X

Knapp St.

Bath Ave.

GRAVESEND

Avenue Y

Cropsey Ave.

Belt Pkwy.

12.6

Emmons Ave.

13.4

Sheepshead Bay

11.7

Neptune Ave.

Corbin
Pl.

Shore Blvd.

West End
Ave.

Oxford
St.

Stillwell Avenue
Subway Terminal

5.6

BRIGHTON
BEACH

Oriental Blvd.

11.6

CONEY
ISLAND

6.7

W. 21st St.

Coney Island
Museum

10.5

Boardwalk

Manhattan
Beach Park

Surf Ave.

New York
Aquarium

10.3

7.6

Brooklyn
Cyclones
Baseball

Wonder
Wheel

Cyclone

0.7 Traverse Church Avenue to swivel right and use the pedestrian sig-nal to reach the west side of Ocean Parkway. Make a quick left on the other side onto the greenway along the southbound median of Ocean Parkway.

5.6 Dismount the sidewalk to your right and turn right (west) to continue onto Surf Avenue.

6.7 Turn left onto West 21st Street. Access the boardwalk ahead. Biking on the boardwalk is only permitted from 5 to 10 a.m. Turn right to explore the western end of the boardwalk.

7.6 At the end of the boardwalk, make a U-turn to return eastward.

8.6 The pier is on your right.

9.9 Optional: Turn left onto Brighton 2nd Street to purchase snacks on Brighton Beach Boulevard. Then return to the boardwalk to enjoy before continuing east.

10.3 At the end of the boardwalk, turn left onto Brighton 14th Street. Veer quickly right to continue onto Brighton 15th Street.

10.5 Turn right onto Brighton Beach Avenue, followed by a quick right onto Corbin Place, and a quick left onto Oriental Boulevard.

11.1 Manhattan Beach Park is on your right. Turn right to enter the park and dismount your bike to explore. (Biking prohibited.) To continue en route, return to Oriental Boulevard, continuing eastward.

11.6 Turn left onto Oxford Street.

11.7 Turn left onto Shore Boulevard.

12.6 Turn right onto West End Avenue, followed by a quick left onto Nep-tune Avenue.

13.4 Cross Ocean Parkway to reach the western side of the parkway. Turn right (north) onto the greenway, retracing your route northward.

18.0 Turn right at Church Avenue to cross Ocean Parkway. Then swivel left to cross Church Avenue. Continue northward along the greenway along the left side of the road.

18.5 Bike counterclockwise around Park Circle.

18.7 Arrive at your starting point.

RIDE INFORMATION

Local Events/Attractions

Coney Island Museum: The museum exhibits a quirky mixture of Coney Island memorabilia. 1208 Surf Ave.; (718) 372-5159; www.coneyisland.com/programs/coney-island-museum

Deno's Wonder Wheel Amusement Park: Home of the nearly century-old Wonder Wheel. 3059 W. 12th St.; (718) 372-2592; www.wonderwheel.com

Luna Park NYC: Home to the landmarked Cyclone roller coaster. 1000 Surf Ave.; (718) 373-5862; www.lunaparknyc.com

New York Aquarium: Home to, among others, sea otters, walrus, penguins, and shark. Surf Avenue and West 8th Street; www.nyaquarium.com

Restaurant

Nathan's Famous: Historic hot dogs, crunchy corn dogs, famous fries; outdoor seating; located a block from the beach, with a stall directly on the boardwalk, too. 1310 Surf Ave. (at Stillwell Avenue), Coney Island; www.nathansfamous.com

Restrooms

Start/end: There are restrooms at the Tennis House on Parkside Avenue. Go clockwise around the traffic circle and exit to your left onto Parkside Avenue. Go 440 feet and the Tennis House will be on your right.

Mile 8.6/9.9: Comfort stations along the boardwalk have restrooms.

Queens

The marina at Little Neck Bay (Ride 25).

Queens is the largest of the five boroughs, encompassing more than a third of New York City's overall area. In terms of geography, it's also the city's center. It counts as the most ethnically diverse county in the country—probably world—with almost half its residents being foreign-born and more than half speaking a language other than English at home.

What this means is that bike rides in Queens are marked by variety. Some rides cover large swaths of ground, revealing a sense of the borough's size. Others hit upon small neighborhood ethnic enclaves, offering glimpses into multiple cultures and various countries. In Jackson Heights, Woodside, and Elmhurst, you'll cycle through South-Asian, Mexican, Chinese, Korean, and Filipino neighborhoods, among others. In Long Island City you'll bike past a rising arts community. Flushing is home to the borough's most famous park and a thriving Chinese community at the end of the 7 line. The Rockaways have been a popular summer getaway for nearly two centuries and exude a relaxing oceanfront vibe. Lastly, a network of parks at the borough's center carries you far away from the challenges of urban cycling. Overall, with about 70 miles of bike lanes added to the borough within six years, Queens offers plenty of rich cycling opportunities for cycling experts and novices alike.

Waterfront Arts Loop

This leisurely route hugs the Queens waterfront, leading you through multiple East River parks—Gantry Plaza State Park, Queensbridge Park, and Astoria Park among them. Along the way, you'll cycle past some of the borough's most noteworthy cultural institutions such as MoMA PS1 and the Socrates Sculpture Park, which exhibits large-scale waterside sculpture and installations. Stop off at any of these cultural spots or simply enjoy the views of the Manhattan skyline and East River you'll get along the way.

Start: Albert E. Short Triangle, at the Court Square-23 Street subway station, at the intersection of 23rd Street and Jackson Avenue

Length: 9.9-mile loop

Approximate riding time: 1.5 hours

Best bike: Hybrid, road, or mountain bike

Terrain and trail surface: The route is paved throughout and the terrain is flat.

Traffic and hazards: The route leads almost exclusively along bike lanes on roads with light to moderate traffic. The intersection at the starting point of your journey, with Jackson Avenue, is the busiest part of the route, so stay especially alert here.

Things to see: MoMA PS1, Gantry Plaza State Park, Queensbridge Park, Noguchi Museum, Socrates Sculpture Park, Astoria Park

Map: *New York City Bike Map*

Getting there: By public transportation: Take the 7, E, M, or G subway to the Court Square-23 Street station. Short Triangle is at the Jackson Avenue/23rd Street exit. By car: Parking is limited. Check MoMA PS1's website for suggested garages. Take the Queensboro Bridge to Queens to exit toward NY-25A W/Jackson Avenue onto Queens Plaza. Go 0.1

mile along Queens Plaza, staying right. Turn right onto Jackson Avenue. After 0.5 mile, 23rd Street and Albert E. Short Triangle will be on your right. GPS coordinates: N40 44.769' / W73 56.725'

THE RIDE

The first noteworthy spot along this cultural waterside jaunt is MoMA PS1, which sits in a low-slung concrete building on 46th Avenue. It's a great place to explore at the end of your tour after you've covered some ground. So to begin, cycle westward along 46th Avenue through a semi-industrial stretch of warehouses and taxi depots toward the skyline. Stay alert here as there's no bike lane. Up ahead, you'll then turn left onto Vernon Boulevard, where a bike lane leads past all-American diners and modish cafes in Long Island City. You'll enter Gantry Plaza State Park's waterfront area up ahead, with the Manhattan skyline, United Nations, and Empire State Building seemingly within arm's reach. Explore the park and piers before catching the waterfront path northward, past playgrounds, stone chess tables, and a towering, iconic Pepsi-Cola sign. You'll exit the park to return to Vernon Boulevard and continue northward toward the Queensboro Bridge. The ivy-covered brick build-

Bike Shop

Spokesman Cycles: 49-04 Vernon Blvd.; (718) 433-0450
A family-friendly full-service bike shop that sells, fixes, and rents bikes and accessories. They have an extensive selection of children's bikes and baby accessories including Leggero trailers.

ing on your right, south of the bridge, is a nineteenth-century former steel foundry that now serves as classy event space. Then, north of the bridge, you'll swing through Queensbridge Park, named for the nearby Queensboro Bridge, and return to the waterfront once more.

Proceeding en route, you'll continue northward along Vernon Boulevard, where you'll pass the Roosevelt Island Bridge before coming to Rainey Park at 34th Avenue. You can enter the park along the waterfront greenway if you wish or continue straight along Vernon Boulevard. On your right just ahead sits the Isamu Noguchi Garden Museum, which displays and interprets works by the Japanese-American artist Isamu Noguchi. The museum, designed by Noguchi himself, helped transform the neighborhood into the culture enclave it is today. Just ahead, another major Queens cultural spot sits on your left—the Socrates Sculpture Park. The sculptor Mark di Suvero led a

Views of the Empire State Building and Manhattan from Gantry Plaza State Park, in Long Island City.

group of like-minded artists and residents in 1986 to transform a neglected landfill into a public art space. The spot now serves both as open-air museum and community park, attracting New Yorkers and tourists alike. Waterfront art installations are shrouded among overgrown trees, and park benches dot the lawns. Created based on the principle that creativity is essential for human life, this is a great spot for a short break.

To proceed, you'll continue along Vernon Boulevard and soon veer left onto another waterfront route just north of 30th Road. The bikeway here follows the contours of the land and juts out next to Goodwill Park and a public housing development. It's a little-known greenway section. The waterside bikeway then veers to the right to deposit you on 1st Street, where you'll continue northward. This soon brings you to a gate off 9th Street, which leads you down to the waterfront once more, here, next to a condo development with backdoor esplanade. Glancing across Pot Cove gives you views of Wards Island Park and the towering Queens-bound RFK Bridge (formerly Triboro Bridge). Then, exiting the gate on the other side, you'll reach Astoria Park—another Queens mainstay with open lawns, playgrounds, and a host of cultural events throughout summer. Catch the greenway along the west edge of the park, leading you underneath the RFK Bridge and giving you river views along the way. To explore the park's interior any further, dismount your bike at any point and walk it along any of the park pathways. (Biking prohibited on park pathways.) Sit back on one of the benches overlooking the water before heading back toward the more bustling part of Queens. Return to your starting point via on-road bike lanes from here and check out MoMA PS1 if you wish.

MILES AND DIRECTIONS

0.0 Cross to the west side of 23rd Street and go south along 23rd Street. Veer immediately right onto Jackson Avenue, followed by a quick right onto 46th Avenue. You'll pass MoMA PS1 on your left.

0.4 Turn left onto Vernon Boulevard.

0.6 Turn right onto 48th Avenue.

0.9 Enter Gantry Plaza State Park straight ahead and explore the park space to your left and piers at your leisure. Then head north, continuing on the bikeway along the waterfront through the park.

1.2 When the waterfront park path ends, turn inland to go right on Center Boulevard, heading south.

1.5 Turn left onto 47th Road, followed by a left onto Vernon Boulevard.

2.4 After passing underneath the Queensboro Bridge, turn left to enter Queensbridge Park via the waterfront route.

2.7 Exit the park, turning left onto Vernon Boulevard.

3.4 Rainey Park is on your left. (Follow the greenway through the park if you wish.)

3.5 The Noguchi Museum is on your right at 33rd Road. Enter if you wish. To proceed, continue north on Vernon Boulevard.

3.7 At Broadway, the Socrates Sculpture Park is on your left. Explore if you wish. To proceed, continue northeast along Vernon Boulevard.

3.9 At 30th Avenue, turn left to catch the waterfront route. The playground will be on your right.

4.2 Follow the path as it veers right to deposit you on 1st Street.

4.3 Exit the waterfront route, turning left onto 1st Street.

4.4 Turn right onto 27th Avenue.

4.7 Turn left onto 9th Street.

4.8 Go through the gate to traverse the courtyard and continue along the waterfront.

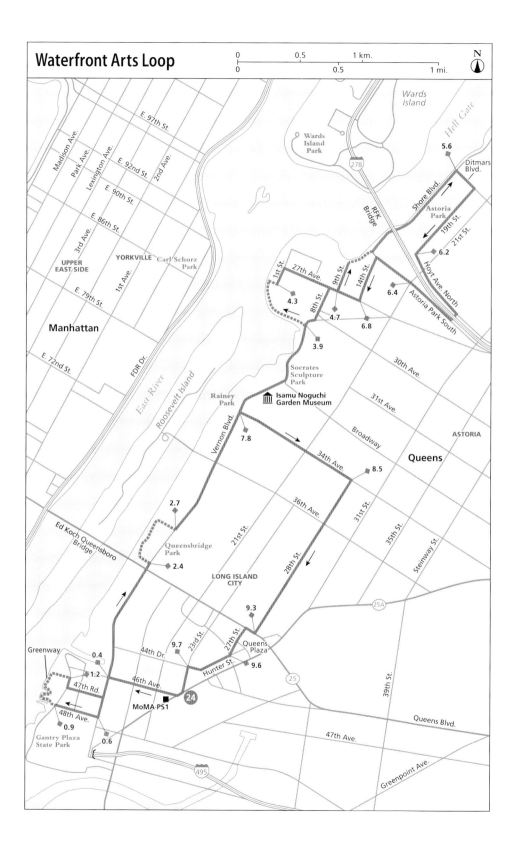

Waterfront Arts Loop

0   0.5   1 km.
0   0.5   1 mi.

N

Wards
Island

Wards
Island
Park

278

Hell Gate

Ditmars
Blvd.

5.6

Shore Blvd.

Astoria
Park

19th St.

21st St.

6.2

RFK
Bridge

E. 97th St.

Madison Ave.
Park Ave.
Lexington Ave.
2nd Ave.

E. 92nd St.

E. 90th St.

E. 86th St.

3rd Ave.

1st St.

27th Ave.

9th St.

14th St.

Hoyt Ave. North

UPPER
EAST SIDE

YORKVILLE

Carl Schurz
Park

1st Ave.

E. 79th St.

4.3

8th St.

4.7

6.4

Astoria Park South

6.8

Manhattan

E. 72nd St.

FDR Dr.

3.9

30th Ave.

Socrates
Sculpture
Park

Isamu Noguchi
Garden Museum

31st Ave.

ASTORIA

East River

Roosevelt Island

Rainey
Park

Vernon Blvd.

7.8

Broadway

34th Ave.

8.5

Queens

2.7

Ed Koch Queensboro
Bridge

Queensbridge
Park

21st St.

36th Ave.

31st St.

35th St.

Steinway St.

2.4

LONG ISLAND
CITY

28th St.

25A

9.3

Greenway

0.4

1.2

44th Dr.

9.7

23rd St.

27th St.

Hunter St.

Queens
Plaza

9.6

25

39th St.

47th Rd.

46th Ave.

MoMA PS1

24

Queens Blvd.

48th Ave.

0.9

0.6

Gantry Plaza
State Park

47th Ave.

Greenpoint Ave.

495

5.0 Exit through the gate onto Shore Boulevard. Continue north onto Shore Boulevard with Astoria Park on your right. (Alternately, catch the greenway along the west edge of Astoria Park, also going north.)

5.6 Turn right onto Ditmars Boulevard, followed by a right onto 19th Street along the edge of the park.

6.2 Turn left onto Hoyt Avenue North, followed by a right onto 21st Street.

6.4 Turn right onto Astoria Park South, followed by a left onto 14th Street.

6.8 Turn right onto 27th Avenue, followed by a left onto 8th Street. Veer right where 8th Street hits Main Avenue. Continue straight onto Vernon Boulevard, going south.

7.8 Turn left onto 34th Avenue.

8.5 Turn right onto 28th Street.

9.3 Access the bikeway straight ahead at Queens Plaza. Then turn right, going west on the bikeway. At 27th Street, swivel left to use the traffic signal to cross to the south side of Queens Plaza. Continue south along 27th Street on the other side.

9.6 Veer right onto Hunter Street. Continue to veer right as Hunter Street turns onto 44th Drive.

9.7 Turn left onto 23rd Street.

9.9 Arrive at your starting point.

RIDE INFORMATION

Local Events/Attractions
Isamu Noguchi Garden Museum: 9-01 33rd Rd.; (718) 204-7088; noguchi.org
MoMA PS1: 22–25 Jackson Ave.; (718) 784-2084; www.momaps1.org
Socrates Sculpture Park: 32-01 Vernon Blvd.; (718) 956-1819; www.socrates sculpturepark.org

Restrooms
Mile 0.9: There are restrooms in Gantry Plaza State Park.
Mile 6.4: There are restrooms in the main park building in Astoria Park, to your right along Astoria Park South.

Queens Greenways to Fort Totten

This greenway route leads through woodlands, wetlands, marshlands, fields, tidal flats, and more to bring you to some of Queens' remotest parks. You'll bike through several park complexes, along Little Neck Bay, stop off at a marina, and arrive at the secluded Civil War–era bastion of Fort Totten, which now serves as public park. Here, tranquil roads amble past weatherworn buildings and a water-front gazebo affords calming views of Long Island Sound. Your return journey leads underneath the towering Throgs Neck Bridge and back to Flushing Meadows Corona Park via residential roads.

Start: Flushing Meadows Corona Park, at the Unisphere

Length: 20.9-mile loop

Approximate riding time: 3 hours

Best bike: Road, hybrid, or mountain bike

Terrain and trail surface: The trail is paved throughout. The terrain has subtly rolling hills, mainly in Cunningham Park.

Traffic and hazards: The first portion of the ride travels along park greenways and on-road bike lanes that connect the greenway segments. Traffic is light to nonexistent along these stretches. The second portion of the journey, after leaving the greenway at the Throgs Neck Bridge, leads along residential streets without bike lanes and mostly light traffic. The final 0.5-mile stretch into Flushing at Main Street has moderate to heavy traffic. The road is a narrow commercial strip, where cars, buses, and bikers vie for space (but at a slow pace). Stay alert for parked car doors opening into the street.

Things to see: Kissena Corridor Park, Vanderbilt Motor Parkway, Cunningham Park, Alley Pond Park, Oakland Lake, Bayside Marina, Fort Totten, Throgs Neck Bridge, Flushing Meadows Corona Park

Maps: *New York City Bike Map,* Fort Totten Map from NYC Parks: www .nycgovparks.org/parks/forttotten, Flushing Meadows Corona Park Map from NYC Parks: www.nycgovparks.org/parks/fmcp

Getting there: By public transportation: Take the 7 subway to the Mets-Willets Point station. There's direct access to Flushing Meadows Corona Park via a ramp heading south. Follow the signs south to the Unisphere and Queens Museum of Art at the park's center. By car: Take the Long Island Expressway E/I-495 E to exit 21 at 108th Street. Turn left onto 108th Street. Turn right onto 52nd Avenue. Park ahead at 111th Street at the park entrance. To get to the starting point from the lot, bike into the park and follow the signs to the Unisphere and Queens Museum of Art at the park's center. GPS coordinates: N40 44.803' / W73 50.661'

THE RIDE

The first part of this journey is a designated greenway route, meaning that small, green roadside markers line the way and help keep you en route. From the Unisphere, you'll bike eastward through Flushing Meadows Corona Park before ducking under the Van Wyck Expressway to follow a greenway connector-stretch toward Kissena Corridor Park. Use the pedestrian crosswalk to your right to cross College Point Boulevard and continue eastward along Booth Memorial Avenue. This soon brings you to Kissena Corridor Park, which

you'll enter at 150th Street, where you turn left into the park. You'll pass baseball diamonds on your left, grasslands on your right, and stay right where the path forks at the grand weeping willow to hug the southern border of Kissena Lake. A short stretch of on-road biking on Underhill Avenue then quickly returns you to the park up ahead.

At the end of Kissena Corridor Park, you'll again follow a greenway connector-stretch, using the pedestrian crosswalk to your left to cross Utopia Parkway and continue eastward on the other side.

Bike Shops

Cigi Bicycle Shop: 42-20 111th St.; (718) 271-1473
Near Flushing Meadows Corona Park, this shop has a thorough selection of brand-name children's and adult bikes for sale. They have flexible layaway options.
Peak Bicycle Pro Shop: 42-42 235th St.; (718) 225-5119
The manager, Kenny, gave me some useful input on biking options in this neck of Queens and into neighboring Long Island. If you're looking for more biking options in this area, this shop is worth the uphill trek to get there.

Oakland Lake, a spring-fed glacial kettle pond located in Alley Pond Park. The lake, once known as Mill Pond, became known as Oakland Lake, named for a nineteenth-century estate here called "The Oaks" after the many oak trees in the area.

You'll pass several baseball diamonds on your right before veering right and traversing the Long Island Expressway. This soon brings you to the western edge of Cunningham Park, where you'll go south along the former Vanderbilt Motor Parkway. Constructed more than a century ago for cars, it's now reserved for bikes and pedestrians only. Follow the greenway through the park's woodlands, across a clearing with baseball diamonds, under an expressway overpass, and back into the woods. After traversing three bridges (to cross roads), slow down to make a near U-turn off the greenway and onto Springfield Boulevard.

A short stretch of on-road biking then brings you to Alley Pond Park, Queens' second-largest park with 635.5 acres of freshwater wetlands, saltwater marshlands, tidal flats, meadows, forests, and more. Follow the main greenway through the park's sloping woodlands. Then exit to your right at the bottom of the hill onto Cloverdale Boulevard. You'll continue to skirt the western edge of Alley Pond Park as you head north along on-road bike lanes. As you reach the end of the park, you'll soon spot Oakland Lake on your left, a tranquil lake surrounded by oaks. Stop off for a short break if you wish and then continue en route.

From the lake, the route goes uphill a short stretch before crossing Northern Boulevard at the top of the hill. Swivel right and use the boulevard's north sidewalk to traverse the Cross Island Parkway. This brings you to the Joe Michaels Mile greenway, named after an early Queens health activist who, after suffering his first heart attack at age 27, went on to run one marathon per year throughout much of his life. He also founded the Cardiac Runners, an organization dedicated to helping others run away from heart disease. Follow the greenway northward alongside languid marshlands on your right and the Cross Island Parkway on your left toward Little Neck. Up ahead, stop off at the Bayside Marina and pier on your right (dismount and walk your bike onto the pier) to check out the fishermen's catch of the day and catch glimpses of the Throgs Neck Bridge in the distance. Then return to the greenway, to continue cycling northward. This soon brings you to Fort Totten, a bastion-turned-park where time seems to stand still. Visit Fort Totten (see sidebar for more information) and then proceed toward the Throgs Neck Bridge.

After traveling underneath the bridge, the greenway ends at Utopia Parkway. This last stretch of journey thus leads along roads with motorists, so stay alert. You'll sweep south along Utopia Parkway's on-road bike lane before accessing smaller, residential roads at 26th Avenue. Your journey then continues along pleasant, tree-lined streets. Bowne Park up ahead is another little-known Queens gem of a park. You'll skirt its edge to then catch 32nd Avenue back toward Flushing. The closer you get to Flushing, the busier the streets get, so stay alert. Sanford Avenue and Main Street lead you through downtown Flushing, where space is tight. Bike cautiously here and stay alert. After

Vanderbilt Motor Parkway

The Vanderbilt Motor Parkway (also known as the Long Island Motor Parkway) was laid out by road race aficionado William K. Vanderbilt Jr. in 1908. Having participated in European Grand Prix races and caused a 1906 car crash which killed a spectator, Vanderbilt envisioned a landscaped long-distance motorway that would traverse cross-roads via bridges and overpasses, whilst keeping race spectators out of harm's way. In addition to serving races, the motorway would allow for scenic drives on race-free days. Today, the parkway is open to bikes (and pedestrians) only and lined with woodlands on either side.

passing the Queens Botanical Garden, you'll skirt the edge of Kissena Corridor Park once more to return to Flushing Meadows Corona Park and your starting point at the Unisphere.

MILES AND DIRECTIONS

0.0 Bike eastward along the Fountain of the Fairs promenade (officially called Dwight Eisenhower Promenade), a series of elongated pools of water.

0.3 At the circular Industry Pond, turn right to hug its southern perimeter. One third of the way around the pond, turn right onto the Path of Discovery to duck underneath the Van Wyck Expressway, following the greenway route. Continue east, with the playground on your right.

0.7 Turn right along the sidewalk at the end of the park. Use the pedestrian crosswalk to cross to the east side of College Point Boulevard. Go east on Booth Memorial Avenue on the other side.

1.0 Turn left onto 137th Street, followed by a right onto 56th Avenue.

1.4 Turn right onto 142nd Street, followed by a left onto Booth Memorial Avenue.

1.8 Turn left onto 150th Street and enter Kissena Corridor Park up ahead.

2.9 Cross 164th Street and hug the park's edge on your right along Underhill Avenue.

3.2 Veer right and back into the park.

3.5 At the end of the park, turn left along the sidewalk and use the pedestrian crosswalk to cross Utopia Parkway. Continue eastward

Queens Greenways to Fort Totten

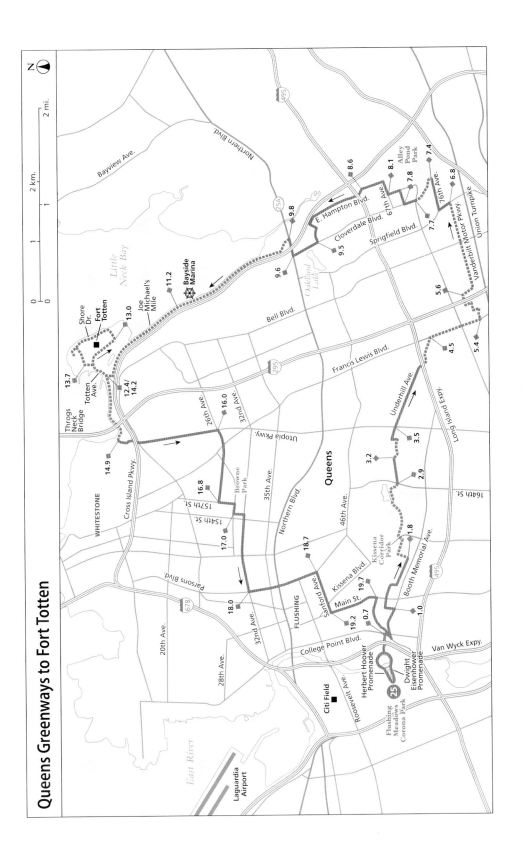

along Underhill Avenue on the other side, with the ball fields on your right.

4.5 Follow the greenway as it makes a sharp right turn and then veers left.

5.4 Stay right of the baseball diamond and turn right under the overpass.

5.6 Turn right along the greenway into the wooded corridor. Follow the greenway as it snakes left and onto the Vanderbilt Motor Parkway rail trail.

6.8 Make a U-turn down the access path to Springfield Boulevard. Turn right to follow Springfield Boulevard northward.

7.0 Turn right onto 76th Avenue.

7.4 Enter Alley Pond Park straight ahead and follow the greenway as it snakes left and then veers right.

7.7 Turn right along the path and out of the park to go north on Cloverdale Boulevard.

7.8 Turn right onto 69th Avenue, followed by a left onto 230th Street.

8.1 Turn right onto 67th Avenue, followed by a right onto 233rd Street.

8.6 Cross East Hampton Boulevard and veer left to follow its bike lane northward.

9.2 Turn left onto 50th Avenue, followed by a quick right onto Horatio Parkway.

9.5 Turn right onto Cloverdale Boulevard. Oakland Lake is just ahead on your left. Stop off if you wish. Then go uphill on Cloverdale Boulevard/233rd Street, continuing northward.

9.6 Cross Northern Boulevard and swivel right to mount the sidewalk along the north edge of the boulevard. Cross the Cross Island Parkway along the sidewalk.

9.8 Turn left onto Joe Michaels Mile.

11.2 The Bayside Marina is on your right. Stop off if you wish. Then continue northward.

12.4 Turn right into Fort Totten.

12.5 Veer right after the gate, onto Totten Avenue. Pass the Bayside Historical Society on your right.

13.0 Turn left onto Sergeant Beers Avenue. Veer left as the avenue becomes Shore Drive.

Fort Totten

Plans for the Civil War–era fortification at Fort Totten were laid out by Robert E. Lee in 1857, but the bastion wasn't completed until five years later. Together with Fort Schuyler, which sits on the opposite side of the East River, Totten's initial role was to help defend New York from eastern attacks. The fort's defensive role was short-lived, however, and it soon came to serve as hospital care facility for the wounded. Since then, the fortification has served an array of purposes, ranging from headquarters for the Eastern Artillery District to Army Reserve post.

Today, most of the compound is owned by the New York City Parks Department and has been developed into a recreational spot with swimming pool, paths for biking, a waterfront walkway, and more. Parts of the area continue to be used by the Army and Coast Guard, and the New York Fire Department uses some of the facilities, too, but neither of their presences detracts from the restful vibe of the spot.

To explore Fort Totten, enter the fort's gates and follow Totten Avenue counterclockwise along the outer perimeter of the former fortification, now a car-free public park space. This brings you past a castlelike building that houses the Bayside Historical Society. Continue onward until you reach Sergeant Beers Avenue at the end of the road. Veer left and follow it onto Shore Drive, which brings you northward again and to an open meadow with wood gazebo and picnic tables. This bayside spot is an ideal place for a mid-ride break. Check out the building along the lawn's northwestern edge, on Weaver Road, that now houses administrative offices for the parks department. To complete your rounds of the grounds, continue north on Shore Drive, heading toward the Throgs Neck Bridge, and visit the Fort Totten Battery at the road's end. After exiting the battery, turn right up the hill, past the visitor's center (where you might stop in). Turn left onto Sylvester Lane at the end of the road, followed by a first right onto Abbott Road. Veer left when it hits Bayside Street, and follow this road back to the entrance gate.

13.4 The gazebo is on your left. Stop off for a break. To continue, return to Shore Drive, continuing north.

13.6 Enter the battery straight ahead. To continue, turn right from the battery entrance (onto Ordinance Road), past the visitor's center.

13.7 Turn left onto Sylvester Lane, followed by a right onto Abbott Road.

13.9 Veer left onto Bayside Street and exit Fort Totten.

14.2 Turn right onto the greenway, heading toward the Throgs Neck Bridge.

14.9 Exit the greenway onto Utopia Parkway. Follow Utopia as it veers left and across the expressway.

16.0 Turn right onto 26th Avenue.

16.8 Turn left onto 157th Street, followed by a right when you hit Bowne Park.

17.0 Turn left onto 155th Street, followed by a right onto 32nd Avenue.

18.0 Turn left onto Parsons Boulevard.

18.7 Turn right onto Sanford Avenue.

19.2 Turn left onto Main Street.

19.7 Turn right onto Peck Avenue. Peck becomes Elder Avenue.

20.0 Turn right onto Booth Memorial Boulevard and then cross College Point Boulevard, using the pedestrian crosswalk. On the other side, turn right along the sidewalk a short stretch before turning left to reenter Flushing Meadows Corona Park. Pass underneath the Van Wyck Expressway.

20.4 Bike around the northern edge of Industry Pond to return to the Unisphere via the Fountain of the Fairs promenade (officially called Herbert Hoover Promenade).

20.9 Arrive at your starting point.

RIDE INFORMATION

Local Events/Attractions
Alley Pond Park: www.nycgovparks.org/parks/alleypondpark
Cunningham Park: www.nycgovparks.org/parks/cunninghampark
Fort Totten: This Civil War–era bastion has a rich military history and is now a peaceful park with weatherworn relics of the past. www.nycgovparks.org/parks/forttotten

Restrooms
Mile 0.7/20.3: There are restrooms in Lawrence Playground (on your right, outbound; on your left, inbound).
Mile 9.4: There are restrooms in Horatio Playground on your right.
Mile 13.6: There are restrooms opposite the Fort Totten Visitor Center.

Jamaica Bay

Jamaica Bay is part of the 26,000-acre Gateway National Recreation Area and one of the most important wildlife refuges in the country, encompassing natural habitats that range from bay waters to salt marsh to upland fields. Taking in an area that's larger than Manhattan, it harbors more than 330 species of migratory birds. This ride circumnavigates the bay along 20 miles of bikeways, crossing creeks and estuaries along the way, and brushing through a range of eco-systems. From the bridgeway peaks you'll catch some singular views of the diminutive skyline and Verrazano-Narrows Bridge in the distance and a stretch of boardwalk biking brings you to the ocean.

Start: The Howard Beach subway station of the A subway line

Length: 20.7-mile loop

Approximate riding time: 3 hours

Best bike: Road or hybrid bike

Terrain and trail surface: The trail is paved throughout except for a 1-mile stretch along the beach, where the boardwalk is made of wooden planks. The terrain is flat except for a slight incline going across the bridges.

Traffic and hazards: This ride travels almost exclusively along the Jamaica Bay Greenway and is thus nearly entirely car-free. One mile of on-road bike route at Howard Beach and on Rockaway Peninsula have light traffic. Hurricane Sandy destroyed much of the Rockaway boardwalk in 2012. If it remains in disrepair, stick to Rockaway Beach Boulevard when you head east on Rockaway Peninsula. Otherwise, take the boardwalk. Take note, though, that biking is officially prohibited after 10 a.m. on summer weekends and holidays.

Things to see: Jamaica Bay Wildlife Refuge, Jacob Riis Park, Flight 587 Memorial, Canarsie Pier, Rockaway Beach

Maps: *New York City Bike Map,* Harbor Parks Jamaica Bay Wildlife Refuge Map: www.harborparks.org, National Parks Service Gateway National Recreation Area Jamaica Bay Bike Map: www.nps.gov/gate/planyourvisit/upload/RGG_map2.pdf

Getting there: By public transportation: Take the Rockaway-bound A subway to the Howard Beach JFK station. Make sure you are on the A train toward Rockaway Peninsula, not Lefferts Boulevard. GPS coordinates: N40 39.633' / W73 49.834'

THE RIDE

From your starting point, you'll bike along on-road bike lanes through the slow-paced residential community of Howard Beach to soon reach the Jamaica Bay Greenway up ahead. Framed by the Belt Parkway on your right and Jamaica Bay on your left, you'll go counterclockwise along the bay-side greenway from here all the way to the Rockaways. This gives you almost 10 miles of uninterrupted car-free biking. You'll cross multiple bridges and waterways along the way, giving you sweeping views across Brooklyn and parts of Queens toward the Manhattan skyline.

Bike Shop

Paul's Bicycle Shop: 163 Beach 116th St.; (718) 318-2000
Newly opened in June 2012, this bike shop sells, rents, and repairs bikes. They specialize in cruisers, which you can rent by the hour, three hours, or day.

Also, farther south, you'll catch sight of the Verrazano-Narrows Bridge, which leads from Brooklyn to Staten Island.

Heading southwest from your greenway access point, the first habitat you'll pass through is Spring Creek Park which encompasses the largest swath of undeveloped wetlands along the bay. Soon thereafter, the first bridge you cross carries you from Queens into Brooklyn. The bridge brings you alongside the Fountain Avenue landfill, a hill that's now covered in prairie grass and is being developed into a public park space. Continuing on, you'll traverse Hendrix Creek, a 7,000-foot tributary of Jamaica Bay. This then soon brings you across the Fresh Creek Basin at the edge of the Fresh Creek Nature Preserve. This protected park space contains more than 40 acres of salt marsh and is a Brooklyn haven for local wildlife.

On the other side of Fresh Creek, you'll then reach Canarsie Pier, a 600-foot pier that attracts anglers from across the five boroughs and next to which a boat launch descends into the bay. Free kayaking is offered here on certain days. (Check the Jamaica Bay website for details.) Heading onward, you'll traverse Paerdagat Basin, pass the Jamaica Bay Riding Academy, and cross your final body of water, Mill Basin. On the other side of the Mill Basin bridge, Four Sparrow Marsh is the home of four native species of sparrows. Continuing onward, follow the greenway as it curves left and runs parallel to Flatbush Avenue, heading southeast and past Floyd Bennett Field on your left. Floyd Bennett Field was New York City's first municipal airport (opened in 1931) and operated as the country's busiest military airport during World War II. It juts up against Jamaica Bay along its eastern border. (See ride 16 for a journey to the airfield.)

At Aviation Road, use the traffic signal to cross to the west side of Flatbush Avenue to access the bike route along the Marine Parkway Gil Hodges Memorial Bridge's western sidewalk. (Official regulations state you must walk your bike across this bridge, but few people pay this rule any heed.) Built in 1937 to connect Brooklyn to the Rockaway Peninsula, Queens, you'll find yourself back in Queens as you descend onto the Rockaways on the other side. Stay alert as you near the end of the bridge. You'll cross a heavily trafficked access road at the end of the bridge. Come to a complete stop before crossing. Then head to the oceanfront along Beach 169th Street.

The next bit of your journey leads along Jacob Riis Park, where you'll head east along Riis Boardwalk, with the entire Rockaway Peninsula stretching out ahead. (See ride 29 for a more complete journey along the Rockaways.) You'll pass a golf course on your left and, during summer months, countless concession stands along the boardwalk. Then, after passing a baseball diamond on your left, the boardwalk ends. You'll reach the on-road bike lane along Rockaway Beach Boulevard via a small path, often sand-covered, that hugs the edge of the ball field. Stay alert as you go east along the boulevard, for buses and cars sometimes travel a rapid pace. At Beach 126th Street you can access the beachfront once more, this time along Rockaway Beach Boardwalk. While biking is officially prohibited after 10 a.m. on summer weekends and holidays, I've never seen this rule being enforced. If the boardwalk is inaccessible (due to hurricane damage or because cycling isn't permitted), stick to Rockaway Beach Boulevard. At the south end of Beach 116th Street, along the boardwalk, sits the Flight 587 Memorial. It commemorates the 265 people who became victims of an American Airlines airplane crash here in 2001. Here, for a tranquil bay-side bite to eat, head north along Beach 116th Street to Jamaica Bay, where The Wharf offers seaside fare on a wood deck overlooking Jamaica Bay. The views here are singular.

To proceed en route, continue eastward along the boardwalk (or Rockaway Beach Boulevard) until you reach Beach 94th Street. This leads you north and across the Veterans Memorial Cross Bay Bridge along its eastern sidewalk.

Bikes locked up along the Rockaway Beach Boardwalk.

(Again, city regulations require that you walk your bike.) On your right in the distance you'll be flanked by the tracks of the A subway traversing Jamaica Bay and planes leaving and landing at JFK. Cross Bay Boulevard then leads through the narrow waterfront neighborhood of Broad Channel. It's one of New York City's lowest-lying neighborhoods and floods on a regular basis (about twice a month). At the north end of the neighborhood, catch the greenway along the west side of the road. This soon brings you to the Jamaica Bay Wildlife Refuge Visitor Center on your left. From here, walking trails lead into the surrounding terrain, giving you an up-close view of flora and fauna. Lock up your bike to explore if you wish. Then, proceeding en route, continue north along the greenway, crossing the Addabbo Bridge and following the bike lane on the other side as it zigzags back to your starting point.

MILES AND DIRECTIONS

0.0 Bike along 159th Avenue and turn quickly right onto 102nd Street.

0.3 Turn left onto 157th Avenue.

1.2 Turn right onto 84th Street. Go 0.5 block. Then cross to the west side of the road and catch the Jamaica Bay Greenway that leads around Jamaica Bay.

Best Bike Rides New York City

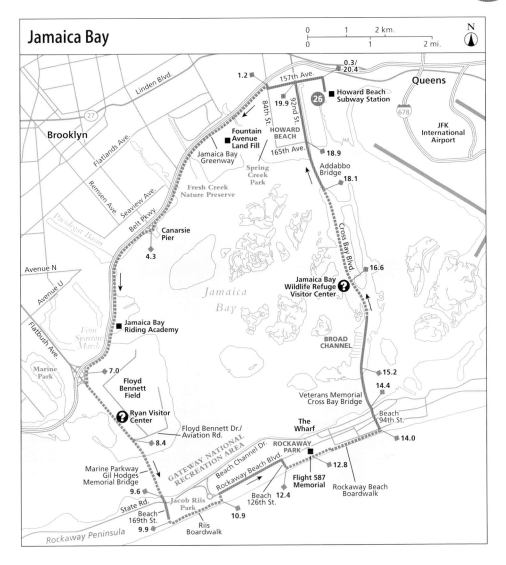

Jamaica Bay

0 1 2 km.
0 1 2 mi.

N

Queens

0.3/20.4

157th Ave.

1.2

19.9

92nd St.

84th St.

26 Howard Beach Subway Station

JFK International Airport

678

Linden Blvd.

27

Brooklyn

Flatlands Ave.

Remsen Ave.

Seaview Ave.

Belt Pkwy.

Paerdegat Basin

Avenue N

Avenue U

Flatbush Ave.

Marine Park

Four Sparrow Marsh

Fountain Avenue Land Fill

Jamaica Bay Greenway

HOWARD BEACH

Spring Creek Park

165th Ave.

Fresh Creek Nature Preserve

18.9

Addabbo Bridge

18.1

Canarsie Pier

4.3

Jamaica Bay

Jamaica Bay Riding Academy

7.0

Floyd Bennett Field

Ryan Visitor Center

Floyd Bennett Dr./ Aviation Rd.

8.4

GATEWAY NATIONAL RECREATION AREA

Marine Parkway Gil Hodges Memorial Bridge

9.6

State Rd.

Beach 169th St.

9.9

Rockaway Peninsula

Jacob Riis Park

Riis Boardwalk

10.9

Beach Channel Dr.

Rockaway Beach Blvd.

Beach 126th St.

12.4

Flight 587 Memorial

ROCKAWAY PARK

12.8

The Wharf

Veterans Memorial Cross Bay Bridge

Jamaica Bay Wildlife Refuge Visitor Center

Cross Bay Blvd.

16.6

BROAD CHANNEL

15.2

14.4

Beach 94th St.

14.0

Rockaway Beach Boardwalk

4.3 Canarsie Pier is on your left.

7.0 Follow the greenway as it curves left, running alongside Flatbush Avenue.

8.4 After crossing Aviation Road, cross to the west side of Flatbush using the pedestrian signal. Access the bikeway along the sidewalk on the other side and swivel left to cross the Marine Parkway Gil Hodges

Memorial Bridge. Dismount and walk your bike across the bridge. Biking is officially prohibited.

9.6 Slow down as you near the end of the bridge and come to a complete stop at its end. Look both ways to check for oncoming traffic before crossing State Road (which is also the car access road for the bridge). Go south on Beach 169th Street toward the beach on the other side.

9.9 Turn left onto Riis Boardwalk.

10.9 Turn left after the baseball fields when the boardwalk ends. The path leads to Rockaway Beach Boulevard's bike lane. Turn right onto the bike lane, going eastward.

12.2 Turn right onto Beach 126th Street to return to the oceanfront.

12.4 Turn left onto the Rockaway Beach Boardwalk, continuing eastward. Biking permitted at all times except weekends and holidays after 10 a.m. May through September. (Take note that Hurricane Sandy destroyed much of the boardwalk in 2012. If the boardwalk is inaccessible, stick to Rockaway Beach Boulevard until you reach Beach 116th Street for an optional left or Beach 94th Street for a definite left—see miles 12.8 and 14.0 for reference.)

12.8 Optionally, turn left onto Beach 116th Street to reach the bay-side restaurant The Wharf. At the end of Beach 116th Street, cross the road and go right around the gas station. The entrance to The Wharf lies behind the lube station. To continue en route, backtrack to the beach along Beach 116th Street and continue east along the boardwalk.

14.0 Turn left onto Beach 94th Street and follow the road as it veers slightly right, meeting up with Beach 92nd Street. Cross to the north side of Beach Channel Drive as soon as you can.

14.4 Mount the sidewalk along the north side of Beach Channel Drive, turning left to access the Veterans Memorial Cross Bay Bridge along its east sidewalk. You must officially walk your bike across this bridge.

15.2 Exit the bridge through the parking lot and continue north along Cross Bay Boulevard.

16.3 Cross to the west side of the road to continue along the greenway.

16.6 The Jamaica Bay Wildlife Refuge Visitor Center is on your left.

18.1 At the end of the greenway, cross to the east side of the road to traverse the Addabbo Bridge.

18.9 At the end of the bridge turn left onto 165th Avenue, followed by a right onto 92nd Street.

19.9 Turn right onto 157th Avenue.

20.4 Turn right onto 101st Street, followed by a quick left onto 158th Avenue.

20.6 Turn right onto 103rd Street.

20.7 Arrive at your starting point.

RIDE INFORMATION

Local Event/Attraction

The Jamaica Bay Wildlife Refuge Visitor Center sheds light on Jamaica Bay's history and displays information on local flora and fauna. It serves as a starting point for short hikes into the surrounding terrain. Cross Bay Boulevard; (718) 318-4340; www.nps.gov/gate; www.nyharborparks.org/visit/jaba.html

Restaurant

The Wharf serves typical waterfront fare on an outdoor wood terrace over-looking Jamaica Bay with excellent views of the Manhattan skyline. 416 Beach 116th St.; (718) 474-8807

Restrooms

Mile 4.3: Canarsie Pier has restrooms.

Mile 10.2: Riis Boardwalk restrooms are here.

Mile 16.6: There are restrooms at the Jamaica Bay Wildlife Refuge Visitor Center.

Quintessential Queens Communities

Queens is the most diverse county in the country, with almost 50 percent foreign-born residents, representing more than 100 nations, and speaking roughly 150 different languages. This sweeping central Queens tour hugs the edge of the borough's extensive cemetery belt and leads through multiple central Queens' communities, where you'll catch glimpses of an array of cultures and lifestyles.

Start: The north side of Queens Plaza, at the junction of Queens Plaza North and 27th Street

Length: 19.4-mile loop

Approximate riding time: 2.5 hours

Best bike: Hybrid, road, or mountain bike

Terrain and trail surface: The trail is paved throughout. There are a few short hills along the way, but no major climbs.

Traffic and hazards: Most of the route follows city streets. Aside from one major bike lane along 34th Avenue and the greenway surrounding Queens Plaza, you'll be sharing the road with motorists, so considerable urban cycling comfort is required. Traffic along the way is moderate. The route leads mainly along neighborhood streets, but a few short stretches follow or cross major traffic arteries. Queens Boulevard, Cooper Avenue, and Woodhaven Boulevard are the busiest. Also, 63rd Drive is a narrow, commercial strip where cars and buses vie for space. Go slowly and keep an eye out for parked car doors opening unexpectedly.

Things to see: Sunnyside, Maspeth, Middle Village, Rego Park, Corona, Jackson Heights, Sunnyside Gardens, Woodside, Louis Armstrong House, Scrabble Avenue, Juniper Valley Park

Map: *New York City Bike Map*

Getting there: By public transportation: Take the 7, N, or Q subway to the Queensboro Plaza station and exit the station onto Queens Plaza North. Your starting point is on the north side of Queens Plaza at 27th Street. Or take the F subway to the 21st Street-Queensbridge station. Cycle south on 21st Street 1 block to reach Queens Plaza. Access the greenway along Queens Plaza North and cycle east to 27th Street. GPS coordinates: N40 45.046' / W73 56.386'

THE RIDE

Heading east from Queens Plaza, you'll soon leave the hectic frenzy of this busy traffic junction behind you as you veer left alongside the tracks of the Long Island Railroad and then right to go east toward Sunnyside. This western Queens neighborhood was farmland into the early 1900s, when the Queensboro Bridge opened and connected the borough to Manhattan, giving residents easy access to the city. Today, 1920s-era six-story apartment buildings mark the multi-ethnic neighborhood.

Heading south from here toward Maspeth, you'll soon hit upon the first of the journey's burial grounds on the south side of Queens Boulevard—New Calvary Cemetery. Queens Boulevard is a busy traffic artery, so stay alert here. New Calvary Cemetery, together with its western progenitor Calvary Cemetery, covers

Bike Shops

Bicycle Repairman Corp: 40-21 35th Ave.; (718) 706-0450
A family-owned and -operated bike shop in Astoria known for its welcoming manner toward cycling novices and experts alike.
Bill's Cyclery: 63-24 Roosevelt Ave.; (718) 335-1906
This full-service Woodside bike shop is great for personalized input.

more than 360 acres of sloping terrain. Like many Queens burial grounds, the graveyard's earliest interment took place in the mid-nineteenth century.

Go uphill along 58th Street, hugging the east edge of New Calvary Cemetery. A short portion of the journey here is lined by car depots and industrial facilities on the left. Then, continuing south, Mount Zion Cemetery soon flanks your journey on the left. This 80-acre cemetery has served the area's Jewish community for more than a century, with its first burial in 1893. Sitting at the top of a hill, views from here reach far.

At the end of 58th Street, veer slightly left, taking the central of three roads to head east and go deeper into Maspeth along Maspeth Avenue. The slight uphill trek leads along one of the neighborhood's pleasant residential strips, with family homes surrounded by well-kept yards. Eastern European immigrants mix with Caribbean, Irish, Italian, and innumerable other nationalities throughout this suburban-feeling middle class community. Along Eliot Avenue your path borders two additional resting spots—Mount Olivet Cemetery on your left and Lutheran All Faith's Cemetery on your right. They, too, have both served the Queens community for more than 150 years. Farther east, you'll soon reach Middle Village's cherished Juniper Valley Park, a popular gathering spot for locals where long-standing residents catch up with friends on tree-covered benches that line the park's paths. It's a great spot for a short break.

Heading onward, you'll come to the last of the ride's cemeteries, Saint John's Cemetery, also in Middle Village. Stay alert as you cycle counterclockwise around the grounds as traffic along 80th Street and Cooper Avenue can be heavy. At the end of Cooper Avenue, traverse the wide intersection with Woodhaven Boulevard by veering slightly left to then veer right onto Yellowstone Boulevard on the other side. From here, Alderton Avenue leads you through the community of Rego Park, another residential community with single-family homes, where Asian immigrants are taking root alongside earlier Eastern European immigrants. Then, as you head north along the short commercial strip on 63rd Drive, stay alert. The road is narrow and cars and buses are often bumper-to-bumper, vying for space. Cyclists are left with a small sliver of a corridor between parked and passing cars. After crossing Queens Boulevard up ahead, traffic decreases again as you head through the northern portion of Forest Hills, an upper-middle class community that borders Flushing Meadows Corona Park in the east.

After ducking underneath the Queens Midtown Expressway along 108th Street, catch the narrow Westside Avenue uphill into Corona, a strongly Ecuadorian neighborhood that abuts Flushing Meadows Corona Park. Heading east on 55th Avenue, the towers from the park's 1964 World's Fair New York State Pavilion suddenly loom large up ahead in the park. The park marks the eastern point of this route. (It's also a nice spot for a rest.)

Proceeding en route, you'll hug the edge of Flushing Meadows Corona Park to soon catch the on-road bike lane on 34th Avenue for your return journey westward. At 106th Street, you can turn left to reach the former Corona home of Louis Armstrong, which now serves as a museum. Continuing west thereafter, you'll then reach the neighborhood of Jackson Heights. This vibrant, residential community is marked by large garden apartment buildings that boast small, private "parks." The "parks" are enclosed by the co-ops that surround them and are accessible only to the residents who live there. Much of the neighborhood, primarily along 35th and 37th Avenues between 88th and 76th Streets is now a national historic district. This part of Jackson Heights

New Calvary Cemetery, one of five cemeteries you'll pass en route, which form part of Queens's extensive cemetery belt.

was developed as one of the first garden city communities, beginning around 1916. At 35th Avenue and 81st Street, you can spot the Community United Methodist Church, where a local architect, Alfred Mosher Butts, invented the word game that eventually became known as Scrabble. A quirky street sign at the corner pays homage to the man and game. Continuing westward, your journey returns to the on-road bike lane on 34th Avenue, travels through Astoria, down to the East River waterfront, and back to your starting point.

MILES AND DIRECTIONS

0.0   Head east on the Queensboro Bridge Greenway along Queens Plaza North.

0.1   Veer slightly right to follow the greenway across Queens Plaza North, using the traffic signal. Follow the greenway along the north sidewalk of Queens Boulevard.

0.4   Turn left onto Skillman Avenue.

0.6   Veer right onto 43rd Avenue.

1.6   Turn right onto 52nd Street.

1.7   Cross Queens Boulevard and turn left, hugging the edge of the cemetery.

2.0   Turn right onto 58th Street.

3.3   Turn left onto Maspeth Avenue.

3.7   Turn right onto 61st Street.

4.1   Continue straight as 61st Street becomes Fresh Pond Road.

4.3   Turn left onto Eliot Avenue.

5.0   Turn right onto 69th Street.

5.3   Turn left onto Juniper Boulevard.

5.5   Juniper Valley Park is at 71st Street. Dismount your bike, enter the park, and explore. (Biking is prohibited on park paths.) Then head south on 71st Street.

5.7   Turn left onto Juniper Valley Road.

6.3   Turn right onto 80th Street.

6.8   Turn left onto Cooper Avenue.

7.4   Veer left across Woodhaven Boulevard. Then make a slight right onto Yellowstone Boulevard.

7.6   Turn left onto Alderton Street.

8.5   Turn right onto 63rd Drive.

8.8   Cross Queens Boulevard.

9.1   Turn right onto 98th Street.

9.2   Turn left onto 64th Avenue.

9.7   Turn left onto 110th Street.

9.9   Turn left onto 62nd Drive.

10.1   Turn right onto 108th Street.

10.4   Veer right onto Westside Avenue.

10.5   Cross Corona Avenue and turn left on the avenue. Make a quick right onto 55th Avenue.

10.6   Turn left onto 111th Street.

11.2   Turn right onto 43rd Avenue.

11.4   Turn left onto 114th Street.

11.7   Turn left onto 37th Avenue.

11.8   Turn right onto 113th Street.

11.9   Turn left onto 34th Avenue.

12.3   To cycle past Louis Armstrong House, turn left onto 106th Street.

12.4   Turn left onto 37th Avenue, followed by a left onto 107th Street.

12.5   Louis Armstrong House is on your left on 107th Street.

Quintessential Queens Communities

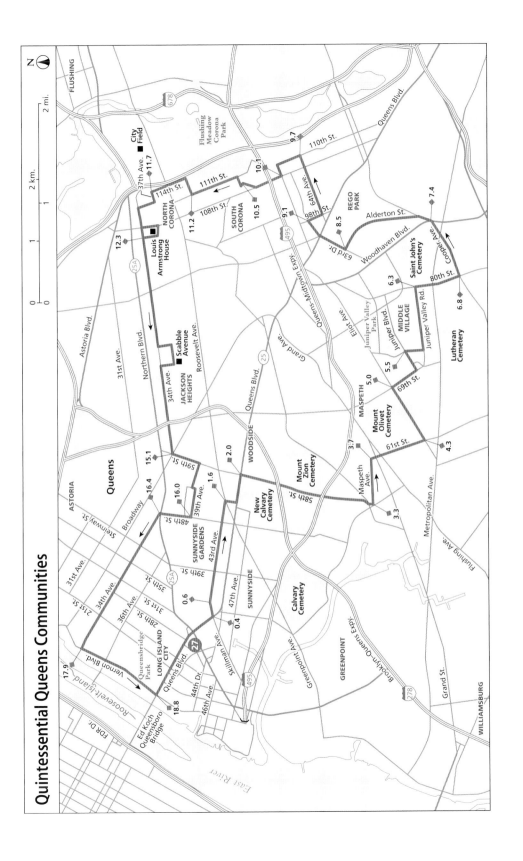

12.6 Turn left onto 34th Avenue.

13.8 To check out Scrabble Avenue, turn left onto 84th Street.

13.9 Turn right onto 35th Avenue.

14.1 Scrabble Avenue is on the corner of 81st Street. Turn right onto 81st Street followed by a left onto 34th Avenue.

15.1 Turn left onto 59th Street.

15.4 Turn right onto 39th Avenue.

15.7 Turn left onto Woodside Avenue, followed by a right onto 39th Avenue.

16.0 Turn right onto 48th Street.

16.4 Turn left onto 34th Avenue.

17.9 Turn left onto Vernon Boulevard.

18.8 At the end of Queensbridge Park, turn left to catch the Queensboro Bridge Greenway.

19.1 Follow the greenway across 21st Street and across Queens Plaza North to continue east along the greenway.

19.4 Arrive at your starting point.

RIDE INFORMATION

Local Events/Attractions

Louis Armstrong House Museum: The former home of Louis and Lucille Armstrong in Corona is now a National Historic Landmark that preserves and exhibits materials related to Armstrong's life. 34-56 107th St., Corona; (718) 478-8274; www.louisarmstronghouse.org

Scrabble Avenue: A creative street sign at the corner of 35th Avenue and 81st Street in Jackson Heights honors the legacy of former Jackson Heights resident Alfred Mosher Butts, who invented the games of Lexiko and Criss-Cross Words, which eventually became Scrabble. Eighty-first Street and 35th Avenue, Jackson Heights

Restrooms

Mile 5.5: There are restrooms in Juniper Valley Park in the park building along the west edge of the park along 71st Street.

Mile 11.8: There are restrooms in Louis Armstrong Playground on your left on 113th Street.

Mile 18.7: There are restrooms in Queensbridge Park along Vernon Boulevard at 41st Avenue.

Flushing Meadows Corona Park and Flushing Bay Promenade

Flushing Meadows Corona Park encompasses almost 900 acres of sprawling lawns, ball fields, a placid lake, and more. This leisurely route leads along tree-covered park alleés and lakeside paths and passes innumerable recreational spots and relics from two twentieth-century World's Fairs. Just north of the park, the route leads to Flushing Bay Promenade, a 1.5-mile greenway with bay views and sea breezes. This park journey is great for anyone looking for a relaxing break from city streets.

Start: The circular plaza at the end of the number 7 subway ramp at the Mets-Willets Point subway station, next to Louis Armstrong Stadium

Length: 10.1-mile loop (6.0-mile loop, short option without Flushing Bay)

Approximate riding time: 2.0 hours (1.5 hours, short option)

Best bike: Hybrid, road, or mountain bike

Terrain and trail surface: The trail is paved throughout and flat.

Traffic and hazards: This route runs along the perimeter of and into Flushing Meadows Corona Park. The interior pathways are entirely car-free. The perimeter roads (Meadow Lake Road, Shea Road, Perimeter Road) have very light traffic. Stay alert as you approach Flushing Bay, north of the park. To reach the bay, you have to duck underneath the Grand Central Expressway, where you'll cross an access road to the expressway. Check for oncoming traffic in both directions before crossing.

Things to see: Flushing Meadows Corona Park, Meadow Lake, Unisphere, Flushing Bay Promenade, Citi Field, World's Fair Marina

Map: *New York City Bike Map*

Getting there: By public transportation: Take the 7 subway to the Mets-Willets Point station. There is direct access to Flushing Meadows Corona Park via a passerelle heading south. Your starting point is at the end of the passerelle, next to Louis Armstrong Stadium. By car: Take the Long Island Expressway E/I-495 E to exit 21 at 108th Street. Turn left onto 108th Street. Turn right onto 52nd Avenue. Parking is at the park, along 111th Street. To get to the starting point from the lot, bike into the park and follow the signs to the number 7 subway (Mets-Willets Point) or the tennis center. Your starting point is the circular plaza beside Louis Armstrong Stadium. GPS coordinates: N40 45.078' / W73 50.548'

THE RIDE

Louis Armstrong Stadium, just west of your starting point, was the US Open tennis tournament's principal match venue until it was replaced by Arthur Ashe Stadium in 1992. To commence your journey from here, turn left (when facing the park), heading northeast and away from the tennis stadium. You'll reach Perimeter Road just ahead, which circumnavigates the entire north portion of the park. While you share the road with motorists here, traffic is light. The first part of your journey orbits the entire park via its perimeter roads. You'll then explore the park's interior at the end of the ride.

Going clockwise along Perimeter Road, you'll soon cross Flushing River along Porpoise Bridge, built for the 1939 World's Fair to keep saltwater from Flushing Bay from inundating the fairgrounds during storm surges. As you round the bend to the right, you'll then pass the park's Ice Rink on your right, with the expressway running parallel to your route overhead on your left. Continuing southward, you can catch sight of the park's most emblematic icon from the 1964 World's Fair, the Unisphere. From the rounded Industry Pond on your right, your sightline stretches westward, across the elongated Fountain of the Fairs, to the 12-story, stainless steel sphere that represents the world.

Continuing onward, when the road begins to veer away from the overhead expressway, keep your eyes peeled for a sharp left turn that takes you south, underneath the expressway, and toward Meadow Lake. Created for the 1939 World's Fair, Meadow Lake is the city's largest freshwater lake. Boats can be rented—paddle boats, rowboats—during summer months, and, on fair-weather days, barbecues and family gatherings dot the lakeside. As you orbit Meadow Lake, you'll pass gently swaying forests of cord grass, sprawling meadows, ball fields, and playgrounds. Then, heading north along the

Boats moored offshore in Flushing Bay, with a plane taking off from LaGuardia Airport overhead.

lake's western shore, Grand Central Parkway will flank your journey on the left. When you reach the north end of the lake, veer slightly right along Sri Chinmoy Street, one of many tree-lined park alleés lined with benches on either side. The benches here and lakeside wooden deck up ahead are great spots for a rest.

To continue en route, circumnavigate the roundabout at the end of Sri Chinmoy Street to catch Amphitheatre Bridge across the Long Island Expressway and head back to the northern section of the park. As you ascend the bridge, the Unisphere will suddenly loom large up ahead once more. A U-turn on the other side of the bridge then brings you back to Perimeter Road, which you'll follow northward along the western edge of the park. Along the way, you'll pass the Queens Museum of Art on your right, approach the park's national tennis center, and soon come to a crossroad, where Perimeter Road forks to the right. You here have the option of bypassing Flushing Bay Promenade by turning right, following Perimeter Road back toward your starting point. If doing so, skip ahead in the route description.

To follow the main route to Flushing Bay Promenade, continue straight, under the train overpass up ahead, onto what becomes Shea Road. When the road dead-ends at the Mets' Citi Field baseball stadium, turn left and duck underneath the Whitestone Expressway toward Flushing Bay. After passing underneath the overpass, use caution as you approach Flushing

The twelve-story tall Unisphere, built for the 1964 World's Fair at the center of Flushing Meadows Corona Park.

Bay for you'll cross a busy access road. Check for oncoming traffic in both directions before crossing the road and turning left. Then veer quickly right into the World's Fair Marina parking area and to the promenade along the water's edge.

From here, the promenade extends a mile to the west and half a mile to the east, making it a popular gathering spot for anglers and bay-side barbecues. Begin by biking westward toward LaGuardia Airport, where you can spot planes taking off and landing in the near distance. Enjoy the salt air and listen for the clanging of ship masts moored offshore (and ignore the rumble of traffic on the expressway overhead on your left). When you hit the western end of promenade, make a U-turn to explore the promenade's eastern end. Then return via Shea Road to connect to Perimeter Road, where you'll turn left toward Arthur Ashe Stadium and through parking lot B at Louis Armstrong Stadium. Bike through the lot and veer left back toward your starting point.

The route now leads into the park's interior toward the Unisphere, an unofficial symbol of Queens that was built to mark the dawning of the space age and has since been featured in innumerable print ads, television shows, and popular films (*Men in Black,* most famously). To get there, take the park lane known as Avenue of Commerce southeastward. Herbert Hoover

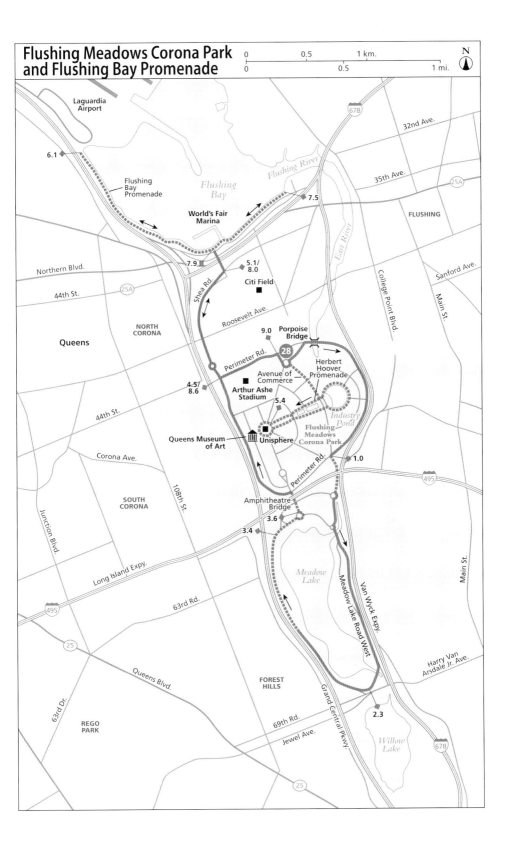

Flushing Meadows Corona Park and Flushing Bay Promenade

0   0.5   1 km.
0   0.5   1 mi.

N

Laguardia Airport

6.1

Flushing Bay Promenade

Flushing River

Flushing Bay

678

32nd Ave.

35th Ave.

25A

FLUSHING

7.5

World's Fair Marina

East River

Northern Blvd.

25A

44th St.

7.9

5.1/ 8.0

Citi Field

College Point Blvd.

Sanford Ave.

Main St.

NORTH CORONA

Queens

Roosevelt Ave.

9.0   Porpoise Bridge

28

Perimeter Rd.

Herbert Hoover Promenade

4.5/ 8.6

Avenue of Commerce

Arthur Ashe Stadium

5.4

Industry Pond

Queens Museum of Art

Unisphere

Flushing Meadows Corona Park

Shea Rd.

44th St.

Perimeter Rd.

1.0

495

Corona Ave.

SOUTH CORONA

108th St.

Amphitheatre Bridge

3.6

3.4

Junction Blvd.

Long Island Expy.

Meadow Lake

Meadow Lake Road West

Van Wyck Expy.

Main St.

495

63rd Rd.

25

Queens Blvd.

FOREST HILLS

Grand Central Pkwy.

Harry Van Arsdale Jr. Ave.

63rd Dr.

REGO PARK

69th Rd.

Jewel Ave.

2.3

Willow Lake

678

25

Promenade then leads you southwest along the Fountain of the Fairs to the Unisphere. Explore the surrounding park space at your leisure, take a break, and then return to your starting point.

MILES AND DIRECTIONS

0.0 From the plaza at the end of the subway passerelle, turn left (when facing the park) to cycle northeastward, in between the tennis courts and toward the northeast edge of the park.

0.2 Veer right across Porpoise Bridge.

1.0 Make a sharp left to head underneath the expressway toward Meadow Lake. After the small bridge, go straight (south) through the parking lot and access Meadow Lake Road West on the other side, continuing south.

2.3 Round the southern tip of the lake to head north along the lake's western edge. Veer right up ahead to stick to the road (and to avoid the on-ramp for the expressway!).

3.4 Go straight along the tree-lined alleé of Sri Chinmoy Street and cir-cumnavigate the roundabout up ahead.

3.6 Exit the roundabout to cross Amphitheatre Bridge, heading north. As soon as you descend on the other side, make a U-turn to your left.

3.8 Turn right onto Perimeter Road.

4.5 To bypass Flushing Bay, turn right to stay on Perimeter Road and skip ahead to mile 8.6. Otherwise, continue straight.

5.1 When the road dead-ends at Citi Field, turn left to duck underneath the expressway. Use caution and stay alert. Cars descending from the expressway on this road travel at a quick tempo. Check both ways for oncoming traffic before crossing.

5.2 After going under the overpass, cross to the north side of the road up ahead and turn left. Veer quickly right and into the World's Fair Marina parking lot and toward the water's edge. Access the bay promenade to head west toward LaGuardia Airport.

6.1 At the end of the promenade, turn around to retrace your prom-enade route and continue to the promenade's eastern end.

7.8 When you reach the eastern end of the promenade, make a U-turn to return toward where you accessed the promenade.

7.9 Stay alert as you descend from the promenade onto the road. Then veer left to turn left underneath the expressway once more, returning toward Citi Field.

8.0 Turn right onto Shea Road.

8.6 Turn left onto Perimeter Road, going east toward Arthur Ashe Stadium. (This is your pick-up point if you bypassed Flushing Bay.)

9.0 Turn right to enter parking lot B at Louis Armstrong Stadium. Veer left at the end of the parking lot to return to your starting point. Once you hit the plaza where you started, catch the second alleé to your right (Avenue of Commerce) into the park's interior.

9.2 At the circular Industry Pond, take your first right onto Herbert Hoover Promenade, putting the elongated fountains on your left, the Fountain of the Fairs.

9.5 Circumnavigate the Unisphere and take a break. To continue, return eastward along the Fountain of the Fairs on Dwight Eisenhower Promenade, with the fountains on your left.

10.0 Loop around Industry Pond and then turn right to return to your starting point via Avenue of Commerce.

10.1 Arrive at your starting point.

RIDE INFORMATION

Restrooms

Start/end: There are restrooms at the foot of the subway passerelle next to the circular plaza.

Mile 3.6: There are restrooms in the park building on the east side of the Amphitheatre Bridge.

29

The Rockaways and Fort Tilden

This relaxing oceanfront route travels through peaceful beachside communities along the Rockaway Peninsula and provides you with sea breezes, ocean views, and beach access along the way. Starting in the east, next to one of the peninsula's most popular surf beaches, it travels along Jacob Riis Park to the westernmost point of the peninsula at Breezy Point. Along the way, the national park of Fort Tilden contains the city's most remote beaches, only accessible by bike or on foot.

Start: The Beach 67 Street-Arverne By The Sea subway station of the A subway line, located at Beach 67th Street and Rockaway Beach Boulevard

Length: 17.0 miles out and back

Approximate riding time: 2 hours

Best bike: Hybrid, road, or mountain bike

Terrain and trail surface: The trail is flat and paved throughout. Hurricane Sandy destroyed much of the boardwalk along the Rockaway Peninsula, so this route runs entirely along paved roads a block inland from the boardwalk. Once (and if) the boardwalk is reconstructed, you can navigate along the boardwalk for portions of this route.

Traffic and hazards: Due to damage sustained during Hurricane Sandy in the fall of 2012, the Rockaways have been in a state of flux over the past couple of years. The terrain will no doubt continue to change in upcoming years, so be on the lookout for beaches, boardwalks, and bikeways that may have become newly accessible since the last riding of this route. Fort Tilden and Breezy Point were particularly heavily damaged.

Rockaway Beach Boulevard from Beach 108th Street to Beach 126th Street is a narrow commercial strip where space is sometimes tight. Stay especially alert here. (West of Beach 126th Street, the road widens and there's an on-road bike lane.) Rockaway Point Boulevard, heading out to Breezy Point, is also a narrow, two-lane road with a narrow border for cyclists. Beach traffic along this stretch is light to moderate (but slow).

Things to see: Rockaway Beach, Fort Tilden, Breezy Point, Jacob Riis Park

Maps: *New York City Bike Map,* Gateway National Recreation Area bike map accessible for download at www.nps.gov/gate/planyourvisit/bike -gateway.htm

Getting there: By public transportation: Take the Far Rockaway-bound A subway to Beach 67 Street-Arverne By the Sea. (Make sure you're not on the Lefferts Avenue-bound A subway.) By car: Take I-495 E to exit 19 onto Woodhaven Boulevard. Go south on Woodhaven Boulevard and continue onto Cross Bay Boulevard. Cross Bay Boulevard becomes Cross Bay Bridge. Exit the bridge straight onto Cross Bay Parkway. Turn left onto Shore Front Parkway and try to find parking on an inland block around Beach 67th Street. With luck, you can find parking on residential streets on the Rockaways or at the public parking between Beach 94th and Beach 95th Streets. GPS coordinates: N40 35.448' / W73 47.764'

THE RIDE

Near your starting point, between Beach 67th and 69th Streets, sits one of the Rockaways' prime surfing spots. Surfers congregate both here and a little farther west, between Beach 87th and 92nd Street, almost year-round to ride the waves. Be sure to stop off to marvel at some of their feats either now or on your return journey.

The first part of your route leads westward along a beachfront road that's framed by bungalow-style beach houses on the right and the ocean on the left, creating a relaxing beach-town vibe. (In the distance, large-scale public housing projects form a striking contrast.) Pre-Hurricane Sandy (2012), a

Bike Shop

Mini Mall: 430 Beach 129th St., Queens; (718) 945-6787
Hidden behind an array of plant stands, this bike shop has a rich 30-year Rockaway history. The owner knows what's happening when and where on the peninsula and will gladly share. He knowingly pointed me toward the day's hot spots (a beachside performance at Beach 80th Street).

beach boardwalk ran the length of the oceanfront and was accessible at innumerable spots between here and Beach 126th Street. Although Hurricane Sandy destroyed much of it, plans are in place to rebuild it and by the summer of 2013 several portions had already been completed. Once the remainder of the boardwalk is complete, you can take the boardwalk westward as far as it goes and then catch Rockaway Beach Boulevard. For the moment, turn inland at Beach 108th Street to reach Rockaway Beach Boulevard.

Heading west along Rockaway Beach Boulevard, stay especially alert along the first stretch, where the road is narrowest and traffic is densest. (It tends to be slow, though.) Then, after crossing the busy commercial strip of Beach 116th Street, the road widens and has an on-road bike lane that affords ample space. You'll cycle through the residential neighborhood of Belle Harbor, marked by tidy, one-family beach-style homes and nicely kept yards. The community made headlines in 2001, when American Airlines Flight 587 crashed here, killing all 260 crew members and passengers on board as well as 5 people on the ground. (A memorial sits at the southern tip of Beach 116th Street.)

Continuing westward, you can spot the arched peaks of the Marine Parkway Gil Hodges Memorial Bridge up head. Built in 1937, it was the first bridge to connect the Rockaways to mainland New York City. A second bridge, the Veterans Memorial Cross Bay Bridge, opened in 1970 at Beach 94th Street farther east. After crossing Beach 149th Street up ahead, your journey veers away from the road and into Jacob Riis Park on your left. Take the small pathway next to the baseball diamond to reach the paved beachside promenade to continue west through Jacob Riis Park. Established more than a century ago as a seaside getaway for city folk, the park was named after Jacob Riis, the early-20th-century muckraking journalist who recorded the plight of the poor. Today, the wide beach and boardwalk, and the adjoining ball courts and golf course, continue to attract New Yorkers seeking an escape from the city heat on summer weekends. From Memorial Day to Labor Day, city lifeguards are here.

Up ahead, Riis Boardwalk ends at the eastern edge of Fort Tilden, which you can reach, if open, via a small lane just off Beach 169th Street. If accessible, explore the grounds via Davis Road, which leads down to some of the area's most serene and secluded beaches. To continue, you'll then head to the northern end of Beach 169th Street to catch State Road. Come to a complete stop before crossing to the north side of the road and check in both directions for oncoming traffic. Cars travel quickly here.

Cycling west along State Road, you will see Fort Tilden ball fields and community gardens on your left and the bay-side ferry dock at Riis Landing on your right. Then, at the end of State Road, you'll reach the private

Bike stands were implemented in Fort Tilden on the Rockaways in recent years to accommodate a growing number of cyclists.

neighborhood of Breezy Point, a 500-acre cooperative-owned community. A security checkpoint guards the entrance to the community, limiting entries to the area. If asked, stop and tell the guard you want to explore. Most of the roads in Breezy Point are private and inaccessible, so stick to the main road of Rockaway Point Boulevard as you head west. You'll then return eastward via a paved beachfront promenade to your entry point to the community at the security gate. Breezy Point was especially hard hit by Hurricane Sandy, so expect to see some beach-side houses in disuse.

After leaving Breezy Point, return eastward via your outbound route, but be sure to take an ocean-front or bay-side break before heading home. The options abound: Grab a bite to eat at one of innumerable snack stands—pizza, dumplings, ice cream—in Jacob Riis Park (during summer months), lock your bike, and head down to the beach for a break. Pick up some provisions at a deli along Beach 116th Street for an ocean-front picnic farther east. Head to the deck-side cafe and bar The Wharf, overlooking Jamaica Bay at the north end of Beach 116th Street. Join the crowds at one of the beachside snack spots east of Beach 108th Street and watch the surfers. Ripper's, at Beach 86th Street, is a popular choice (open during summer months). Relax and replenish; then return to your starting point.

0.0 Head south on Beach 67th Street, toward the ocean.

0.2 Turn right onto Shore Front Parkway.

0.5 Circumnavigate the roundabout and continue west along the ocean-front on the other side.

1.1 The popular beachfront cafe Rippers is on your left.

2.1 Turn right onto Beach 108th Street.

2.2 Turn left onto Rockaway Beach Boulevard.

4.2 At Beach 149th Street, veer left to continue west along the southern edge of Rockaway Beach Boulevard. Turn left just ahead to take the narrow pathway to the left of the ball fields toward the beachfront.

4.4 Turn right to head west along Riis Boardwalk.

5.3 Turn right onto Beach 169th Street.

5.5 You can access Fort Tilden along the lane to your left. If you enter, the lane becomes Davis Road. To continue toward Breezy Point, head to the northern end of Beach 169th Street.

5.7 Turn left onto State Road.

5.8 Riis Landing is on your right.

6.8 You can access Fort Tilden, if open, via Beach 193rd Street on your left. Alternately, continue straight toward Breezy Point.

Fort Tilden

Fort Tilden was established in 1917 to help protect New York Harbor from naval attack during World War I. It continued with military duties throughout World War II and served as a Nike missile station during the Cold War. The Army transferred Fort Tilden to the National Park Service in 1974. Today, the former military base is a protected national historic site and offers a unique mix of decommissioned military structures and spots of natural beauty. Biking the pathways that crisscross the grounds, you're surrounded by dunes, cord grass, and beach shrubbery on all sides. Although Fort Tilden has become increasingly popular in recent years, it still stands out for its untouched beaches.

The Rockaways and Fort Tilden

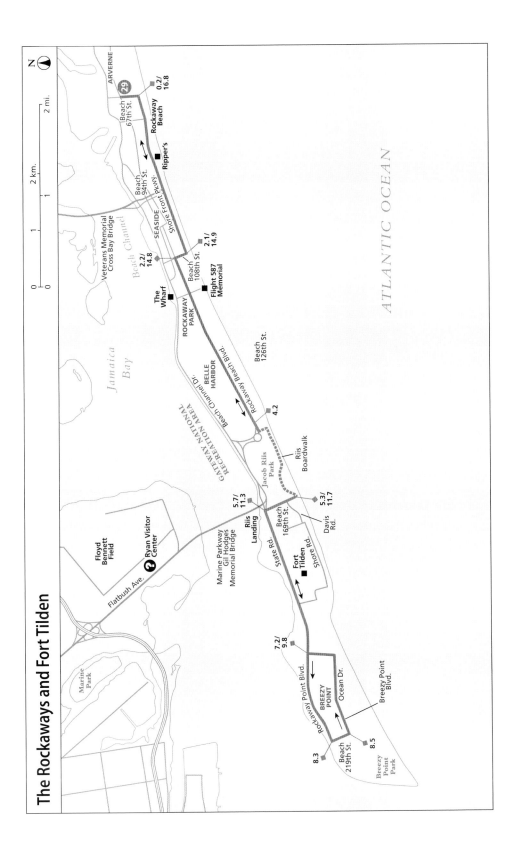

ARVERNE

29   Beach 67th St.

Rockaway Beach   0.2/16.8

Ripper's

Beach 94th St.   Shore Front Pkwy.

SEASIDE

Veterans Memorial Cross Bay Bridge

Beach Channel

The Wharf   2.2/14.8

Beach 108th St.   2.1/14.9

ROCKAWAY PARK

Flight 587 Memorial

BELLE HARBOR

Beach Channel Dr.

Rockaway Beach Blvd.

GATEWAY NATIONAL RECREATION AREA

Beach 126th St.

4.2

Jacob Riis Park

Riis Boardwalk

ATLANTIC OCEAN

Jamaica Bay

Floyd Bennett Field

Ryan Visitor Center

Flatbush Ave.

Marine Park

Riis Landing   5.7/11.3

Beach 169th St.   5.3/11.7

Davis Rd.

State Rd.

Fort Tilden

Shore Rd.

Marine Parkway Gil Hodges Memorial Bridge

7.2/9.8

Rockaway Point Blvd.

BREEZY POINT

Ocean Dr.

Breezy Point Blvd.

8.3

Beach 219th St.   8.5

Breezy Point Park

N

0   1   2 km.

0   1   2 mi.

7.2 State Road becomes Rockaway Point Boulevard. The security checkpoint to Breezy Point is here.

8.3 Turn left onto Beach 219th Street.

8.5 Turn left onto Breezy Point Boulevard.

8.8 Continue straight onto the beach promenade of Ocean Drive.

9.5 Turn left, following the promenade as it exits through the parking area and returns to the security checkpoint.

9.8 Turn right to exit Breezy Point onto State Road. Head east on State Road.

11.3 Turn right onto Beach 169th Street.

11.7 Turn left onto Riis Boardwalk.

12.6 When the promenade ends, turn left alongside the baseball field to return to Rockaway Beach Boulevard.

12.7 Turn right onto Rockaway Beach Boulevard.

14.8 Turn right onto Beach 108th Street.

14.9 Turn left onto Shore Front Parkway.

16.0 Rippers is on your right.

16.8 Turn left onto Beach 67th Street.

17.0 Arrive at your starting point.

RIDE INFORMATION

Restaurants

Rippers: A popular beach cafe on the boardwalk at Beach 86th Street. (718) 634-3034; 86badvibes.com

The Wharf: A serene bay-side cafe with outdoor terrace that serves typical waterfront fare and offers excellent views across Jamaica Bay to the Manhattan skyline. To get there, head to the northern end of Beach 116th Street, cross the road, and go right around the gas station. The entrance to The Wharf sits behind the lube station. 416 Beach 116th St.; (718) 474-8807

Restrooms

Mile 1.1/16.0: There are restrooms and water fountains at the beach building at Beach 86th Street and other spots along the beachfront.

Mile 5.1: There are restrooms in the park building in Jacob Riis Park on your right.

Mile 11.9: There are restrooms in the park building in Jacob Riis Park on your left.

Forest Park and Forest Hills Gardens

Forest Park comprises 540 acres of woodlands, wetlands, and outdoor recreational terrain. This route leads through the park's peaceful pine grove, amongst majestic oaks, and over softly rolling forest terrain. On weekends, the park attracts cyclists, joggers, families, and other outdoor enthusiasts, but rarely gets overly crowded. The second part of the journey, through Forest Hills Gardens at the northeastern corner of Forest Park, leads through a century-old planned community of red-roofed houses, sculpted gardens, and tree-lined streets, reminiscent of Tudor-style Europe. This peaceful, nearly car-free bike route through shaded woodlands is a great option for those with limited city cycling experience, too.

Start: The Overlook, at the east end of Forest Park

Length: 8.0 miles out and back

Approximate riding time: 1.5 hours

Best bike: Road, hybrid, or mountain bike

Terrain and trail surface: Streets along the trail are paved. The terrain is softly rolling.

Traffic and hazards: This route crosses two heavily trafficked intersections—Woodhaven Boulevard and Union Turnpike—but is otherwise nearly car-free. The greenway through Forest Park's east section is entirely car-free and the western portion has only light traffic. In Forest Hills Gardens, you'll bike along residential streets with very few cars.

Things to see: Forest Park, Pine Grove, Carousel, Forest Hills Gardens, Seuffert Bandshell, Station Square

Maps: *New York City Bike Map,* City of New York Parks and Recreation Map: www.nycgovparks.org/parks/forestpark/map

Getting there: By public transportation: Take the F or E subway to the Kew Gardens/Union Turnpike station. Exit the station onto 80th Road.

Bike southwest on 80th Road about 0.3 mile to reach Park Lane. Turn right onto Park Lane and enter Forest Park at Forest Park Drive on your left. The Overlook is on your left. GPS coordinates: N40 42.649' / W73 50.181'

THE RIDE

Forest Park comprises 540 acres of woodlands, wetlands, flora, and fauna, and is known for its hilly "knob and kettle" terrain, formed by the edge of the Harbor Hill Moraine left behind by the massive Wisconsin glacier some 20,000 years ago. The Overlook, your starting point, is named for what were once far-reaching views across the park, but trees obscure much of the view today. From here, catch the car-free Forest Park Drive westward. The park drive, like so many other city green spaces, was designed by Frederick Law Olmsted in the 1890s.

Heading west, you'll cycle through a tranquil pine grove, sowed in 1912. The city planted 2,500 pines after a fungus killed 15,000 chestnut trees in the forest that year. Some of these original pines stand up to 100 feet high today. Continuing westward, you'll scale several gentle hills before reaching Victory Field on your right at Woodhaven Boulevard. Heed the traffic signal to cross this boulevard, where traffic can be dense.

Bike Shops

Gray's Bicycle: 82-34 Lefferts Blvd.; (718) 441-9767
A bike shop with a half-century-long history and a neighborhood feel, where the owner is likely to greet you warmly with "honey." They fix bikes, sell bikes, and have bikes for rent (by the hour or day).
Spokesman Cycles: 80-16 Cooper Ave.; (718) 366-0450
Located in the Atlas Park shopping mall, Spokesman Cycles is a large full-service bike shop with an extensive selection of brand-name bikes as well as bike parts, clothing, and accessories. A great place for high-tech gear.

The next stretch westward along Forest Park Drive shares the road with cars, but traffic is very light. Stop off to explore any of the park's walking trails that lead off from the main drive. Strack Pond, for example, opposite the Forest Park Carousel, is a peaceful freshwater haven where herons, wranglers, and butterflies abound. To check out the Carousel, turn right toward the park's picnic area, where you can access the carousel via the stone steps on the right side of the drive. The intricately carved horses, lions, and unicorns

The bike trail that skirts the edge of Forest Park Golf Course.

The Overlook

The Overlook was designed in 1911 to house the headquarters of the newly established Queens Parks Department. Until then, the Brooklyn Parks Department had managed all Queens parks, including Forest Park, called Brooklyn Forest Park at the time. The Spanish Mission–style building was named for its sweeping views across Forest Park and originally was just a one-room house. One of its most noteworthy residents was the author Henry Miller (1892–1980), who worked for the Queens Parks Department for some time, first as grave digger and later as office assistant. One anguished night in 1927, after his wife, June, had left him for Paris, he reputedly stayed up all, tormentedly typing thirty-two pages that shaped much of his literary work to come.

that populate this merry-go-round were carved more than a century ago by Daniel Carl Muller, a German immigrant who was renowned for his ornate wood-carving. Continuing en route, you'll pass the Seuffert Bandshell on your right, named after the Brooklyn-born son of Bavarian immigrants who began hosting concerts here in the early twentieth century. It can host up to 3,500 people and continues to provide free concerts during summer months.

When you reach the Forest Park Golf Course up ahead, stay right to cycle through the golf course parking lot, continuing westward. Then follow the bikeway to the right, skirting the edge of the golf course, and cycling through a grove of red and black oaks. After ducking underneath a shallow overpass up ahead, you'll turn left and reach the playground and park building that mark the western end of the park. Make a U-turn here to retrace your route along Forest Park Drive back to the Overlook.

When you reach the Overlook once more, the second part of your journey ensues. To visit the planned community of Forest Hills Gardens, exit Forest Park onto Park Lane and enter through the gates at Union Turnpike. Designed by Frederick Law Olmsted Jr. (Olmsted's son) and Grosvenor Atterbury, this planned community was established in 1909 and feels far removed from New York City. Bike along tree-lined streets with Tudor-style, red-roofed houses, passing manicured yards and picturesque stone churches along the way. You'll then soon reach Station Square, a redbrick town plaza where the Long Island Railroad makes a stop. Stop off for a drink at one of the cafe terraces along the square before retracing your route through Forest Hills Gardens back to Forest Park's Overlook.

Forest Park and Forest Hills Gardens

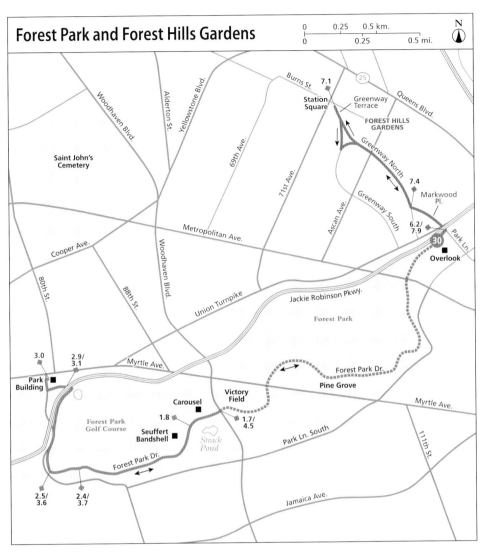

0   0.25   0.5 km.

0   0.25   0.5 mi.

N

Burns St.   **7.1**   (25)

Station Square

Greenway Terrace

FOREST HILLS GARDENS

Greenway North

7.4

Markwood Pl.

Greenway South

6.2/7.9

30

Overlook

Park Ln

Woodhaven Blvd.

Alderton St.

Yellowstone Blvd.

69th Ave.

71st Ave.

Ascan Ave.

Queens Blvd.

Saint John's Cemetery

Metropolitan Ave.

Cooper Ave.

Woodhaven Blvd.

80th St.

88th St.

Union Turnpike

Jackie Robinson Pkwy.

Forest Park

Myrtle Ave.

Forest Park Dr.

Pine Grove

Myrtle Ave.

111th St.

3.0

2.9/3.1

Park Building

Forest Park Golf Course

Carousel

1.8

Seuffert Bandshell

Strack Pond

Victory Field

1.7/4.5

Park Ln. South

Forest Park Dr.

2.5/3.6

2.4/3.7

Jamaica Ave.

MILES AND DIRECTIONS

0.0   From the Overlook, turn left onto Forest Park Drive.

1.7   Cross Woodhaven Boulevard and catch the greenway on the other side.

1.8 The Carousel is on your right.

2.4 Veer slightly right off Forest Park Drive to go straight through the golf course parking lot (with the golf course on your right).

2.5 At the end of the parking lot, follow the bikeway to the right, continuing along the golf course. Follow the bikeway as it veers right up ahead.

2.9 After the underpass, turn left.

3.0 The park building at the west end of the park is your turnaround point. Make a U-turn to retrace your route to the overlook.

3.1 Duck underneath the overpass. Follow the greenway as it skirts the edge of the golf course.

3.6 Turn left through the parking lot, continuing along the greenway.

3.7 Exit the parking lot straight ahead onto Forest Park Drive.

4.5 Cross Woodhaven Boulevard and enter the east section of the park next to Victory Field.

6.2 Exit Forest Park and turn left onto Park Lane.

6.3 Cross Union Turnpike and enter Forrest Hills Gardens on Markwood Place. Markwood Place becomes Greenway North. Continue straight as Greenway North becomes Greenway Terrace.

7.1 Circumnavigate redbrick square of Greenway Terrace, also called Station Square. Take a break here. Then make a U-turn to return across Greenway Terrace square. Stay right of the triangular island at the center of the road. Turn sharply left and then right at its end to catch Greenway North back toward Markwood Place.

7.4 Stay left when the road splits to take Markwood Place back to the entrance of Forest Hills Gardens.

7.7 Cross Union Turnpike onto Park Lane.

7.9 Turn left onto Forest Park Drive.

8.0 Arrive at your starting point.

RIDE INFORMATION

Restrooms
Start/end: There are restrooms at the Overlook.
Mile 3.0: There are restrooms in the park building at the west end of Forest Park.

Staten Island

The greenway through LaTourette Park, part of the Staten Island Greenbelt (Ride 33).

Separated from the other four boroughs by Upper New York Bay, Staten Island can feel far removed from New York City. It's the most suburban of the five boroughs, with fewer bike lanes and more motor vehicles. This means that cyclists on shared roads here should use extra caution whilst taking in the island's relaxed residential vibe. One of the great rewards of venturing across the Bay onto Staten Island is that it allows you to discover some of the city's less-cycled paths. The island's 2,800-acre Staten Island Greenbelt connects seven city parks and affords ample cycling opportunities surrounded by nature. Miles of multi-use bike paths through parks and along beaches afford car-free cycling opportunities without worry. Also, the island's hilly terrain provides a interesting change from the relatively flat landscape throughout most of the other boroughs. And of course, getting there by ferry is one of the joys of these rides, too.

Bike shops are relatively few and far between, here, so be sure to bring flat fixings.

This ride takes you to three very distinct Staten Island parks. The first, Snug Harbor, is a cultural center and botanical garden that started off as a hospital for aging seamen. The second, Clove Lakes Park, is a "forever wild" site, a designation the city's parks department bestows to preserve natural spots that are of unique ecological value. The third, Silver Lake Park, is Staten Island's Central Park, with a serene lake at its heart. Spring bloom and fall foliage make this ride particularly enjoyable, so try to go in spring or fall.

Start: St. George Ferry Terminal, opposite Staten Island Borough Hall

Length: 11.9-mile loop

Approximate riding time: 2 hours

Best bike: Hybrid, road, or mountain bike

Terrain and trail surface: The trail is paved throughout and hilly. Bement Avenue takes you up 130 feet. From the north end of Clove Lakes Park to Victory Boulevard, it goes up another 100 feet along a steady upward slog. Victory Boulevard then takes you downhill, only to go up again toward Silver Lake Park.

Traffic and hazards: While this route visits three Staten Island Parks, it also travels along residential and urban roads with light to moderate traffic, so some urban cycling comfort is required. Victory Boulevard has no bike lane and moderate traffic, but the road's breadth gives bikers ample space.

Things to see: Snug Harbor, Chinese Scholar Garden, Clove Lakes Park, Silver Lake Park

Maps: *New York City Bike Map,* Snug Harbor Cultural Center map: www .snug-harbor.org/plan-your-visit

Getting there: By public transportation: Take the Staten Island Ferry from Manhattan's Whitehall Terminal to Staten Island's St. George

Terminal. To get to Manhattan's Whitehall Terminal, take the R subway to the Whitehall Street station or the 1 subway to the South Ferry station. By car: If using the Verrazano-Narrows Bridge, exit toward I-278 W / New Jersey and take exit 14 on the left toward Narrows Road W/Hylan Boulevard. Turn right onto Fingerboard Road. Turn left onto Bay Street and follow Bay Street until you reach the St. George Ferry Terminal where there's parking.

If using the Bayonne Bridge, take exit 13 to turn right onto Morningstar Road toward Richmond Terrace. Turn right onto Richmond Terrace, heading east. Follow Richmond Terrace to the ferry terminal. GPS coordinates: N40 38.555' / W74 04.512'

THE RIDE

From the Staten Island ferry terminal, you'll head north toward the Staten Island Yankees baseball stadium, home of Staten Island's minor league baseball team. You'll cycle down to the water's edge from here, where a waterfront esplanade takes you northwest along Staten Island's north shore. You'll pass the borough's September 11 Memorial along the water's edge on your right and have sweeping views in multiple directions. Across Upper New York Bay to the east you can spot the Brooklyn shore. To the north, if you strain, you might see the Statue of Liberty and Ellis Island. Across Kill Van Kull, glancing northwest, you'll see industrial harbors of New Jersey.

At the western end of the esplanade, the route returns to Richmond Terrace, where a bike lane continues westward. You'll pass Gerardi's Farmers Market on your right and then soon reach Snug Harbor Cultural Center up ahead on your left. You can enter Snug Harbor via the gate on Snug Harbor Road and follow the road as it veers to the right and past a string of red cottages along Cottage Row. The cottages once housed bakers, butchers, sailors, and other merchants. Today, they serve as residencies for interns and emerging artists. Heading east along Chapel Road, you'll then pass Snug Harbor's Sailors Chapel before veering left along a narrow pathway that leads toward the heroic Neptune Fountain, where Neptune sits atop a serpent, poised to tackle.

Returning westward along a park pathway, you'll travel past five landmarked Greek Revival–style buildings (Snug Harbor Buildings A through E) on your left, the first of which—Building C in the middle—stems from 1830. Once you're back on Cottage Row, you'll continue southward through the park, past a Chinese Scholar Garden on your right and a lovely archway of hornbeam trees on your left. Lock up or walk your bike to explore other parts

Biking through Clove Lakes Park. The park is home to a more-than-300-year-old tulip tree.

The Largest Living Thing

Clove Lakes Park is dotted with lakes and ponds, all of which were created by a series of dams built across Clove Brook beginning in the 1600s. The water pressure from some of the earliest dams was used to operate the local mills. Today the park's claim to fame is a 300-plus-year-old, more than 100 foot-tall tulip tree in its northwest section—it's Staten Island's largest living thing.

of the park—the glass house, the herb garden—before exiting the park at its southern edge onto Henderson Avenue.

A left onto Bement Avenue soon takes you into the residential neighborhood of West Brighton, where you'll go steadily uphill along one-family houses with pleasant front yards. Next, you'll reach Clove Lakes Park on Martling Avenue. Before crossing the bridge, turn right into the park, with the lake on your left. Heading north along the pathway, yield to pedestrians and joggers along the way. You'll then cross the lake via a picturesque red-railinged bridge to head south along the lake's opposite shore. You'll pass another quaintly arched bridge on your left before following the path as it climbs back up to road level to your right, returning you to Martling Avenue.

The next leg of your journey leads along the western edge of Clove Lakes Park. To explore the woods and wetlands in the southern portion of Clove Lakes Park before heading on, turn left onto Martling Avenue and, before crossing the bridge, enter the park to your right (the water will be on your left). Walk your bike as biking is prohibited in this southern portion of the park. When you're ready to continue, return to Martling Avenue to then go uphill along Slosson Avenue, brushing the park's western edge.

From the top of the hill, you'll then go downhill along Victory Boulevard. Stay alert here. Traffic is moderate and travels at a quicker pace. In front of you in the distance, you'll have sweeping views of Staten Island's woodlands as they roll into the distance. After passing Woodland Cemetery on your right, the route then goes uphill toward Silver Lake Park. Grab a snack at one of the delis along the way to enjoy in Silver Lake Park just ahead.

Enter Silver Lake Park next to the golf course along the car-free (on weekends) park road. Heading north, the golf course will frame your ride on the left, and you'll have views across the reservoir on your right. Then, after biking about halfway around the reservoir, turn right to bike across the bridge to the benches along the eastern edge of the water; it's a lovely spot for a break. To proceed en route, bike back across the reservoir and continue north along

Fall foliage in Clove Lakes Park.

Silver Lake Park Road. Brighton Avenue then carries you northward back to the waterfront esplanade via mostly residential roads. Follow the waterfront back to your starting point.

MILES AND DIRECTIONS

0.0 From the Staten Island ferry terminal, turn right onto Richmond Terrace.

0.2 Turn right onto Wall Street, followed by a left at the water's edge to bike along the water along the North Shore Esplanade.

1.2 Turn left onto Jersey Street, followed by a quick right onto Richmond Terrace.

2.1 Turn left onto Snug Harbor Road, followed by a quick left into the gates of Snug Harbor. Follow the road (unmarked, but officially called Cottage Row) as it veers right, slightly uphill.

2.2 Turn left onto Chapel Road. After passing the chapel (playhouse) on your right, turn left at the parking lot, onto Melville Road. Veer right when the path splits, heading toward the fountain (the fountain will be on your right).

2.6 Turn left to go up Randall Way, followed by a right onto Chapel Road.

Best Bike Rides New York City

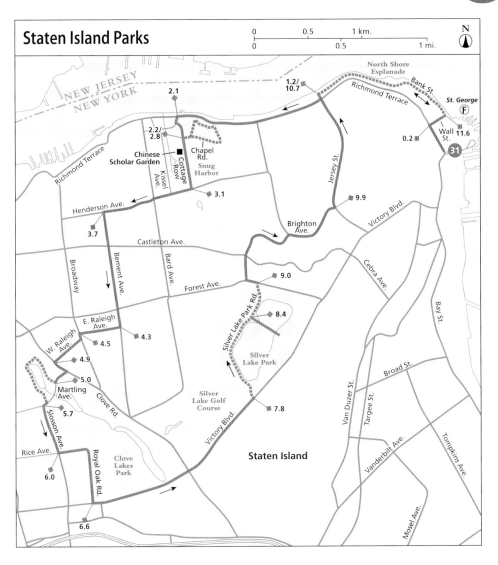

Staten Island Parks

0   0.5   1 km.

0   0.5   1 mi.

N

NEW JERSEY
NEW YORK

Richmond Terrace

North Shore Esplanade

Bank St.

Richmond Terrace

St. George
F

1.2/10.7

2.1

2.2/2.8

0.2

Wall St. 11.6

31

Chinese Scholar Garden

Chapel Rd.

Cottage Row

Snug Harbor

Kissel Ave.

3.1

Jersey St.

9.9

Victory Blvd.

Henderson Ave.

3.7

Castleton Ave.

Brighton Ave.

Broadway

Bement Ave.

Bard Ave.

Forest Ave.

9.0

Cebra Ave.

Bay St.

E. Raleigh Ave.

4.3

4.5

W. Raleigh Ave.

Silver Lake Park Rd.

8.4

Silver Lake Park

Broad St.

4.9

5.0

Martling Ave.

Clove Rd.

Silver Lake Golf Course

7.8

Van Duzer St.

Targee St.

Vanderbilt Ave.

Tompkins Ave.

5.7

Slosson Ave.

Rice Ave.

6.0

Royal Oak Rd.

Clove Lakes Park

Victory Blvd.

Staten Island

6.6

Mosel Ave.

2.8 Turn left to catch Cottage Row, going south.

2.9 The entrance to the Chinese Scholar Garden is on your right.

3.1 Exit Snug Harbor and turn right onto Henderson Avenue.

3.7 Turn left onto Bement Avenue.

4.3 Turn right onto East Raleigh Avenue.

Snug Harbor

When a former sea captain (Robert Richard Randall) died in 1801, his will specified that his estate near Washington Square in Manhattan serve as a hospital for tired and aging seamen and be named Sailors Snug Harbor. At the time, the site was rural. Due to a challenge to his will, however, it took another three decades before his will could be set in motion. By that time, the landscape around Washington Square had changed considerably, making it unsuitable for the endeavor. (And it was deemed more profitable to use the land for other purposes.) The will's trustees thus relocated the site to Staten Island, where the first buildings opened in the 1830s. Over the years, more buildings were added and the site accommodated dormitories, a chapel, music hall, and main hall, among other structures.

When the trustees of Snug Harbor spoke of destroying the old buildings in the 1960s, the City Landmarks committee intervened and named Buildings A through E official historic landmarks. The wrought-iron fence that surrounds the site and the gatehouse on Richmond Terrace have since then also been named landmarks. Shortly thereafter, in a series of purchases throughout the 1970s, the City of New York acquired the 83-acre site, and by 1976 all of the remaining sailors at the site were moved to other locations.

By 1976 volunteers had managed to raise enough money to open Snug Harbor as a cultural center, hosting its first arts exhibit one year later. Today, the Snug Harbor Cultural Center hosts film series, readings, arts exhibits, concerts, dance, and theater performances year-round. These performances and the site's many gardens bring over 250,000 visitors to the center each year.

4.5 Turn left onto Broadway, followed by a quick right onto West Raleigh Avenue.

4.9 Turn left onto Clove Road, followed by a right onto Martling Avenue.

5.0 Before crossing the bridge, enter Clove Lakes Park on your right on the park path. Yield to pedestrians.

5.2 Turn left to cross the red-railinged bridge. On the other side, turn left to head south along the west side of the lake.

5.3 When the path splits, veer left along the lake.

5.7 At the end of this northern portion of the park, use the pedestrian signal to cross Martling Avenue. If you wish to explore the southern portion of the park, turn left onto Martling and enter the park on your right. Dismount and walk your bike as biking is prohibited in this part of the park. To continue, catch Slosson Avenue from Martling Avenue, going uphill along the park's western edge.

6.0 Turn left onto Rice Avenue, and follow the road as it veers right and becomes Royal Oak Road.

6.6 Turn left onto Victory Boulevard.

7.8 After passing Silver Lake Golf Course, turn left to enter Silver Lake Park on Silver Lake Park Road. The reservoir will be on your right.

8.4 Turn right onto the bridge across Silver Lake. The benches along the east shore of the reservoir are a great spot for a break. To continue, backtrack across the bridge and turn right to continue north on Silver Lake Park Road.

9.0 Turn left onto Forest Avenue, followed by a quick right onto Brighton Avenue. Follow Brighton Avenue as it veers right.

9.9 Turn left onto Jersey Street.

10.7 At the end of Jersey Street, turn right onto Bank Street and retrace your route back toward the Staten Island ferry terminal.

11.6 After the ballpark, turn right onto Wall Street, followed by a left onto Richmond Terrace.

11.9 Arrive at the ferry terminal.

RIDE INFORMATION

Local Event/Attraction
Snug Harbor Cultural Center: A cultural center and botanical garden located in what used to be a home for retired sailors. 1000 Richmond Ter.; (718) 448-2500; www.snug-harbor.org

Restrooms
Start/end: There are restrooms at the ferry terminal.
Mile 2.9: There are restrooms in numerous buildings throughout Snug Harbor, for example in the entrance building to the Chinese Scholar Garden.

Beaches and Bastions

This route leads past Staten Island's prime coastal defense bastion of Fort Wadsworth, where fortification remnants stand tall beside the towering Verrazano-Narrows Bridge. You'll then cycle along the island's sweeping South Beach coast all the way south to Miller Field, a former Air Force airfield turned recreational spot. Bay views and beach breezes accompany you along most of this ride, making it a great option for anyone in need of a city getaway. It's also a good option for those less confident with city cycling as most of the journey is on separated greenways.

Start: St. George Ferry Terminal, in front of Staten Island Borough Hall

Length: 14.4 miles out and back

Approximate riding time: 2 hours

Best bike: Road, hybrid, or mountain bike

Terrain and trail surface: The trail is paved throughout most of the journey, except for the boardwalk portion. Along the Staten Island beachfront you have the option of taking the paved bikeway or the boardwalk. The boardwalk is made of wooden planks. The terrain is flat, except for the area surrounding Fort Wadsworth, which sits on a bluff and has one steep hill.

Traffic and hazards: About one fourth of this route leads along an on-road bike lane on Bay Street, where traffic is lightest on Sunday mornings. The rest of the route is on a separated bikeway where there's no traffic.

Things to see: Alice Austen House, Fort Wadsworth, Miller Field, Staten Island Beaches, Verrazano-Narrows Bridge

Maps: *New York City Bike Map,* National Park Service Gateway National Recreation Area Staten Island Bike Map: www.nps.gov/gate/planyourvisit/upload/Staten_Island_Bike_Map_Low_Rez.pdf

Getting there: By public transportation: Take the Staten Island Ferry from Manhattan's Whitehall Terminal to Staten Island's St. George Terminal. To get to Manhattan's Whitehall Terminal, take the R subway to the Whitehall Street station or the 1 subway to the South Ferry station. By car: If using the Verrazano-Narrows Bridge, exit toward I-278 W / New Jersey and take exit 14 on the left toward Narrows Road W/Hylan Boulevard. Turn right onto Fingerboard Road. Turn left onto Bay Street and follow Bay Street until you reach the St. George Ferry Terminal where there's parking.

If using the Bayonne Bridge, take exit 13 to turn right onto Morningstar Road toward Richmond Terrace. Turn right onto Richmond Terrace, heading east. Follow Richmond Terrace to the ferry terminal. GPS coordinates: N40 38.539' / W74 04.530'

THE RIDE

The start of your journey leads southward along Bay Street, the main road along Staten Island's eastern shore. It first leads through the waterfront neighborhood of Tompkinsville, established in 1816 and considered the island's oldest European village. You'll pass Tappen Park on your right, a picturesque town square complete with graceful gazebo, elegant brickwork, and wrought-iron lanterns. If you glance to your left along the way, you'll get occasional glimpses of the elevated Staten Island Railway, which runs the length of the island to its southern tip at Tottenville.

After ducking underneath the railroad, Edgewater Street then leads you through a semi-

Bike Shop

NYC Bicycle Shop: 1178 Bay St.; (718) 569-0333
New to Staten Island in 2012, this bike shop branched out from a Manhattan mainstay with a long-established history. Satisfy all your biking needs here, from sales to repairs, from rentals to parts.

industrial stretch for a short spurt before bringing you to the panoramic waterfront promenade of Bruno Beach. Here, you'll have sweeping bay views that are framed by the Verrazano-Narrows Bridge in the south, the Manhattan skyline in the north, and the Brooklyn waterfront across the bay. At the end of the road sits the landmark Alice Austen House, where the pioneering photographer Alice Austen once lived. Today it's a museum that displays selections of Austen's work. Stop off if you wish. Then continue southward on Bay Street.

Goats grazing and serving as living lawn mowers at Fort Wadsworth, an area first fortified by the Dutch in the seventeenth century. The Verrazano-Narrows Bridge looms overhead.

Bay Street then soon leads to the gates of Fort Wadsworth, part of the Gateway National Recreation Area. After passing the site's visitor center up ahead on your left, you'll reach the enclave's main sites along Tompkins Avenue. You'll pass a fort on your left, a battery on your right, and have the Verrazano-Narrows Bridge towering over you. The Overlook at the road's end gives you a bird's-eye view of the fort's main battery at the foot of the hill. Across the water sits Bay Ridge, Brooklyn. You'll reach the Battery via a steep descent along Hudson Road to your left. Explore the site at your leisure and then scale the opposite hill to go underneath the Verrazano-Narrows Bridge. You'll then skirt the edge of a ball field before turning left onto USS North Carolina Road, which leads downhill to the waterside. You can here access an unprotected beach area across the dunes on your left. Up ahead, keep your eyes peeled for a narrow bikeway that leads off to the left and toward the main boardwalk along Staten Island's South Beach shore.

When the bikeway reaches the boardwalk up ahead, you have two options. You can either continue along the paved bikeway you're on or access the boardwalk bikeway for 2.5 miles of boardwalk biking, but boardwalk biking is officially only permitted from 5 to 10 a.m. I took the paved pathway out, the boardwalk back, and this route description does the same. At the Vanderbilt hotel, stay right of the hotel, cycling along the hotel drive to follow

Best Bike Rides New York City

Going north along the South Beach boardwalk toward the Verrazano-Narrows Bridge.

the bikeway. The coastal bikeway ends at Miller Field, a former Army Air Force Base that boasted grass runways in its heyday. It's now a recreational spot operated by the National Park Service. Explore the former airfield along the bikeways that crisscross the field at your leisure before returning to the coast to retrace your route northward.

When you reach Freedom Circle, the circular, flag-bedecked platform along the boardwalk, veer right to stay on the boardwalk. Follow the marked bike lane and yield to pedestrians as you head north toward the ever-larger Verrazano-Narrows Bridge. Stop off along the boardwalk benches or board-walk cafe for a break before retracing your route to the ferry terminal.

MILES AND DIRECTIONS

- **0.0** Cross to the west side of Bay Street to turn left, going south on Bay Street.
- **1.7** Veer left onto Edgewater Street.
- **2.2** To explore Alice Austen Park, dismount and explore the park straight ahead. To continue, turn right, going uphill on Hylan Boulevard, followed by a left onto Bay Street.

Beaches and Bastions

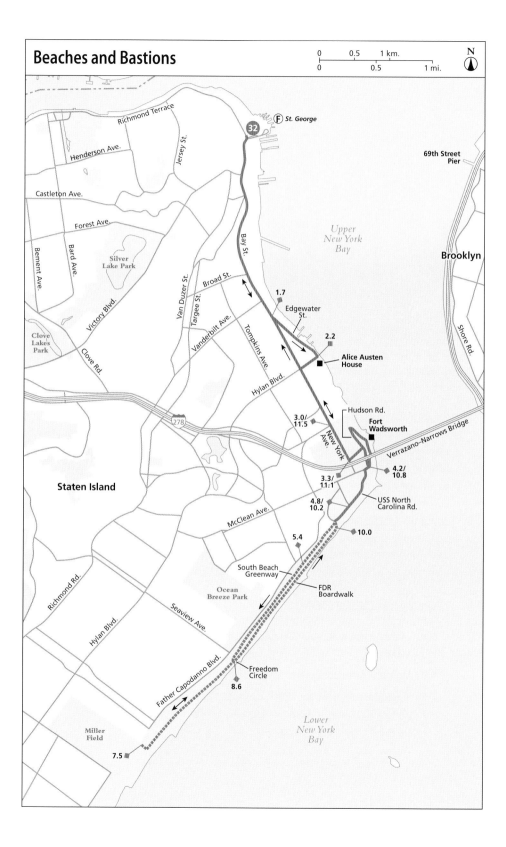

0   0.5   1 km.
0   0.5   1 mi.

N

F St. George

32

69th Street Pier

Richmond Terrace

Henderson Ave.

Jersey St.

Castleton Ave.

Forest Ave.

Silver Lake Park

Bard Ave.

Bement Ave.

Victory Blvd.

Clove Lakes Park

Clove Rd.

Van Duzer St.

Targee St.

Vanderbilt Ave.

Broad St.

Bay St.

Tompkins Ave.

Hylan Blvd.

Upper New York Bay

Brooklyn

Shore Rd.

1.7

Edgewater St.

2.2

Alice Austen House

Hudson Rd.

Fort Wadsworth

Verrazano–Narrows Bridge

New York Ave.

3.0/ 11.5

Staten Island

278

3.3/ 11:1

4.8/ 10.2

McClean Ave.

5.4

4.2/ 10.8

USS North Carolina Rd.

10.0

South Beach Greenway

Ocean Breeze Park

Seaview Ave.

FDR Boardwalk

Richmond Rd.

Hylan Blvd.

Father Capodanno Blvd.

Freedom Circle

8.6

Miller Field

7.5

Lower New York Bay

A Fort with a Continuous History

Fort Wadsworth stands tall atop the Narrows, the narrow straight between Staten Island and Brooklyn that forms the entrance to New York Harbor. The area was fortified by the Dutch in the seventeenth century and distinguishes itself with a prolonged uninterrupted military role.

Most of the structural remnants you can see today were built by the British in the eighteenth century and had a prime defensive function throughout the Revolutionary War. After the war, the US military took over the fortification and it served the armed forces in the Civil War.

The fortification comprises innumerable smaller structures, most significantly Fort Tompkins and Battery Weed, and is today known as Fort Wadsworth, renamed in 1865 to honor a fallen Major General Wadsworth. Touring Fort Tompkins allows you to explore cavernous corridors that protected the city for centuries. At the bottom of the hill that Fort Tompkins stands upon, you can visit Battery Weed, a four-story military fortress that faces the water.

The fort continued in the hands of the US Army or Navy until 1994, when the Navy submitted it to the National Park Service. It now forms part of the 26,000-acre Gateway National Recreation Area, which also comprises Jamaica Bay in Queens and Brooklyn (see ride 26), and terrain at Sandy Hook, New Jersey.

During summer months, you might come upon a flock of goats grazing on the steep slopes surrounding the fort. A sustainable resource project began employing goats as living lawn mowers here every summer in 2007.

3.0 Enter the gate to Fort Wadsworth and continue straight as Bay Street becomes New York Avenue.

3.3 After passing the visitor center parking lot, turn left onto Tompkins Avenue.

3.5 At the Overlook, turn left onto Hudson Road, going downhill, and make a U-turn as soon as you can onto Battery Weed Road.

3.9 Arrive at the Battery. To proceed, continue south on Battery Weed Road, going uphill toward the bridge. Turn right onto Hudson Road, skirting the ball field.

4.2 Turn left onto USS North Carolina Road.

4.8 Turn left onto the narrow bikeway.

Alice Austen: A Pioneer

One of the earliest women to document life on the streets with a camera, Alice Austen (1866–1952) was a pioneer in many realms of life. As a young girl, she'd carry her glass plates and prints from her family's home to a water pump in the backyard to rinse them in frigid water because the home lacked running water. Later she'd lug her camera equipment, weighing up to 50 pounds, by horse carriage across Staten Island, photographing life at large. In the early twentieth century, her travels took her beyond the bounds of the boroughs to Vermont, Illinois, Massachusetts, and perhaps Europe. She also cowrote a book, *Bicycling for Ladies,* and was the first woman on Staten Island to own a car. She spent fifty years of her life living with a female friend, Gertrude Tate, and never married.

5.4 Veer to the right of the beachside Vanderbilt hotel—through what resembles the hotel driveway—and return to the beachfront paved bikeway thereafter.

7.5 The bikeway ends at Miller Field. Explore the former airfield at your leisure along the bikeways that crisscross the space. To proceed en route, return to the beachside bikeway.

8.6 At Freedom Circle, stay right to stick to the boardwalk.

10.0 Exit the boardwalk back onto the bikeway, continuing north toward the Verrazano-Narrows Bridge.

10.2 Turn right onto USS North Carolina Road.

10.8 Turn right onto Hudson Road, followed by a quick left to return underneath the bridge to Fort Wadsworth.

11.0 At the Overlook, turn left onto Tompkins Avenue.

11.1 Turn right onto New York Avenue.

11.5 Continue straight onto Bay Street.

14.4 Arrive at your starting point.

RIDE INFORMATION

Local Events/Attractions

Alice Austen House: This landmark house houses a permanent collection of photography by the pioneering early-twentieth-century female photographer Alice Austen. 2 Hylan Blvd.; (718) 816-4506; aliceausten.org

Miller Field: A former Army Air Force Base with more than 187 acres of open recreational terrain and ball fields galore. www.nyharborparks.org/visit/mifi.html, www.nps.gov

Fort Wadsworth: A Revolutionary War–era fortification. www.nyharborparks.org/visit/fowa.html, www.nps.gov

Restrooms

Start/End: Restrooms and water fountains are located in the St. George Ferry Terminal.

Mile 5.3–10.3: There are numerous restrooms and water fountains along the boardwalk.

33

Greenbelt Parks and Parishes

This ride leads through residential neighborhoods with a suburban feeling to the Staten Island Greenbelt, 2,800 acres of interconnected natural and sculpted green spaces. Along the way, stop off at the College of Staten Island's parklike campus, skirt the edge of Freshkills Park, and explore LaTourette Park's woodlands and wetlands. Cycle through the historic seventeenth-century parish of Richmond Town, test your uphill biking powers on Lighthouse Hill, and dig deeper into Staten Island's flora and fauna at the Greenbelt Nature Center. Return to your starting point via railway or beachfront bikeway.

Start: St. George Ferry Terminal, opposite Staten Island Borough Hall

Length: 23.9-mile loop (main route)/15.5-mile loop (railway option)

Side trips around the College of Staten Island's campus and to the Greenbelt Nature Center add up to 3.6 miles to either option.

Approximate riding time: 3.5 hours (main option)

Best bike: Road, hybrid, or mountain bike

Terrain and trail surface: The trail is paved throughout except for a 2-mile stretch of greenway through LaTourette Park, which is brushed gravel. The terrain is hilly, with several gentle slopes and one steep incline at Lighthouse Hill.

Traffic and hazards: Some portions of this ride lead through residential neighborhoods on urban roads without bike lanes. While most of the roads have only light traffic, stay alert at all times, especially when crossing the busy intersections of Richmond Avenue and Richmond Hill Road. There's a short stretch along Richmond Terrace where traffic is moderate to heavy. An optional trip to the Greenbelt Nature Center along Rockland Avenue shares the road with moderate traffic. The route requires city cycling comfort.

Things to see: Staten Island Greenbelt, College of Staten Island, Willowbrook Park, Freshkills Park, LaTourette Park, Staten Island Range Lighthouse, Jacques Marchais Museum of Tibetan Art, Greenbelt Nature Center, Historic Richmond Town

Maps: *New York City Bike Map,* Historic Richmond Town Map: historicrichmondtown.org/village-map, Staten Island Greenbelt Trails: www.sigreenbelt.org/Trails/trailmap.pdf, College of Staten Island Map: www.csi.cuny.edu/prospectivestudents/maps.html

Getting there: By public transportation: Take the Staten Island Ferry from Manhattan's Whitehall Terminal to Staten Island's St. George Terminal. To get to Manhattan's Whitehall Terminal, take the R subway to the Whitehall Street station or the 1 subway to the South Ferry station. By car: If using the Verrazano-Narrows Bridge, exit toward I-278 W / New Jersey and take exit 14 on the left toward Narrows Road W/Hylan Boulevard. Turn right onto Fingerboard Road. Turn left onto Bay Street and follow Bay Street until you reach the St. George Ferry Terminal where there's parking.

If using the Bayonne Bridge, take exit 13 to turn right onto Morningstar Road toward Richmond Terrace. Turn right onto Richmond Terrace, heading east. Follow Richmond Terrace to the ferry terminal. GPS coordinates: N40 38.567' / W74 04.525'

THE RIDE

Staten Island's suburban landscape is both a blessing and a curse when it comes to cycling culture—a blessing because it means the island is peppered with tranquil residential neighborhoods along pleasant tree-lined streets that make for lovely cycling experiences; a curse because it means getting to these neighborhoods requires some skilled urban cycling. This journey emphasizes the former and tries to avoid the latter.

The first stretch of this journey leads along the tranquil North Shore Waterfront Esplanade, with views of New Jersey's industrial port across the water, the Manhattan skyline in the distance, and Brooklyn's skyline behind you. When the esplanade ends, you'll continue westward along Richmond Terrace, which leads you through semi-industrial terrain with car washes and auto repair shops lining the way. Jewett Avenue up ahead then brings you to more relaxed, residential neighborhoods, and the farther inland you get, the more suburban it feels. College Avenue soon takes you past one-family homes with nicely trimmed lawns. As you bike uphill along Woolley Avenue, be sure to glance behind you for striking views of the Bayonne Bridge, which connects Staten Island to New Jersey.

Up ahead, after crossing the Staten Island Expressway and passing West-wood Park, you'll soon be able to access the College of Staten Island's leafy campus. When you hit Victory Boulevard, the campus entrance sits on your left. To reach the entrance, dismount your bike and walk it 100 feet along the sidewalk. Enter the campus if you wish and follow the 2-mile Loop Road as it circumnavigates the campus. To continue en route, follow Victory Boulevard westward. The road here has heavy traffic, so stay alert. And if you prefer, stick to the sidewalk (walking your bike) until you reach Willowbrook Park on your left circa 0.1 mile down the road. Enter the park, which forms part of the Staten Island Greenbelt, and hug the edge of Willowbrook Lake, where lakeside benches are a lovely spot for a short break. Then, continue toward the Carousel to turn right and exit the park.

Stay alert as you cross Richmond Avenue up ahead, where traffic can be heavy. Residential roads then soon bring you to another greenbelt park on your right—Freshkills Park. A landfill for fifty years until 2001, the "park" is still under development and being completed in segments. Skirt the park's edge, checking out any portions you can, and then return eastward. Use caution once more crossing Richmond Avenue and then enjoy the ride along residential Travis Avenue toward LaTourette Park. Enter the 840-acre park, also part of the greenbelt, via a small footpath just across Forest Hill Road. A brushed-gravel greenway then leads you south through the park, hugging the golf course on your left and leading through swaths of dense woodlands a little farther south. When the pathway forks up ahead, veer left to go eastward. You'll skirt the park's wetlands, where you'll have sweeping views of the marshes surrounding Richmond Creek.

From Landfill to Park
Freshkills functioned as a landfill from its establishment in 1948 by
Robert Moses until its closure in 2001. Shortly thereafter, the city
launched a design competition to convert the landfill into a park
space, and a New York- and Philadelphia-based landscape design
firm was selected as the main design consultant. Upon its comple-
tion within the next thirty years, Freshkills Park will cover 2,200 acres
and be almost three times as big as Central Park.

You'll then exit LaTourette Park next to historic Saint Andrew's Church, established in 1712 and part of Historic Richmond Town. At Center Street, turn left to enter this historic site, a recreation of the seventeenth-century settlement that began as Richmond in the 1690s. Twenty-eight historic buildings dating back to the seventeenth century lay scattered across 100 acres of land here. Explore at your leisure. Then continue eastward through the site along Center Street.

Proceeding en route, you'll soon reach Lighthouse Avenue, which snakes to the top of Lighthouse Hill, a neighborhood bedecked in lavish homes and offering prime water views. Along the way, you'll pass the Jacques Marchais Museum of Tibetan Art. Housed in a building resembling a Tibetan Monastery—complete with lotus ponds, gold fish, meditation cells, and terraced gardens—it's a serene getaway. An optional jaunt left on Edinboro Road

Saint Andrew's Church of Historic Richmond Town, established in 1712.

The general merchandise store at Historic Richmond Town.

brings you to the Staten Island Range Lighthouse, which first shone its light more than a century ago. Continuing onward, use your breaks as you descend Meisner Avenue. It's steep!

At the bottom of the hill, take an optional excursion left onto Rockland Avenue to the Greenbelt Nature Center, the nexus of the Staten Island Greenbelt with nature trails leading you up close to Staten Island's flora and fauna. Use caution, though, as cars sometimes travel quickly on Rockland Avenue. Then retrace your route to continue southeastward on Rockland Avenue, heading toward the final leg of your journey.

After crossing Richmond Road, you'll soon reach South Railroad Avenue's on-road bike lane, heading north. At New Dorp Lane, you have the option of catching the Staten Island Railway back to the St. George Ferry Terminal. Alternately, continue en route to the coast, where you'll bike north along the shorefront. Take either the wood-planked boardwalk or paved bikeway adjacent to the boardwalk toward the Verrazano-Narrows Bridge. (Take note that boardwalk biking is officially permitted between 5 and 10 a.m. only.) When the boardwalk ends, continue toward the bridge along the bikeway, past dunes on your right and going uphill along USS North Carolina Road, which becomes Hudson Road. You'll then duck underneath the bridge, and soon thereafter catch Bay Street back to your starting point.

MILES AND DIRECTIONS

0.0 Turn right to head northwest on Richmond Terrace.

0.2 Turn right onto Wall Street, followed by a left onto the North Shore Esplanade when you hit the water.

1.2 Turn left onto Jersey Street, followed by a quick right onto Richmond Terrace.

3.6 Turn left onto Jewett Avenue.

4.8 Turn right onto College Avenue.

5.1 Turn left onto Woolley Avenue.

6.3 Turn right onto Westwood Avenue.

6.7 Turn right onto Willowbrook Road, followed by a quick left onto Dreyer Avenue, and a right onto Canterbury Avenue when Dreyer comes to an end.

7.1 To reach the College of Staten Island, don't cross Victory Boulevard. Instead, dismount your bike and walk it along the sidewalk to your left. The campus entrance is just ahead. Optional: Explore the 200-acre parklike campus along its perimeter road, circumnavigating

Greenbelt Parks and Parishes

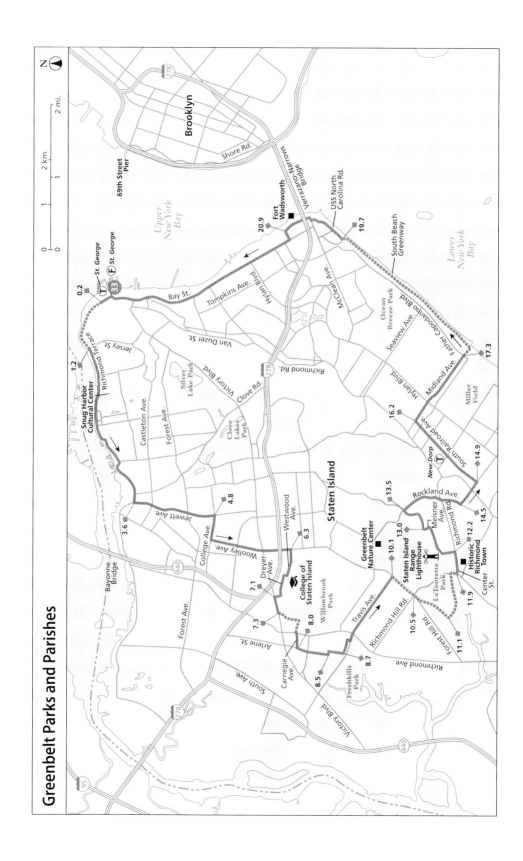

N

Brooklyn

Shore Rd.

69th Street Pier

Upper New York Bay

St. George
F St. George
0.2
33 T

Verrazano-Narrows Bridge

Fort Wadsworth
20.9

USS North Carolina Rd.
19.7

South Beach Greenway

Lower New York Bay

Bay St.

Tompkins Ave.

Hylan Blvd.

McClean Ave.

Ocean Breeze Park

Seaview Ave.

Father Capodanno Blvd.

Snug Harbor Cultural Center
1.2
Richmond Terrace

Jersey St.

Van Duzer St.

Silver Lake Park

Victory Blvd.

Clove Rd.

278

Richmond Rd.

Hylan Blvd.

Midland Ave.

17.3

Miller Field

Castleton Ave.

Forest Ave.

Clove Lakes Park

South Railroad Ave.

16.2

New Dorp
T

14.9

Bayonne Bridge

Jewett Ave.

3.6

College Ave.

Woolley Ave.

4.8

Westwood Ave.

6.3

Staten Island

13.5

Rockland Ave.

Meisner Ave.

14.5

440

Dreyer Ave.

7.1

College of Staten Island

Willowbrook Park

Greenbelt Nature Center

13.0

10.1

Staten Island Range Lighthouse

La Tourette Park

12.2

Historic Richmond Town

Richmond Rd.

11.9

Center St.

Forest Ave.

7.3

8.0

Travis Ave.

Richmond Hill Rd.

10.5

Forest Hill Rd.

11.1

Carnegie Ave.

8.5

Arlene St.

8.7

Freshkills Park

Richmond Ave.

South Ave.

Victory Blvd.

440

278

95

0   1   2 km.
0   1   2 mi.

the campus (about 2 miles). To continue, go west on Victory Boulevard 2 blocks. Traffic is heavy. Stay alert (or walk your bike along the sidewalk).

7.3 Enter Willowbrook Park on your left. Bike through the parking lot to turn right along the pathway, going counterclockwise around the lake.

7.7 Turn right onto Eton Place, exiting the park. Cross Richmond Avenue to go left circa 50 feet before making a quick right onto Carnegie Avenue.

8.0 Turn left onto Arlene Street. Continue straight as Arlene Street becomes North Park Drive. Freshkills Park is on your right.

8.5 Turn left onto Rivington Avenue, followed by a quick right onto Mulberry Avenue.

8.7 Turn left onto Sleepy Hollow Road, followed by a right onto Freedom Avenue, and a quick left onto Travis Avenue.

9.0 Veer right onto Draper Place and stay left when it splits just ahead to cross Richmond Avenue. Go left along Richmond Avenue circa 80 feet to make a quick right onto Travis Avenue.

10.1 Cross Forest Hill Road and take the footpath straight ahead into LaTourette Park. Turn right to bike south along the park greenway.

10.5 Cross Richmond Hill Road to continue along the greenway.

11.1 Veer left when the greenway forks, going east.

11.7 Exit the park with the churchyard on your right. Turn right onto Richmond Hill Road up ahead. Richmond Hill Road becomes Arthur Kill Road.

11.9 Turn left onto Center Street and into Historic Richmond Town. Explore the site at your leisure if you wish. Then continue eastward on Center Street.

12.2 Turn left onto Moore Street, followed by a right onto Richmond Road, and a quick left onto Lighthouse Avenue. Follow Lighthouse Avenue as it veers right up the hill. It's steep!!

12.9 To visit the Staten Island Range Lighthouse, turn left onto Edinboro Road and go circa 0.4 mile (and retrace your route afterward). Otherwise continue on Lighthouse Avenue (which becomes Terrace Court).

13.0 Veer right onto Meisner Avenue, going downhill. Use caution—it is steep!

13.5 To visit the Greenbelt Nature Center, turn left onto Rockland Avenue and go circa 0.7 mile (and retrace your route afterward). Otherwise turn right onto Rockland Avenue.

14.1 When the road forks at Richmond Avenue, veer right, followed by a quick, sharp left onto Morley Avenue (a near U-turn). Then take a quick right onto Dalton Avenue.

14.5 Turn left onto Tysens Lane.

14.9 Turn left onto South Railroad Avenue.

15.5 To abbreviate the route, board the Staten Island Railway at the New Dorp Lane station to return to your starting point at the St. George Ferry Terminal. To ride the complete route, stick to South Railroad Avenue.

16.2 Turn right onto Midland Avenue.

17.3 Turn right onto Father Capodanno Boulevard. After circa 450 feet, turn left to access the beach boardwalk. Take note that biking is officially only permitted on the boardwalk from 5 to 10 a.m. At Freedom Circle, the circular cement outcrop with flags, you can either stick to the boardwalk to the right, or dismount the boardwalk onto the paved bikeway, which runs parallel to the boardwalk.

19.7 The boardwalk ends. Descend onto the paved bikeway, continuing toward the Verrazano-Narrows Bridge. Turn right onto USS North Carolina Road, continuing toward the bridge. USS North Carolina Road becomes Hudson Road.

20.4 Follow Hudson Road to the right, followed by a quick left to bike underneath the bridge.

20.9 Turn left onto Mont Sec Avenue, followed by a right onto Bay Street.

23.9 Arrive at your starting point.

RIDE INFORMATION

Local Events/Attractions

Greenbelt Nature Center: The hub of many Staten Island Greenbelt activities including a pleasant 1-mile nature hike. 700 Rockland Ave.; (718) 351-3450; sigreenbelt.org

Jacques Marchais Museum of Tibetan Art: A museum devoted entirely to Tibetan art and housed in a building that represents Himalayan architecture. 338 Lighthouse Ave.; (718) 987-3500; tibetanmuseum.org

Historic Richmond Town: A reconstructed seventeenth-century hamlet. 441 Clarke Ave.; (718) 351-1611; historicrichmondtown.org

Restrooms

Start/End: Restrooms and water fountains are located in the St. George Ferry Terminal.

Mile 7.7: Restrooms are located at the visitor's center beside the pond in Willowbrook Park, opposite the Carousel.

Mile 11.9: Restrooms are located behind the museum at Historic Richmond Town.

Mile 17.5–19.7: There are restrooms along the beach boardwalk.

Staten Island North to South

This ride spans Staten Island from north to south, starting at the St. George Ferry Terminal and ending in Conference House Park, home to the "South Pole," New York State's southernmost point. Traversing Staten Island along its southern flank, it runs parallel to the more than 150-year-old Staten Island Railway and swings into Great Kills Park, a 580-acre swath of wetlands, woodlands, and beachfront. Conference House Park, at the end of your journey, contains several historic build-ings (dating as far back as circa 1680) worth checking out and some lovely water-front picnic spots. Your northbound journey returns to St. George via Staten Island Railway.

Start: St. George Ferry Terminal, opposite Staten Island Borough Hall

Length: 21.7 miles, one way

Approximate riding time: 3 hours

Best bike: Hybrid, road, or mountain bike

Terrain and trail surface: The trail is paved throughout and relatively flat.

Traffic and hazards: Staten Island is the city's most car-dependent of the five boroughs. It's also the most suburban and, like many a suburban enclave, still has miles to go in terms of cycling infrastructure. Bike lanes are scarce. Much of the ride thus shares the road with motorists and buses and requires considerable city cycling comfort. Use caution and stay alert at all times. The heaviest traffic is along Hylan Boulevard, which you'll access near Great Kills Park. Hylan Boulevard's heaviest traffic lies to the north—you've bypassed this—but the first 0.5 mile or so of your route here at times also has heavy traffic. As you head farther south, the traffic thins and the boulevard eventually also bears a painted bike lane.

Things to see: Great Kills Park, Great Kills Harbor, Conference House Park, South Pole, Conference House, Biddle House, Rutan-Beckett House, Staten Island Railway

Maps: *New York City Bike Map,* Conference House Park map: www .nycgovparks.org/parks/R006/map/ConferenceHousebrochure.pdf

Getting there: By public transportation: Take the Staten Island Ferry from Manhattan's Whitehall Terminal to Staten Island's St. George Terminal. To get to Manhattan's Whitehall Terminal, take the R subway to the Whitehall Street station or the 1 subway to the South Ferry station. By car: If using the Verrazano-Narrows Bridge, exit toward I-278 W / New Jersey and take exit 14 on the left toward Narrows Road W/Hylan Boulevard. Turn right onto Fingerboard Road. Turn left onto Bay Street and follow Bay Street until you reach the St. George Ferry Terminal where there's parking.

If using the Bayonne Bridge, take exit 13 to turn right onto Morningstar Road toward Richmond Terrace. Turn right onto Richmond Terrace, heading east. Follow Richmond Terrace to the ferry terminal. GPS coordinates: N40 38.551' / W74 04.502'

THE RIDE

To begin this grand sweep from north to south, you'll catch Bay Street at the ferry terminal, the main drag along Staten Island's eastern shore. As you head south, on your left you can catch glimpses of the Staten Island Railway, established in the mid-nineteenth century and predating the city's subway system. The north-south track along which you are riding is the railway's sole remaining passenger line. Upper New York Bay and the Brooklyn shorefront across the water are also visible intermittently. You'll cycle through the eastern shore neighborhoods of St. George, Tompkinsville, Clifton, and Rosebank before turning right at Von Briesen Park, heading inland. While most of the roads here are residential, the first two—School Road and Lily Pond Road, both of which have bike lanes—have the heaviest traffic, so stay alert. After that, McClean Avenue brings you to more peaceful residential roads with one-family homes and manicured lawns in the neighborhoods of Grasmere, Dongan Hills, and Grant City. Then, the Staten Island Railway accompanies you once more as it runs parallel to your journey overhead along North Railroad Avenue.

Heading toward Great Kills Park from here, you'll be on a major road for about 0.5 mile—Hylan Boulevard. This boulevard is known for heavy traffic,

Views of bay waters from the Great Kills Park picnic area. The park covers 580 acres of wetlands, woodlands, and beachfront and forms part of the Gateway National Recreation Area.

especially north of your access point. Still, while traffic is lighter and slower here than up north, stay alert for turning vehicles and halting buses.

Up ahead, as you enter Great Kills Park along Buffalo Street, gentle sea breezes, placid wetlands, and a beachy vibe of leisure greet you. The park is part of the 26,000-acre Gateway National Recreation Area, which encompasses marshlands, beaches, wildlife sanctuaries, and recreational spots along Jamaica Bay in Queens, Sandy Hook in New Jersey, and the Staten Island waterfront. Great Kills Park also houses Staten Island's only osprey nesting site. Take a water-side break at one of the park's two beach access points—the picnic area or Beach Center. Both spots give access to the waters of Lower New York Bay and afford views, due east, of Queens's westernmost point, Breezy Point on the Rockaways. When you're ready to continue, retrace your path along Buffalo Street to Hylan Boulevard.

Heading southwestward along Hylan Boulevard, traffic decreases slightly and commercial neighborhoods give way to residential and natural zones with native habitats. Much of the route here is framed by nature preserves and park spaces. South of Barclay Avenue, you'll hug the edge of the Blue Heron Nature Preserve, 200 acres of wetlands, swamps, woodlands, and streams where the *chirr* of cicadas and call of birds can be heard from the road. Just beyond, southwest of Luten Avenue, you'll brush up against Wolfe's

Pond Park. The woodlands that abut your route here are filled with white oak, hickory, and sweet gum. You'll traverse the salt marsh of the Lemon Creek Wetlands, which harbor New York City's only colony of purple martins (the largest North American swallow). Lastly, you'll skirt the edges of North Mount Loretto State Forest, Butler Manor Woods, and Long Pond Park, all of which sit west of Sharrott Avenue and are important stopover spots for various migratory bird species.

Sprague Avenue up ahead then soon brings you toward the final stretch of your journey at Conference House Park. A bikeway leads through the 286-acre park, with innumerable smaller paths leading deeper into the natural environs. From the bikeway's right-hand turn, follow the signs to the "South Pole," walking your bike along one of the nature trails. Then, continue north along the bikeway to check out some of the park's historic buildings that shed light on three centuries of Staten Island history. The oldest, the Conference House, built in circa 1680, was named for failed peace negotiations of 1776. Check out this or the park's other historic houses. Then find a spot on the lawn overlooking Arthur Kill, the tidal strait that separates Staten Island from mainland New Jersey, and take a break before hopping on the Staten Island Railway at Tottenville to journey back to St. George.

MILES AND DIRECTIONS

0.0 From the Staten Island Ferry Viaduct, cross to the west side of Bay Street using the traffic signals. Turn left to head south along Bay Street.

2.7 Turn right onto School Road.

3.0 Turn left onto Lily Pond Road.

3.4 Turn right onto McClean Avenue.

4.3 Veer slightly right to continue onto Reid Avenue.

4.5 Veer right to stay on Reid Avenue.

4.7 Turn left onto Laconia Avenue.

4.9 Turn right onto Burgher Avenue.

5.2 Turn left onto North Railroad Avenue.

5.7 Turn right onto Liberty Avenue, followed by a quick left onto North Railroad Avenue.

5.8 Turn right onto Dongan Hills Avenue, followed by a left onto Jefferson Street. Jefferson Street becomes North Railroad Avenue just ahead.

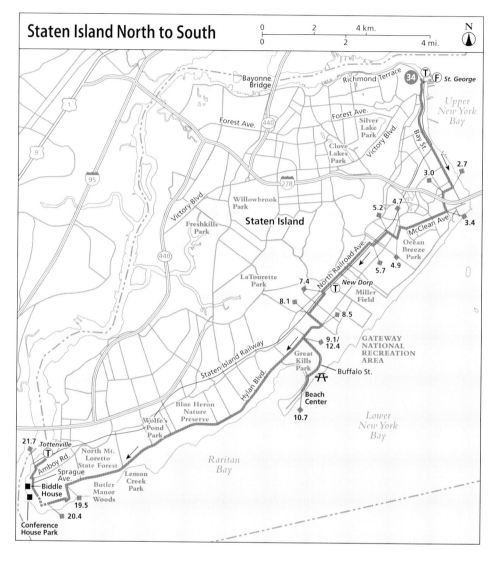

Staten Island North to South

Staten Island

7.3 North Railroad Avenue becomes Anthony J. Crecca Jr. Plaza.

7.4 Turn left onto Beach Avenue, followed by a quick right onto South Railroad Avenue.

8.1 Turn left onto Guyon Avenue.

8.5 Turn right onto Hylan Boulevard.

9.1 Look behind you before veering left to get ready to make a left turn. Turn left onto Buffalo Street and enter Great Kills Park.

10.1 The first beach picnic area is on your left. Take a waterside break here or continue south along Buffalo Street to Beach Center up ahead.

10.7 Beach Center is on your left. Enter through the parking lot and access the beach area if you wish. Then make a U-turn at the park pavilion to return northward along Buffalo Street.

12.4 Turn left onto Hylan Boulevard.

15.8 Hylan Boulevard's on-road bike lane begins here.

19.5 Turn left onto Sprague Avenue.

19.8 Turn right onto Surf Avenue, followed by a right onto Loretto Street.

20.0 Turn left onto Billop Avenue.

20.4 Continue straight onto the greenway through Conference House Park.

20.6 Follow the bikeway as it turns right.

20.8 Veer left, hugging the edge of the park along Satterlee Street.

21.0 The Conference House museum is on your left at Hylan Boulevard. The lawns surrounding the house are a lovely spot for a break. To proceed en route, continue northward along Satterlee Street.

21.2 The Biddle House and the Rutan-Beckett House are accessible on your left at Shore Road. To proceed en route, continue northward on Satterlee Street.

21.3 Turn left onto Amboy Road, followed by a right onto Hopping Avenue.

21.6 Turn left onto Bentley Street.

21.7 Arrive at the Tottenville Station of the Staten Island Railway and hop on the train back to the ferry at the north end of Staten Island, the last stop on the train.

RIDE INFORMATION

Local Events/Attractions

The Conference House: Now a historic house museum, this two-story stone manor was constructed around 1680 by Captain Christopher Billop. 298 Satterlee St.; (718) 984-6046; www.conferencehouse.org

Great Kills Park: 580 acres of wetlands, woodlands, beachland, and more, forming part of the Gateway National Recreation Area. www.nyharborparks .org/visit/grki.html; www.nycgovparks.org/parks/greatkillspark

Restrooms

Start/end: There are restrooms in the Staten Island ferry terminal.
Mile 10.7: There are restrooms at the beach pavilion at Beach Center in Great Kills Park.
Mile 21.0: There are restrooms in Conference House Park in the park building.

The Bronx

Heading north along the South County Trailway, next to Tibbetts Brook Park. The trailway connects to North County Trailway at its northern end (Ride 40).

The Bronx is probably the city's best-kept cycling secret, with a rapidly growing bike culture that still has an exhilarating, pioneering feel. The fourth-largest of the boroughs, the Bronx received 18 percent of all new bike lanes built in the city since 2007. (Compare that to 20 percent in Queens, which is almost three times the size of the Bronx.) The northernmost of the five boroughs, the Bronx comprises hilly terrain in the west that offers expansive views across the Hudson, and a flatter region extending toward Long Island in the east. While people often associate the Bronx with inner-city congestion and over-population, about 25 percent of the borough's area is open space—including Pelham Bay Park and Van Cortlandt Park—with multi-use greenways affording car-free cycling opportunities. An extended greenway connects many of these various green spots, extending from Van Cortlandt Park at the borough's center to Pelham Bay Park and Orchard Beach in the east. Additionally, cyclists who are comfortable biking alongside motor vehicles can explore multiple quirky inner-city parks with creative designs, visit the homes of founding fathers, explore the borough's wealthier northern neighborhoods of Riverdale and Fieldston, and more.

Bike shops are still relatively few and far between here, though, so be sure to bring flat fixings.

35

Orchard Beach and City Island

This ride travels along greenways through New York City's largest park system, Pelham Bay Park. At three times the size of Central Park, the park contains miles of walking trails and bridle paths, golf courses, an architectural landmark, and 13 miles of shorefront along the Long Island Sound that includes Orchard Beach. Conceived as the "Riviera of New York" by Robert Moses in the 1930s, Orchard Beach continues as Pelham Bay Park's most popular attraction, with a beachfront esplanade. On this ride, you'll skirt the edge of all of these sites before heading to the historical seaport community of City Island, surrounded by the waters of the Longs Island Sound on all sides. This ride is a great, mostly car-free, city getaway. Head out early, before the crowds.

Start: Senator Abraham Bernstein Square, at the intersection of Pelham Parkway and White Plains Road

Length: 17.5 miles out and back

Approximate riding time: 2.5 hours

Best bike: Hybrid, road, or mountain bike

Terrain and trail surface: The trail is paved throughout and relatively flat. The eastbound journey to the beach goes slightly downhill. The westbound journey goes slightly uphill. There are a few small hills in Pelham Bay Park.

Traffic and hazards: Most of this route travels on the NYC Greenway, which is car-free. The greenway crosses multiple access roads along Pelham Parkway, though, so stay alert. Come to a complete stop and check for oncoming traffic before crossing. City Island Avenue, on City Island, is the only route section that's on-road without a bike lane. It's a popular cycling route and traffic is light, but stay alert. (To avoid this on-road section, make City Island's northern end your turnaround spot at Catherine Scott Promenade. Don't head to the southern tip.)

Things to see: Orchard Beach, Pelham Bay Park, Bronx Victory Memorial, Bartow-Pell Mansion Museum, City Island, City Island Historical Society and Nautical Museum

Maps: *New York City Bike Map,* Department of City Planning *Bike the Bronx* map, New York City Parks Map of Pelham Bay Park: www .nycgovparks.org/sub_your_park/vt_pelham_bay_park/images/ Pelham%20map-rev2005.pdf

Getting there: By public transportation: Take the 2 subway to the Pelham Parkway station. Senator Abraham Bernstein Square is at the north edge of Pelham Parkway. GPS coordinates: N40 51.455' / W73 52.040'

THE RIDE

The Bronx is often overlooked when it comes to recreational biking, but the borough has an ever-increasing number of greenway miles, including along Pelham Parkway (officially called the Bronx and Pelham Parkway) leading out to Orchard Beach. When the parkway was constructed over a century ago, a series of rules governed what could be built along its borders: no buildings within 150 feet and no bars along the route. For years on Sunday mornings, the central lane was closed to cars and used for professional bicycle racing.

Today, a greenway leads along the north edge of the westbound lane from White Plains Road eastward toward Orchard Beach. When cycling along the greenway, more than 100 feet of green space still separate you from the houses that flank the northern parkway edge. Going slightly downhill as you head eastward, check out the residence that's popularly referred to as the "Christmas House" at 1601 Pelham Pkwy. on your left. This pink-hued home, with year-round life-size reindeer out front, is hard to miss.

At Stillwell Avenue, the greenway switches parkway sides. Use the pedestrian signal to cross Pelham Parkway and continue eastward. This soon leads you across a series of access roads. While there's a designated bike- and pedestrian-crossing at each, there's no traffic signal, so come to a complete stop before crossing. After crossing the Bruckner Expressway, the greenway crosses its final access road to deposit you at Pelham Bay Park. To your right stands the Bronx Victory Column (which honors Bronx soldiers killed during World War I) and a labyrinthine web of pathways extends into the park, snaking around ball fields, playgrounds, picnic spots, and more. You could spend a

City Island boats moored offshore at Catherine Scott Promenade on City Island.

whole day exploring this part of the park alone, but our route presses onward toward the beach.

Follow the greenway northeastward, across the Hutchinson River and toward the north section of Pelham Bay Park. When you hit the first intersection, cross to the north side City Island Road. Then swivel left to cross Shore Road and follow the greenway northward along its west flank. You'll pass the park's equestrian center on your left, glide through wooded terrain, and swerve along the edge of two pristine golf courses. Just beyond, after crossing to the east side of the road, you can access the entrance to the Bartow-Pell Mansion Museum, a nineteenth-century landmark building made of local stone and equipped with sculpted gardens. Explore the mansion at your leisure and then retrace your route past the golf courses and equestrian center to City Island Road, where you'll stick to the greenway along the north edge of the road to continue toward Orchard Beach.

You'll traverse sloping woodlands and come to clearings that provide bay-water views on both sides of the road. You'll then veer left, cross to the east side of Park Drive, and continue northward toward Orchard Beach. You can then access the beachfront just past the bus terminal, where a mile-long bay-side esplanade extends northward. (If required, dismount and walk your bike along this esplanade.) Playgrounds, ball courts, and food stands (during summer months) line the esplanade, which offers sweeping views of Pelham

The City Island Historical Society and Nautical Museum sheds light on the island's maritime roots.

Bay, and a nature center sits at its northern end. From there, you can access the Kazimiroff Nature Trail if you wish. Short and long loop paths lead around Hunter Island, just north of here, where you can wander alongside the island's wetlands and rocky shoreline.

To continue en route, return to the greenway to retrace your route a short jaunt before veering left to follow the greenway across City Island Bridge and onto City Island, a seaport community with a New England feel. As you descend the bridge, you'll pass Catherine Scott Promenade on your left, where benches look out toward Eastchester Bay.

From here, to reach the south end of the island, you'll have to do some on-road cycling along City Island Avenue. Stay alert as the road is narrow. Along the way, you'll pass emblematic island establishments like Jack's Bait and Tackle, the Lickety Split ice creamery, and the Black Whale restaurant. The narrow mile-long avenue culminates at the island's southern tip next to bayside restaurants with classic waterfront fare. If you glance to the east, you can catch sight of Hart Island, just a mile long and a quarter-mile wide.

Make a U-turn at the island's southern tip to retrace your route northward. If you wish, check out the quirky Nautical Museum to your right on Fordham Street to learn some island history. Then, to proceed en route, continue northward to leave City Island via the bikeway on the southern side of City Island Bridge. This soon brings you via greenway back to Shore Road, where a left-hand turn returns you to Pelham Parkway's greenway. Retrace your route from here to your starting point.

MILES AND DIRECTIONS

0.0 Catch the greenway eastward along the north edge of Pelham Parkway's westbound lane.

1.7 At Stillwell Avenue, use the pedestrian signal to cross to the south side of Pelham Parkway. Continue east along the greenway.

1.8 Come to a complete stop before crossing the access ramps at the Hutchinson River Parkway and the Bruckner Expressway just beyond.

2.6 Stop at the end of Pelham Parkway to cross to the south side of the parkway at Pelham Bay Park. Turn right along the greenway to reach the Bronx Victory Column.

2.7 Make a U-turn around the monument to return to the park entrance and continue northeastward along Shore Road, crossing the Pelham Bridge toward Orchard Beach.

3.6 Cross City Island Road. Then swivel left to cross Shore Road and catch the greenway along its western flank, heading north.

Orchard Beach and City Island

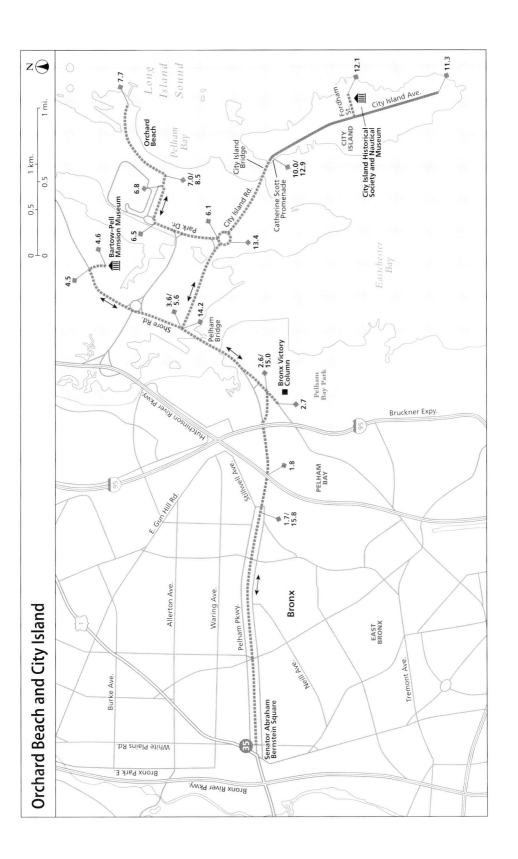

> **Hart Island**
>
> Sitting on just 130 acres in the Long Island Sound, Hart Island served as prisoner of war camp for four months in 1865. The City of New York then purchased the island to serve as potter's field, burial grounds for unidentified or indigent people. Today, with up to one million people buried in Hart Island Cemetery, the island holds the nation's largest potter's field. Prison labor has been used to perform these burials.

4.5 Turn right to cross Shore Road and access the Bartow-Pell Mansion Museum across the road.

4.6 Check out the mansion if you wish. Then make a U-turn and return to Shore Road, cross back to the greenway along its western flank, and return south to City Island Road.

5.6 After passing the equestrian center, cross to the east edge of Shore Road and follow the greenway along the north edge of City Island Road, heading east.

6.1 Follow the greenway as it veers left and then switches to the east side of Park Drive. Continue north.

6.5 Enter the gate to Orchard Beach and follow the greenway to the right toward the waterfront.

6.8 After passing the bus terminal, turn right into the park space and follow the path to the beach esplanade.

7.0 Turn left along the promenade and bike to the end. (Walk your bike if required.)

7.7 Make a U-turn to retrace your route along the promenade.

8.5 Turn right, exiting the promenade through the park area and past the bus terminal.

8.6 After the bus terminal, turn left onto the greenway and follow the bikeway as it veers left. Cross City Island Bridge onto City Island.

10.0 Catherine Scott Promenade is on your right. To continue, head south along City Island Avenue.

11.3 When you reach the water, make a U-turn to bike north along City Island Avenue.

12.0 Turn right onto Fordham Street to reach the Historical Society and Nautical Museum.

12.1 The museum is on your right. To continue, backtrack to City Island Avenue and continue north.

12.9 Turn left, crossing City Island Avenue, to access the bikeway along the south side of City Island Bridge, leading west.

13.4 Follow the bikeway around the traffic circle, continuing west.

14.2 At Shore Road, turn left along the greenway (east side of the road) to return toward Pelham Bay Park.

15.0 After crossing Pelham Bridge, turn right to cross the road and continue westward along the Pelham Parkway greenway (south side of the road).

15.8 The greenway switches parkway sides. Use the pedestrian signal to cross to the north side and continue westward.

17.5 Arrive at your starting point.

RIDE INFORMATION

Local Events/Attractions

Bartow-Pell Mansion Museum: Pelham Bay used to be peppered with grand mansions, but today this nineteenth-century landmark mansion is the only one still standing. 895 Shore Rd.; (718) 885-1461; www.bartowpellmansion museum.org

City Island Historical Society & Nautical Museum: This landmark building houses a quirky collection of artifacts and exhibits that shed light on the community's nautical history. 190 Fordham St.; (718) 885-0008; www.cityisland museum.org

Restrooms

Mile 7.0/8.5: There are restrooms and water fountains along the promenade at Orchard Beach.

The Grand Concourse

This ride travels along the Bronx's more than 100 year-old Grand Concourse, a majestic boulevard modeled after Paris's Champs Elysées, initially with separate lanes for separate forms of locomotion. Today, a bike lane lines the entire 4-mile artery, and your journey is framed by ornate Art Deco- and Art Moderne–style buildings. You'll pass Poe Cottage, where the poet Edgar Allan Poe spent his final years, and an idiosyncratic Queen of the Universe Shrine. The route then leads through the Bronx's Little Italy, where pastry shops, pasta makers, butchers, and pizza parlors are likely to tempt you to stop off for a taste.

Start: The Heinrich Heine Fountain in Joyce Kilmer Park on the Grand Concourse and East 161st Street

Length: 11.1-mile loop

Approximate riding time: 1.5 hours

Best bike: Hybrid, road, or mountain bike

Terrain and trail surface: The terrain is paved and mainly flat. There's one steep ascent at East 175th Street toward Crotona Park. It then goes downhill through the park.

Traffic and hazards: Most of this route leads along on-road bike lanes on wide city streets. While traffic is moderate, the streets are wide enough to allow for comfortable biking. The 1.5-mile stretch through Little Italy takes you onto city streets without bike lanes, so urban cycling comfort is required. Remain especially alert for car doors opening and vehicles turning during this portion of the journey, starting at East 188th Street.

Things to see: Bronx Borough Hall, Heinrich Heine Fountain, Bronx Museum of the Arts, Queen of the Universe Shrine, Grand Concourse, Little Italy, Crotona Park

Maps: *New York City Bike Map*, Department of City Planning *Bike the Bronx* map

Getting there: By public transportation: Take the B, D, or 4 subway to the 161st Street/Yankee Stadium station. Bike east 3 blocks on East 161st Street to reach Joyce Kilmer Park on the north side of the road. Use the pedestrian crosswalk to reach the park. By car: Take the FDR Drive north to exit 18 (at the Willis Avenue Bridge). After crossing the bridge, access I-87 N/Major Deegan Expressway. Take exit 5 onto East 161st Street, going east. Concourse Plaza Garage is at 200 E. 161st St. between Sheridan and Morris Avenues. GPS coordinates: N40 49.641' / W73 55.394'

THE RIDE

Your starting point for this journey, the Heinrich Heine Fountain, perched high on a knoll in Joyce Kilmer Park, offers prime views of the colonnaded façade of the Bronx's imposing borough hall just across the street. To begin your journey, you'll cross to the east side of the Grand Concourse to cycle northward along its on-road bike. Along the way, elaborate façades of five- and six-story Art Deco- and Art Moderne–style buildings frame your journey.

You'll pass the Bronx Museum of the Arts, which sits in a converted synagogue on your right, and continue northward past innumerable architectural marvels. One of them sits just north of East Fordham Road—the ten-story former Dollar Saving Bank, now the Emigrant Savings Bank, was constructed over a period of twenty years beginning in 1932. Just beyond sits Poe Cottage, where the poet Edgar Allan Poe spent his last years from 1846 to 1849. The modest white-wooden farmhouse was built around 1812 and, when Poe lived here, was surrounded by sloping farmlands that stretched eastward to Long Island.

Continuing north, when you hit Van Cortland Avenue East you've reached the end of the Grand Concourse. Use the traffic signal to cross to the boulevard's west side and bike southward, continuing along the bike lane. Stop off for a quick visit to the Queen of the Universe Shrine, a memorial that commemorates the spot where a 9-year-old boy purportedly was graced with an appearance by the Virgin Mary in 1945. Occurring just at the end of World War II, she told him to pray for world peace. Climb the narrow stone staircase to your right that leads up to the shrine.

Continuing south, you'll soon leave the Grand Concourse behind to cycle toward Belmont, the Bronx's Little Italy. Beginning with a left onto East 188th Street and ending with a right onto Southern Boulevard, this 1.5-mile part of the journey has no bike lanes, so stay especially alert. A short stretch along

The Grand Concourse

Some of the many Art Deco- and Moderne–style buildings along the Bronx's Grand Concourse. The concourse was modeled after Paris's Champs-Elysées.

East 188th Street has moderate traffic and soon brings you to Arthur Avenue, the heart of Little Italy, where you'll find a host of cafes, *pasticcerías,* and *prosciutterías.* The Arthur Avenue Retail Market, just south of East 186th Street, is an ideal place to still a craving for the tastes of Italy. The indoor market houses an array of Italian pastry shops, pasta makers, butchers, coffee specialists, and wine connoisseurs, among others. Pick up some provisions here for a break in Crotona Park up ahead. The Madonia Brothers Bakery next door and Dominick's Restaurant across the road are also Belmont mainstays.

Heading onward, you'll make a sharp left at Crescent Avenue, bringing you to a series of smaller residential roads. A left onto East 182nd Street then soon brings you to Southern Boulevard, where you'll find a bike lane once more.

The next jaunt of journey leads through Crotona Park at East 175th Street. A bikeway enters the park at the top of the hill and swerves past a tranquil 3-acre lake, picnic areas, innumerable ball fields, tennis courts, and a pool. Stay left of the tennis courts, going in between the courts and the lake. The lake-side benches are a great spot to take a break and enjoy your Italian provisions. To continue, exit Crotona Park onto the on-road bike lane on Crotona Avenue and follow the bike lane as it zigzags along a series of streets back to your starting point.

MILES AND DIRECTIONS

0.0 Use the pedestrian crossing to reach the east side of the Grand Concourse. Then go north along the on-road bike lane.

3.1 The former Dollar Savings Bank Building is on your right.

3.2 Poe Cottage is on your right.

The Grand Concourse—the Bronx's Champs Elysées

In the 1800s, the Bronx was a rural community of farmland and green space where agricultural swaths of land produced most of the fruit, vegetables, and grain that nourished its neighbors to the south in Manhattan. Considered a pastoral haven, the writer Edgar Allen Poe is just one of many who were drawn to the area for the clean, fresh air that could be found here. The Grand Concourse itself was built in the early twentieth century to give escape-seeking Manhattanites convenient access to the Bronx's parks and green spaces. Designed by the engineer Louis Risse, a French immigrant, the boulevard was intended to resemble the Champs-Elysées in Paris, with separate arteries for pedestrians, horse carts, and cyclists, and underpasses at each major intersection.

After the Grand Concourse was completed in 1909, affluent Manhattanites began moving to the area, seeking respite from the stifling Manhattan tenements down south. Development throughout the district increased rapidly thereafter throughout the 1920s and '30s. This building boom was guided by the idea that the architecture of a community greatly affects the character of its residents: elegant urban design would lead to stable communities, with enhanced quality of life and fewer social hardships. The elaborate Art Deco- and Art Moderne-style buildings with ornate façades that line the Grand Concourse are a result of this belief.

A few decades later, during the 1970s, the South Bronx went through a period of social restructuring, with 30 percent of its residents moving away, and poorer residents moving in. This led to an overall decrease in city services, bringing with it a strong sense of social unrest. By the mid-1980s, community advocates and political leaders attempted to revive the area by rebuilding some of the local infrastructure and thus attracting new residents once more. Today, the Concourse closely resembles what it looked like decades ago during the first half of the twentieth century.

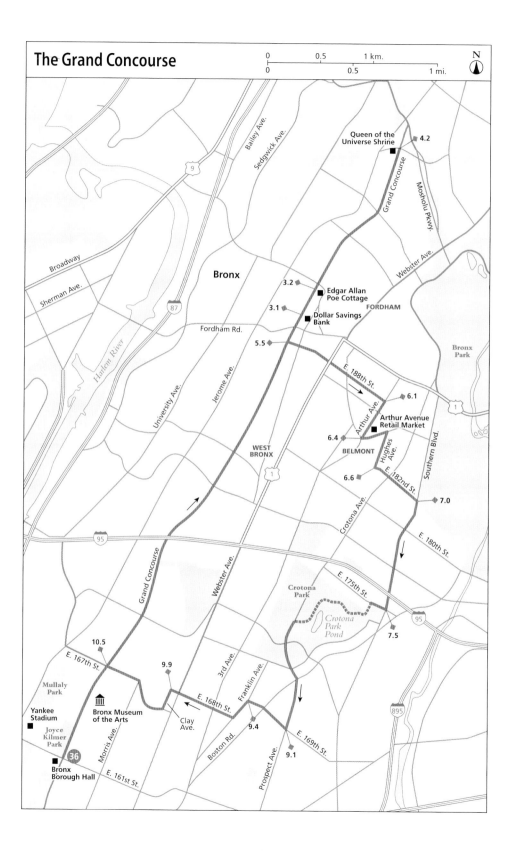

The Grand Concourse

0   0.5   1 km.
0   0.5   1 mi.

N

Queen of the
Universe Shrine   4.2

Grand Concourse

Mosholu Pkwy.

Bailey Ave.

Sedgwick Ave.

9

Broadway

Bronx

3.2

Edgar Allan
Poe Cottage

Webster Ave.

FORDHAM

Sherman Ave.

87

3.1

Dollar Savings
Bank

Bronx
Park

Fordham Rd.

5.5

Harlem River

E. 188th St.

6.1

University Ave.

Jerome Ave.

Arthur Ave.

Arthur Avenue
Retail Market

6.4

Hughes Ave.

Southern Blvd.

WEST
BRONX

BELMONT

1

6.6

E. 182nd St.

7.0

Crotona Ave.

95

E. 180th St.

Grand Concourse

Webster Ave.

Crotona
Park

E. 175th St.

Crotona
Park
Pond

95

10.5

7.5

E. 167th St.

9.9

3rd Ave.

Franklin Ave.

Mullaly
Park

Yankee
Stadium

Bronx Museum
of the Arts

E. 168th St.

Clay
Ave.

9.4

895

Joyce
Kilmer
Park

36

Morris Ave.

Boston Rd.

Prospect Ave.

E. 169th St.

9.1

Bronx
Borough Hall

E. 161st St.

4.2 Make a U-turn at Van Cortland Avenue East, traversing the Grand Concourse to go south along its west side.

5.5 Turn left onto East 188th Street.

6.1 Turn right onto Arthur Avenue.

6.4 Turn left onto Crescent Avenue, followed by a right onto Hughes Avenue.

6.6 Turn left onto East 182nd Street.

7.0 Turn right onto Southern Boulevard.

7.7 Turn right onto East 175th Street, going uphill. At the top of the hill, enter Crotona Park on your left. Follow the greenway as it curves through the park.

8.2 Veer left, with the tennis courts on your right. Take a break by the lake on your left.

8.5 Exit the park and turn left onto Crotona Avenue. Crotona Avenue becomes Prospect Avenue up ahead.

9.1 Turn right onto East 169th Street.

9.4 Turn left onto Franklin Avenue, followed by a quick right onto East 168th Street.

9.9 Turn left onto Clay Avenue, followed by a quick right onto East 167th Street.

10.5 Turn left onto the Grand Concourse.

11.1 Arrive at your starting point.

RIDE INFORMATION

Local Events/Attractions

Bronx Museum of the Arts: A converted synagogue with a three-story glass atrium that displays works by artists of African, Asian, and Latin American descent. 1040 Grand Concourse; (718) 681-6000; www.bronxmuseum.org

Arthur Avenue: The Bronx's Little Italy is centered around Arthur Avenue in Belmont. www.arthuravenuebronx.com

Poe Cottage: The poet Edgar Allen Poe's home from 1846 to 1849. 2640 Grand Concourse; (718) 881-8900; www.bronxhistoricalsociety.org/poecottage

Restrooms

Mile 8.3: There are restrooms in the park buildings in Crotona Park, next to the tennis courts and on the lake's shore.

37

A Grid of Greenways

This journey travels along more than 9 miles of the Bronx's extensive grid of car-free greenways, which connect park spaces throughout the borough. Cutting through Van Cortlandt Park, you'll cycle past the borough's largest freshwater lake, the country's oldest public golf course, and along wooded pathways. A major greenway artery along Mosholu Parkway then leads you south to another major Bronx park, Bronx Park, where you'll cycle to the borough's northern border along the Bronx River. On your return journey, stop off at the New York Botanical Garden, if you wish, before returning to Van Cortlandt Park.

Start: The West 242nd Street entrance to Van Cortlandt Park, at West 242nd Street and Broadway

Length: 9.7 miles out and back (partial)

Approximate riding time: 1.5 hours

Best bike: Hybrid, road, or mountain bike

Terrain and trail surface: The trail is paved throughout. The terrain is slightly hilly. The outward journey goes uphill through Van Cortlandt Park and downhill along the Mosholu Parkway Greenway. The return journey does the opposite. There's also one short, steep climb in Bronx Park.

Traffic and hazards: The entire route runs along car-free greenways that extend from Van Cortlandt Park to Bronx Park and beyond. To access the Mosholu Parkway Greenway from Van Cortlandt Park, you have to cross Mosholu Parkway itself, where traffic is heavy. Use the traffic signals and stay alert. The Mosholu Parkway Greenway then crosses several crossroads. Come to a complete stop before traversing them.

Things to see: Van Cortlandt Park, Bronx Park, Allerton Ballfields, Bronx River, New York Botanical Garden, Van Cortlandt Lake

Maps: *New York City Bike Map,* Van Cortlandt Park map available for download at vcpark.org/park/park_map.html, Department of City Planning *Bike the Bronx* map available for download at www.nyc.gov/html/dcp/html/transportation/bike_bronx_greenway.shtml

Getting there: By public transportation: Take the 1 subway to the Van Cortlandt Park-242nd Street station. Descend from the elevated tracks on the east side of Broadway and enter the park at West 242nd Street. By car: From Midtown take the West Side Highway (NY 9A) north. Take exit 17 toward Dyckman Street and merge onto Riverside Drive. Go about 0.2 mile. Veer slightly right along Riverside Drive and then turn left onto Broadway to go north about 2.2 miles. Turn left onto Van Cortlandt Park South. Go 0.3 mile. Turn left at Bailey Avenue and proceed to Van Cortlandt Park's golf course parking area. Start your cycling route at mile 0.3 in the route description below. GPS coordinates: N40 53.380' / W73 53.881'

THE RIDE

The Van Cortlandt Park Greenway cuts across the southwestern part of the park's more than 1,000 acres of woodlands, wetlands, and meadows. To catch the greenway eastward, cycle in between the ball fields on your right and the picnic and pool area on your left. When the path splits at the northeast corner of the ball fields, you'll veer left, away from the playing fields to head underneath an archway. (For the past couple of years a few dozen feet of the path here have been dirt.) You'll skirt the edge of the parking lot up ahead, veering toward the lake. Then follow the greenway as it crosses the parking lot

Bike Shop

United Spokes: 207 W. 242nd St.; (718) 432-2453
A great bike shop with a friendly staff just steps from Van Cortlandt Park. They organize repair clinics and are a good spot to find out about rides and other cycling events.

to the right and picks up on the sidewalk on the other side. This soon brings you toward two golf courses—the Van Cortlandt Golf Course, which opened as the country's first public course in 1895, and the Mosholu Golf Course.

Continuing eastward, you'll skirt the edge of Van Cortlandt Lake, an 18-acre body of water known for its high density of yellow perch. When the

Biking east through Van Cortlandt Park, alongside Van Cortlandt Lake.

path splits, you'll then make a sharp right turn to follow the greenway as it spirals up and around 470 degrees to send you south through more densely forested swaths of the park. The Mosholu Golf Course will be on your left. At the southern edge of Van Cortlandt Park, stay alert and use the traffic signals to cross Dickinson Avenue and Mosholu Parkway to catch the next greenway—the Mosholu Parkway Greenway, which heads south along the west edge of Mosholu Parkway. Enjoy the downhill ride toward Bronx Park, but stay alert for crossroads along the way. Stop before crossing.

After traversing Hull Avenue, you can spot the redbrick 52nd Police Precinct station, a city landmark complete with gabled roof and clock tower, on your left. The greenway then veers slightly left, going across a bridge and turning sharply left when you hit Southern Boulevard (also called Dr. Theodore Kazimiroff Boulevard). On the other side of the boulevard you can catch glimpses of the New York Botanical Garden, one of the Bronx Park's best-known features. (Stop off at the gardens on your return journey if you wish.) The park is also home to the Bronx Zoo and contains one of few remaining natural waterside landscapes, alongside the Bronx River.

After entering Bronx Park, veer left of the Allerton Ballfields, named after Daniel Allerton, an early Bronx settler who was a direct descendant of a signer of the Mayflower Compact. At the northeastern corner of the ball fields, swing right and then left again toward and across the Bronx River. You'll then head north along the riverside greenway toward the north edge of the borough. The 24-mile Bronx River begins north of here in Westchester County and empties into the East River farther south. There are numerous river access points along the way as you head north, with riverside benches that are nice resting spots. If you go down to the river, dismount and walk your bike as cycling is prohibited on these paths.

At East 229th Street, when you hit upon the access road to the Bronx River Parkway, the greenway discontinues. It picks up farther north again, heading—in spurts—through Westchester County. Make a U-turn here to return southward to your entry point to the Bronx River Greenway. From there, you'll continue south, heading uphill through a swath of wooded wilderness. Then, from the top of the hill, you'll cut westward through the park's interior. Use caution here and come to a complete stop before crossing the access and exit roads for the Bronx River Parkway. Up ahead, when the greenway (now sidewalk) narrows, crossing the Bronx River, stay alert for oncoming cyclists.

When you hit the Allerton Ballfields once more, skirt their western edge to return towards the Mosholu Parkway Greenway. (From that greenway you have the option of visiting the New York Botanical Gardens; see directions below.) Retrace your route along the Mosholu Parkway Greenway back to Van Cortlandt Park and your starting point.

MILES AND DIRECTIONS

0.0 Go east along the greenway into Van Cortlandt Park, in between the ball fields on your right and the picnic area on your left.

0.1 When the path forks, veer left, heading under an archway. Continue veering left to hug the edge of the parking lot (on your right).

0.3 Before reaching the lake, swivel right to follow the greenway across the parking lot and along the road on the other side. Head east along the greenway, with Van Cortlandt Lake on your left.

0.6 Turn right, looping up and around 470 degrees to the right. Then follow the greenway southward.

1.2 Cross Dickinson Avenue along the crosswalk straight ahead. Then swivel left to cross Mosholu Parkway. Access the Mosholu Parkway Greenway on the east side of the parkway to go southward.

2.4 Turn left at Southern Boulevard (Dr. Theodore Kazimiroff Boulevard), following the greenway. Stay left of the Allerton Ballfields up ahead.

2.7 From the northeast edge of the ball fields, veer right and then left again to continue along the greenway.

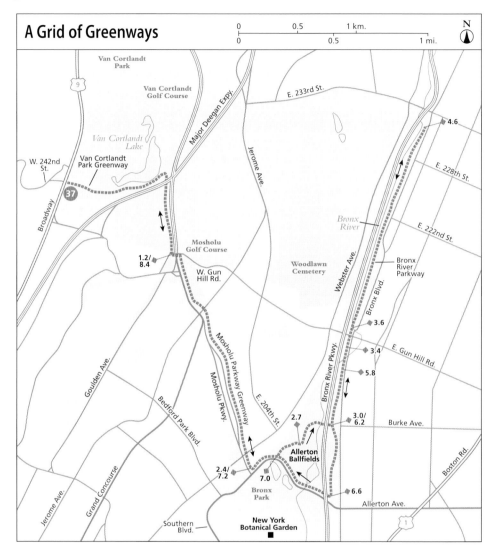

A Grid of Greenways

0   0.5   1 km.
0   0.5   1 mi.

N

Van Cortlandt
Park

9

Van Cortlandt
Golf Course

E. 233rd St.

Van Cortlandt
Lake

Major Deegan Expy.

Jerome Ave.

4.6

E. 228th St.

W. 242nd
St.

Van Cortlandt
Park Greenway

37

Broadway

Bronx
River

E. 222nd St.

Bronx
River
Parkway

Mosholu
Golf Course

1.2/
8.4

W. Gun
Hill Rd.

Woodlawn
Cemetery

Webster Ave.

Bronx Blvd.

3.6

3.4

E. Gun Hill Rd.

5.8

Goulden Ave.

Bedford Park Blvd.

Mosholu Pkwy.

Mosholu Parkway Greenway

E. 204th St.

Bronx River Pkwy.

2.7

3.0/
6.2

Burke Ave.

Boston Rd.

Jerome Ave.

Grand Concourse

2.4/
7.2

7.0

Allerton
Ballfields

6.6

Bronx
Park

Allerton Ave.

Southern
Blvd.

New York
Botanical Garden ■

1

3.0 After traveling underneath the bridge, turn left to go north along the Bronx River Greenway.

3.4 Go over the bridge and through the parking area.

3.6 Access the northern portion of the greenway via the roundabout at East 211th Street.

4.6 Make a U-turn to return southward.

5.8 After the bridge, access the greenway on your right.

6.2 Veer left to continue south. Take the path on the far left when the path forks into three arms.

6.6 After passing the skate park and hitting upon Allerton Avenue (don't cross), turn right to take the greenway westward. Come to a complete stop before crossing the access roads to the Bronx River Parkway.

7.0 Veer left to go west from the Allerton Ballfields.

7.2 Turn right onto the Mosholu Parkway Greenway. (To visit the New York Botanical Garden, turn left onto Hull/Marion Avenue, the first cross street. Then take the third left onto Bedford Park Boulevard, which leads to the entrance of the gardens.)

8.4 When the greenway ends at West Gun Hill Road, swivel left to traverse Mosholu Parkway along the pedestrian crosswalk. Then cross Dickinson Avenue and access the Van Cortlandt Park Greenway through the park.

9.0 Follow the greenway as it loops around 470 degrees to the left. Then head west alongside Van Cortlandt Lake.

9.4 Turn right to cross the road and then continue along the right side of the parking lot. Head underneath the bridge on your right, cross the path of dirt.

9.6 Go west in between the playing fields and picnic area.

9.7 Arrive at your starting point.

RIDE INFORMATION

Restrooms
Start/finish: There are restrooms just north of the West 242nd Street entrance to Van Cortlandt Park, accessible from the sidewalk along Broadway.
Mile 2.6/7.0: There are restrooms in the park building beside the Allerton Ballfields.

38

South Bronx Treasures

Probably green spaces and waterside parks aren't the first thing you think of when you think of the southeast Bronx, but this area is filled with innumerable verdant jewel-like parks, complete with water views. The route leads along greenways through Soundview, Pugsley Creek, Concrete Plant, and Crotona Park. These park portions of the route are connected to one another via short, on-road stretches, making this is a great ride for urban explorers who feel comfortable cycling on city streets and are eager to discover some of New York's best-kept secrets.

Start: The Prospect Avenue subway station of the 2 and 5 subways, on the southwest corner of the intersection at Prospect Avenue and Westchester Avenue

Length: 15.1-mile loop

Approximate riding time: 2.5 hours

Best bike: Hybrid or mountain bike

Terrain and trail surface: The trail is paved throughout except for a 0.3-mile stretch of crushed gravel in Castle Hill Park. The terrain is flat, except for a short ascent to Crotona Park along East 175th Street, and a descent from the park to your end point.

Traffic and hazards: This route runs mainly along park greenways (no traffic) and on-road bike lanes (light or moderate traffic). About 2.5 miles of the route have no bike lanes. When crossing the Bronx River along the sidewalk of the Bruckner Expressway, walk your bike (and avoid potential shards of glass along the way). Stay especially alert when making left-hand turns (on Bronx River Avenue and Westchester Avenue, for instance) and use pedestrian crosswalks for added safety.

Things to see: Barretto Point Park, Soundview Park, Pugsley Creek Park, Castle Hill Park, Concrete Plant Park, Crotona Park

Map: *New York City Bike Map*

Getting there: By public transportation: Take the 2 or 5 subway to the Prospect Avenue stop in the Bronx, an elevated station. Descend to ground level, where you'll be on the corner of Prospect and Westchester Avenues, your starting point for this ride. GPS coordinates: N40 49.164' / W73 54.115'

THE RIDE

On this journey, you'll cycle through an array of city- and green-scapes that take you off the beaten path—from the semi-industrial swath at your starting point to waterfront parks along much of the rest of your journey. To begin, go south on Prospect Avenue's on-road bike lane. You'll then soon make a sharp left turn onto Southern Boulevard. Use the crosswalk if traffic seems heavy. Up ahead, you'll duck underneath the Sheridan Expressway and cycle through a semi-industrial section of warehouses and depots. Tiffany Street then carries

Looking south from Tiffany Street Pier in Barretto Point Park in Hunts Point.

you to the first waterside reprieve, Barretto Point Park, an impeccable little park with a pier that feels worlds away from the semi-industrial terrain you just biked through.

Continuing en route, you'll bike past warehouses and car service stations once more before reaching the Bruckner Expressway. Dismount your bike here to walk it across the Bronx River along the expressway's sidewalk (biking officially prohibited). Then, remount your bike on the other side to zigzag your way along streets to Soundview Park, another little-known waterfront park. Following the greenway through the park, you'll pass ball fields, sprawling lawns, and have sweeping views of the Bronx River's entry point into the East River. The waterfront benches are lovely resting spots.

Up ahead, you'll exit Soundview Park and then cycle through a laid-back residential neighborhood for a short stretch. This brings you to the Shorehaven bikeway on your right, which hugs the East River and culminates beside Clason Point Park (also known as Kane's Park). Local anglers toss their lines into the East River, here, with up-close views of the Whitestone Bridge.

Proceeding en route, you'll follow a short on-road stretch with light traffic to your next park-scape—Pugsley Creek Park. A greenway here snakes along the northern edge of the park, offering glimpses of freshwater wetlands and, with any luck, an osprey or two. This leads directly to the crushed gravel greenway along the wetlands of Castle Hill Park. When you reach the east edge of this park, you have two options. You can make a U-turn to retrace your route through the parks back to Soundview Park. This is the more scenic route. Alternately, for a more direct—and urban—route, take the 2-mile on-road route described here. It leads mainly along on-road bike lanes back to Soundview Park.

Either way, from Soundview Park (via either route option), you'll return toward the Bruckner Expressway, where you'll cross the Bronx River once more, but this time along the expressway's northern sidewalk. From atop the bridge, keep your eyes peeled for the ramp down to Concrete Plant Park, which stretches northward along the Bronx River on your right. Remount your bike to enter the park along the greenway. Home to a former concrete plant, several of the structures in which concrete was produced—so-called hoppers—remain standing in rusty red throughout the park today. (The park won a design award a few years back for successful integration of past and present into an urban park space.) The benches along the river are lovely spots for a break.

From the northern end of the park, dismount your bike to walk it a short stretch along the sidewalk to your left. Then cross to the north side of Westchester Avenue along the pedestrian crossing and swivel left to go west along Westchester Avenue. Traffic can be heavy here, so remain especially alert until

Concrete Point Park, home to a former concrete plant along the Bronx River. The park won a design award for successful integration of past and present into an urban park space.

you reach the on-road bike lane on Longfellow Avenue up ahead. The next and final part of your journey goes through Crotona Park. Enter the park from the top of the hill at East 175th Street and follow the greenway as it snakes downhill, swerving right and then left again. When the bikeway splits, veer left, staying left of the tennis courts and heading toward the lake. Take a break along the lakeside benches, if you wish, before returning to your starting point.

MILES AND DIRECTIONS

0.0 Go south along Prospect Avenue.

0.5 Turn sharply left onto Southern Boulevard.

0.9 Veer right onto Leggett Avenue. Stay on Leggett Avenue as it becomes Randall Avenue and veers slightly left.

1.4 Turn right onto Tiffany Street.

1.8 Enter Barretto Point Park and circumnavigate its perimeter counterclockwise along the water. Then exit the park back onto Tiffany Street, heading north.

2.9 Turn right onto Garrison Avenue.

3.4   Turn left onto Edgewater Road. At Bruckner Expressway just ahead, dismount and walk your bike along the expressway's southern sidewalk across the Bronx River on your right.

3.6   On the other side of the river, remount your bike and turn right onto Bronx River Avenue.

3.7   Turn left onto Story Avenue, followed by a right onto Colgate Avenue.

4.1   Enter Soundview Park along the greenway and follow it through the park. Stay right whenever the road forks.

5.5   Exit Soundview Park, turning right onto Harding Park/Bronx River Avenue.

6.0   Turn right onto the Shorehaven bikeway.

6.5   Turn right onto Soundview Avenue.

6.6   Enter Clason Point Park straight ahead. To continue en route, go northwest on Soundview Avenue.

6.8   Veer right onto Stephens Avenue.

7.1   Turn right to access the greenway through Pugsley Creek Park.

7.9   Continue straight into Castle Hill Park along the crushed gravel path.

8.2   Turn left onto Castle Hill Avenue.

9.1   Turn left onto Lafayette Avenue.

10.2   Go straight to enter Soundview Park. Exit the other side to continue along Lafayette Avenue.

10.7   Turn right onto Colgate Avenue, followed by a left onto Story Avenue, and a right onto Bronx River Avenue.

11.1   After passing underneath the expressway, swivel left, to access the northern sidewalk of Bruckner Expressway to cross the Bronx River. Walk your bike on the sidewalk.

11.3   After crossing the river, turn right to enter Concrete Plant Park along the bikeway ramp. Remount your bike.

11.7   When you exit Concrete Plant Park, turn left along the sidewalk (walk your bike). Cross to the north side of Westchester Avenue up ahead along the pedestrian crossing, then swivel left, remount your bike, and go west along Westchester Avenue.

11.8   Turn right onto Longfellow Avenue.

12.5   Turn left onto East 174th Street.

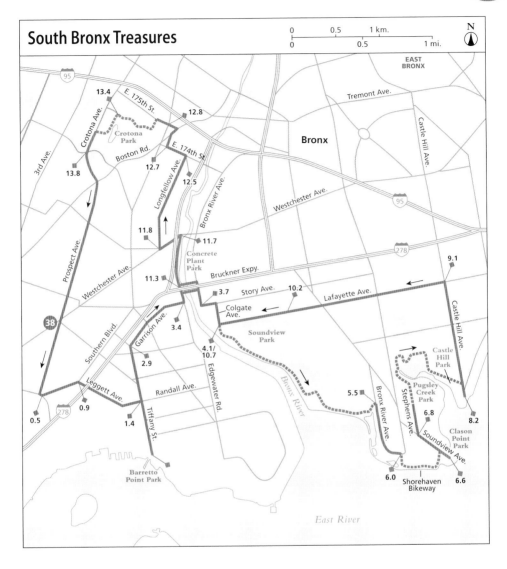

South Bronx Treasures

12.7 Turn right onto Hoe Avenue and veer right just ahead onto Boston Road.

12.8 Use the pedestrian crosswalk at East 175th Street to cross Boston Road and go west on East 175th Street.

13.0 At the top of the hill at Waterloo Place, turn left onto the greenway through Crotona Park. Cross Crotona Park East just ahead to continue along the greenway on the other side.

13.4 When the greenway forks, veer left, with the tennis courts on your right and the lake on your left up ahead.

13.8 Exit the park onto Crotona Avenue, going south. Crotona Avenue becomes Prospect Avenue.

15.1 Arrive at your starting point.

RIDE INFORMATION

Restrooms

Mile 1.8: There are restrooms in Barretto Point Park.

Mile 13.4: There are restrooms in Crotona Park in the park building by the lake.

39

A Bronx Rumble to Wave Hill

This bike route leads you from the pulsating southern Bronx to the calm of the Bronx's more exclusive northern neighborhoods of Fieldston and Riverdale. You'll shoot north along multiple miles of on-road bike lanes, through various Bronx communities, past numerous colleges, and alongside striking old stone churches. You'll then enter the hilly terrain of Fieldston and Riverdale, where winding, tree-lined roads lead past lavish stone residences. Stop off at Wave Hill, a public garden and cultural center, if you wish, for sweeping views of the Hudson River and Palisades. Then return along the Harlem River to your starting point.

Start: Hostos Community College, at the intersection of East 149th Street and the Grand Concourse

Length: 19.6-mile loop

Approximate riding time: 3.5 hours

Best bike: Road or mountain bike

Terrain and trail surface: The trail is paved throughout. The terrain has steep hills throughout Fieldston and Riverdale. Check your brakes especially carefully before heading out on this ride.

Traffic and hazards: Most of the route follows on-road bike lanes that run along wide city streets with moderate traffic, giving cyclists ample space. Still, stay alert at all times, especially for turning vehicles. The north section of this route, through Fieldston and Riverdale, runs along steep and narrow curving roads without bike lanes. Traffic is very light here and cars drive slowly. The route requires some urban cycling comfort.

Things to see: Lehman College, Jerome Park Reservoir, Fieldston, Riverdale, Wave Hill, Inwood Hill Park, Harlem River, Yankee Stadium

Maps: *New York City Bike Map,* Department of City Planning *Bike the Bronx* map

Getting there: By public transportation: Take the 4, 5, or 2 subway to the 149th Street/Grand Concourse stop. By car: Take the FDR Drive north to exit 18 (at the Willis Avenue Bridge). After crossing the bridge, follow the signs to I-87 N/Major Deegan Expressway. Take exit 5 from I-87 N (at East 161st Street). Go east on East 161st Street where the Concourse Plaza Garage is on your right at 200 E. 161st St. (between Sheridan and Morris Avenues). GPS coordinates: N40 49.108' / W73 55.636'

THE RIDE

The first stretch of your journey leads northward along an on-road bike lane through residential city blocks, where, during summer months, children play outdoors and fire hydrants are apt to serve as sprinklers. This soon brings you to a busy intersection at East 167th Street, where multiple roads intersect. Stay alert and follow the bike lane onto Edward L. Grant Highway, a broad avenue that passes through a motley neighborhood of charming churches and run-down buildings. University Avenue then leads northward toward Lehman College. Marked by Gothic-style buildings, the college sits just across from the Jerome Park Reservoir, a 100-year-old reservoir that still hydrates parts of the city today. Hugging the reservoir's eastern edge, you'll cycle past athletic fields and college yards to Sedgwick Avenue.

Bike Shop

Tread Bike Shop: 250 Dyckman St.; (212) 544-7055
One of the friendliest bike shops in the five boroughs, where the staff truly take their time to meet your needs. The day I was there, the staff pulled up bike maps on the computer to show me the best routes through the Bronx, from south to north, and west to east.

Stay alert on Sedgwick Avenue, where you'll follow an on-road segment a short spurt. When the road splits into three arms, continue straight, along the middle lane, to stay on Sedgwick Avenue. A short stretch of zigzagged biking downhill at West 238th Street soon brings you toward the elevated tracks of the 1 subway and past a much-loved Bronx establishment on your left, S&S Cheesecake. For more than five decades it's brought cheesecake lovers to the Bronx.

Continuing onward, you'll catch a narrow, uphill bikeway to your right at Irwin Avenue and continue uphill past Manhattan College, established in 1853, on your right. This brings you into the exclusive neighborhood of

Pathway through Wave Hill, a public garden and cultural center in Riverdale in the Bronx.

Views from Wave Hill, a public garden and cultural center in Riverdale in the Bronx, south toward the George Washington Bridge.

Fieldston, a suburban community of stately single-family homes along hilly tree-lined streets. Snake your way through this corner of country in the city.

Then, crossing the Henry Hudson Parkway at West 252nd Street will lead you to Riverdale, another stately neighborhood on a slope. With landmarked estates, it feels far removed from city life. Sitting high on a bluff in the northwestern corner of the Bronx, it affords sweeping views of the Hudson River and Palisades across the water. Independence Avenue then carries you past Wave Hill, a 28-acre public garden and cultural center. Once a private estate, it now houses gardens, walkways through forested terrain, a gallery, and environmental center. It's a must spot for a mid-route break. (There's a fee to enter.)

Proceeding en route, you'll continue south on Independence Avenue and then skirt the edge of Riverdale Park, a slim park on the Hudson River. A steep ascent on West 232nd Street then soon brings you to more throbbing Bronx neighborhoods again. As you wind your way downhill from here, glance into the distance occasionally for far-reaching views of the city skyline. This brings you away from the Bronx's suburban neighborhoods for good, toward Marble Hill. Officially part of Manhattan, this community is geographically seemingly on Bronx terrain. Just ahead, walk your bike across the Broadway Bridge along the sidewalk to access mainland Manhattan. (Bridge biking prohibited.)

After the bridge, you'll skirt the edge of Inwood Hill Park and head south along Seaman Avenue toward Fort Tryon Park. This final stretch of your journey leads along on-road bike lanes on city streets to the Harlem River Greenway. Heading south along the Harlem River, multiple bridges then neatly frame the city skyline in the distance and your journey is flanked by Highbridge Park's rocky terrain on your right. Follow the greenway as it leads uphill to your right, alongside Harlem River Drive, to reach West 155th Street where you access the Macombs Dam Bridge across the Harlem River. Walk your bike along the northern sidewalk. (Bridge biking officially prohibited.) At the end of the bridge, stay alert. Come to a complete stop before crossing a motor-vehicle access ramp and continuing toward Yankee Stadium. A final on-road section, mostly along bike lanes, then leads back to your starting point.

MILES AND DIRECTIONS

0.0 Bike west on East 149th Street. Take the second right onto Gerard Avenue.

1.4 Turn left onto East 167th Street.

1.5 Cross Jerome Avenue and turn right onto Edward L. Grant Highway, which later becomes University Avenue.

4.4 Turn right onto Strong Street, followed by a left onto Goulden Avenue/Reservoir Avenue. When the road splits, stay right, sticking to Goulden Avenue.

5.6 Turn left onto Sedgwick Avenue.

5.9 When the road splits into three, take the middle lane to stay on Sedgwick Avenue.

6.1 Turn right onto West 238th Street, followed by a quick right onto Cannon Place, and a first left to connect to Orloff Avenue, going left.

6.4 Turn right onto West 238th Street.

6.7 Turn right onto Tibbett Avenue, followed by a left onto West 240th Street.

6.9 Turn right onto the Irwin Avenue bikeway. Exit the trail straight ahead, going uphill on Waldo Avenue (called Manhattan College Parkway at places). Continue straight to stay on Waldo Avenue.

7.4 Turn left onto West 246th Street. Continue straight through the roundabout.

7.7 Turn right onto Delafield Avenue. Stay left when the road splits, continuing on Delafield Avenue.

A Bronx Rumble to Wave Hill

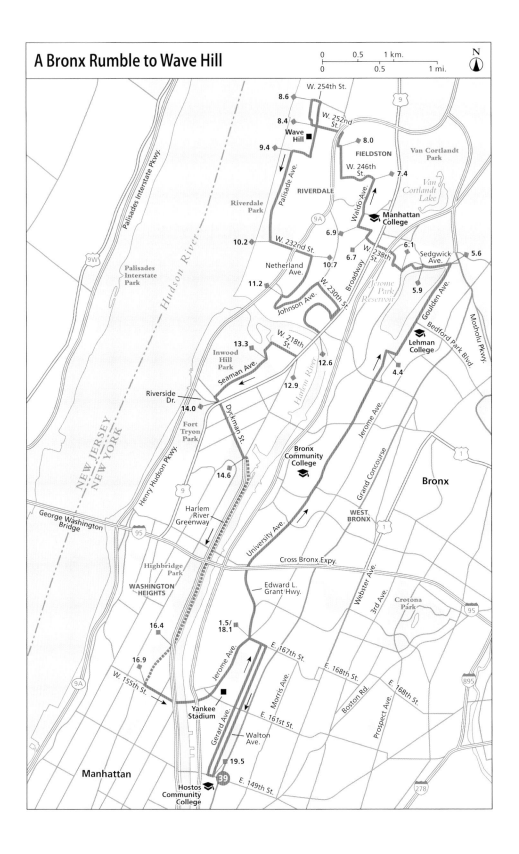

Scale:
0   0.5   1 km.
0   0.5   1 mi.

N

Labels and markers:

W. 254th St.
8.6
8.4
W. 252nd St.
Wave Hill
8.0
9.4
FIELDSTON
Van Cortlandt Park
W. 246th St.
7.4
Van Cortlandt Lake
RIVERDALE
Waldo Ave.
Palisades Interstate Pkwy.
Riverdale Park
Palisade Ave.
Manhattan College
6.9
6.1
Sedgwick Ave.
5.6
Riverdale Park
10.2
W. 232nd St.
9A
6.7
10.7
5.9
Hudson River
Palisades Interstate Park
Netherland Ave.
Broadway
W. 238th St.
Jerome Park Reservoir
Goulden Ave.
Mosholu Pkwy.
9W
11.2
Johnson Ave.
W. 230th St.
Bedford Park Blvd.
Lehman College
13.3
W. 218th St.
12.6
4.4
Inwood Hill Park
Seaman Ave.
12.9
Harlem River
Jerome Ave.
Riverside Dr.
14.0
Dyckman St.
Fort Tryon Park
Bronx Community College
Grand Concourse
Bronx
NEW JERSEY
NEW YORK
Henry Hudson Pkwy.
9
14.6
Harlem River Greenway
WEST BRONX
1
1
George Washington Bridge
95
University Ave.
Cross Bronx Expy.
Highbridge Park
WASHINGTON HEIGHTS
Edward L. Grant Hwy.
Webster Ave.
3rd Ave.
Crotona Park
95
16.4
Jerome Ave.
E. 167th St.
E. 168th St.
895
16.9
1.5/18.1
Morris Ave.
Boston Rd.
Prospect Ave.
E. 168th St.
9A
W. 155th St.
Yankee Stadium
Gerard Ave.
E. 161st St.
Manhattan
Walton Ave.
19.5
39
E. 149th St.
278
Hostos Community College

8.0 Turn left onto West 250th Street, followed by a quick right along Henry Hudson Parkway.

8.2 Turn left onto West 252nd Street to cross the parkway.

8.4 Turn right onto Sycamore Avenue.

8.6 Turn right onto West 254th Street and go uphill. It's steep! At the top of the hill turn right onto Independence Avenue.

9.1 The entrance to Wave Hill is on your right. Dismount, lock up, take a break, and explore. To proceed en route, continue south on Independence Avenue.

9.3 When the road ends, turn right onto Spaulding Lane (unmarked, downhill).

9.4 Turn left onto Palisade Avenue, with Riverdale Park on your right.

10.2 Turn left onto West 232nd Street.

10.7 Turn right onto Netherland Avenue.

11.2 Turn left onto Kappock Street, followed by a sharp left onto Johnson Avenue.

11.9 Turn right onto West 230th Street.

12.0 Turn right at Kingsbridge Avenue onto Marble Hill Avenue, followed by a right onto West 228th Street/Terrace View Avenue. Stay left when the road forks to continue onto West 225th Street.

12.6 Dismount your bike to walk your bike across the west sidewalk of the bridge. (Bridge biking officially prohibited.) Remount your bike on the other side, going south.

12.9 Turn right onto West 218th Street. Inwood Hill Park is at the end of the road. (Explore if you wish.) Turn left onto Indian Road, hugging the edge of the park. Follow the road as it veers left onto West 214th Street.

13.3 Turn right onto Seaman Avenue.

14.0 Turn left onto Riverside Drive and veer right onto Dyckman Street just ahead.

14.6 Cross 10th Avenue to access the Harlem River Greenway straight ahead. Turn right to go south.

16.4 Follow the bikeway as it veers up to the right and away from the water.

16.9 At West 155th Street, dismount to walk your bike along the northern sidewalk across the Macombs Dam Bridge. (Biking officially prohibited.) Toward the end of the bridge, use the pedestrian crossing to cross the motorist access road. Use caution. There's no traffic signal here.

17.6 The bridge sidewalk leads onto Jerome Avenue, across from Yankee Stadium. Use the pedestrian crosswalk to cross to the east side of Jerome Avenue and continue north on Jerome Avenue.

18.1 Turn right onto East 167th Street, followed by a right onto Walton Avenue.

19.5 Turn left onto East 149th Street.

19.6 Arrive at your starting point.

RIDE INFORMATION

Local Events/Attractions

S&S Cheesecake Inc.: Cheesecake with a five-decade history. 222 W. 238th St.; (718) 549-3888; www.sscheesecake.com

Wave Hill: A 28-acre public garden and cultural center overlooking the Hudson River and Palisades. W. 249th St. and Independence Avenue; (718) 549-3200; www.wavehill.org

Restrooms

Mile 6.1: There are restrooms in Fort Independence Playground on your left.
Mile 9.1: There are restrooms at Wave Hill.
Mile 13.2: There are restrooms in Inwood Hill Park.

Old Putnam Trail and South County Trailway

This ride journeys along the Putnam Trail through Van Cortlandt Park and connects to the South County Trailway in Westchester County. Both trails run alongside a former railway line—the Old Put—which carried passengers from the Bronx to Brewster in the late nineteenth century. Today, the trails are popular car-free biking and hiking treks. In Van Cortlandt Park, the dirt-track Putnam Trail bumbles over railroad cross-ties, through an oak-hickory forest, past a lake, and alongside wetlands on what is one of the park's major nature corridors. In Westchester County, the trail is paved and framed by a narrow border of deciduous trees along much of the way. This route is out-and-back, so you can go as far north as you wish before turning back. The car-free ride is a great respite from city cycling.

Start: The West 242nd Street entrance to Van Cortlandt Park, at West 242nd Street and Broadway

Length: 17.1 miles out and back (to Mount Hope)

Approximate riding time: 2.5 hours

Best bike: Mountain or hybrid bike (for the dirt Putnam Trail)

Terrain and trail surface: The 1.3-mile Putnam Trail through Van Cortlandt Park runs along a former railroad bed, now made of dirt and containing protruding railroad cross-ties that make for a bumpy ride. Stay alert along the way. The South County Trailway leading north from Van Cortlandt Park is paved. The terrain is flat.

Traffic and hazards: The trail is entirely car-free, but stay alert for numerous crossroads along the South County Trailway. Come to a complete stop before crossing them. Also, along the Putnam Trail in Van Cortlandt Park, stay alert for remnants of railroad cross-ties and other obstacles (rocks, tree roots) that protrude along the dirt trail. Avoid them.

Things to see: Putnam Trail, South County Trailway, Old Put Stations, Van Cortlandt Park, Van Cortlandt Lake, Tibbetts Brook Park

Maps: *New York City Bike Map,* North and South County Trailway Bike Map accessible at www.nycbikemaps.com/maps/north-and-south-county-trailways-bike-map

Getting there: By public transportation: Take the 1 subway to the Van Cortlandt Park-242nd Street station. Descend from the elevated tracks on the east side of Broadway and enter the park at West 242nd Street. By car: From Midtown take the West Side Highway (NY 9A) north. Take exit 17 toward Dyckman Street and merge onto Riverside Drive. Go 0.2 mile. Veer right along Riverside Drive to turn left onto Broadway. Go north 2.2 miles. Turn left onto Van Cortlandt Park South. Go 0.3 mile. Turn left at Bailey Avenue and proceed to Van Cortlandt Park's golf course parking area. Start your cycling route at mile 0.3 in the route description below. GPS coordinates: N40 53.380' / W73 53.881'

THE RIDE

To begin your journey, you'll access the Putnam Trail in Van Cortlandt Park next to the golf course parking lot, just south of the lake. The former railroad bridge at the lake's southwest corner marks the beginning of the 1.3-mile dirt trail. Remnants of the old rail line dot the way as you head north alongside Van Cortlandt Lake on your right and Tibbetts Brook and surrounding wetlands on your left. Cycle through an oak-hickory forest and brush up against the Van Cortlandt Golf Course, which opened in 1895 as the country's first public golf course. You might spot skunks, rabbits, raccoons, and even foxes as you head north on this quiet nature corridor. Along the way, yield to hikers and remain alert for roots, stones, cross-ties, and other protrusions.

The Putnam Trail meets up with the South County Trailway at the north edge of the park. This paved, car-free trail extends 14 miles northward through Westchester County alongside the Old Put with railway signposts sharing local railway lore along the way. Going north, the trail is framed by a narrow border of forest and meanders through a patchwork of commercial and residential zones. Running parallel to the Saw Mill River Parkway, however, the murmur of traffic is never far away.

A nice stop-off spot just north of Van Cortlandt Park is Tibbetts Brook Park, accessible on your right. The 160-acre park contains two artificial lakes, which you can circumnavigate via a path that loops along their perimeter.

A former railroad bridge at the southern end of the Putnam Trail through Van Cortlandt Park.

Go slowly and yield to walkers along the way. The park also holds remnants of the Old Croton Aqueduct, which carried water from the Croton River in Westchester County to Manhattan reservoirs beginning in the first half of the nineteenth century. Sit by the lake, sprawl on the meadow, or simply cycle the park's circumference before returning to the South County Trailway.

From here, this ride continues north to the former Mount Hope railway station. Given that the route is out-and-back, though, you can turn around at any point (or here). The journey north continues along a fencerow of trees, past suburban homes with manicured yards, and next to commercial strips. The trail takes you past the former railway stations of Dunwoodie, Bryn Mawr Park, Nepperhan, Gray Oaks, and Nepera Park, before reaching Mount Hope, where a small clearing allows for partial access to the Saw Mill River and makes for a good turnaround spot. Take a short break by the trail-side clearing before retracing your route southward back to Van Cortlandt Park.

MILES AND DIRECTIONS

0.0 Go east along the greenway into Van Cortlandt Park, in between the ball fields and the picnic area.

0.1 When the path forks, veer left, heading under an archway. Continue veering left to hug the edge of the parking lot (on your right).

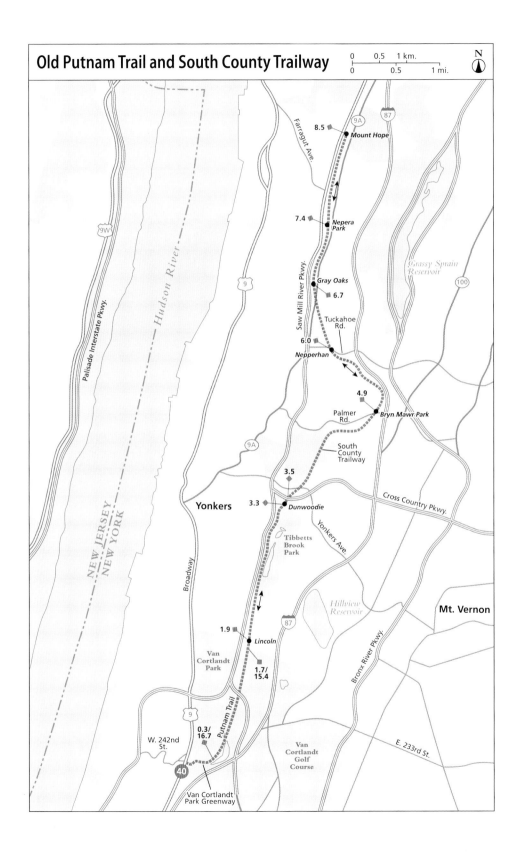

Old Putnam Trail and South County Trailway

0	0.5	1 km.
0	0.5	1 mi.

N

8.5 *Mount Hope*

Farragut Ave.

9A

87

7.4 *Nepera Park*

9W

Hudson River

9

Saw Mill River Pkwy.

Grassy Sprain Reservoir

100

Gray Oaks **6.7**

Tuckahoe Rd.

6.0

Nepperhan

4.9

Palmer Rd.

Bryn Mawr Park

Palisade Interstate Pkwy.

9A

South County Trailway

3.5

Yonkers

3.3 *Dunwoodie*

Cross Country Pkwy.

Yonkers Ave.

NEW JERSEY
NEW YORK

Tibbetts Brook Park

Hillview Reservoir

Mt. Vernon

Broadway

87

1.9

Lincoln

1.7/ 15.4

Bronx River Pkwy.

Van Cortlandt Park

9

Putnam Trail

0.3/ 16.7

W. 242nd St.

40

Van Cortlandt Park Greenway

Van Cortlandt Golf Course

E. 233rd St.

0.3 Veer left of the lake, and cross the former railroad bridge to go north along the Putnam Trail, with the lake on your right.

1.7 Continue onto the South County Trailway. Stay alert for crossroads (stop before crossing) and look out for signposts indicating former Old Putnam Railraod stations. (Approximate locations indicated below.)

1.9 The Lincoln station sign is here.

3.3 Turn right and go downhill to enter Tibbetts Brook Park. Careful; it's steep! When you've finished exploring—or if you bypass the park—return to the South County Trailway to continue north. The Dunwoodie station is marked just ahead.

3.5 Cross the Yonkers Avenue Railroad Bridge and follow the trail as it bends right.

4.9 The Bryn Mawr Park station sign is here.

6.0 After passing the shopping plaza on your right, follow the trail as it bends right and over an overpass. The Nepperhan station sign is here.

6.7 The Gray Oaks station sign is here.

7.4 The Nepera Park station sign is here.

8.5 The Mount Hope station sign is here. A trail to your right leads down toward the Saw Mill River. It's one of the few entry points toward the river and makes for a good turnaround spot. Take a break and then turn around to follow South County Trailway back to Van Cortlandt Park.

13.8 The entrance to Tibbetts Brook Park is on your left.

15.4 Continue onto the Putnam Trail.

16.7 Cross the former railroad bridge and veer right under the overpass up ahead.

17.1 Arrive at your starting point.

RIDE INFORMATION

Restrooms
Start/end: There are restrooms just north of the West 242nd Street entrance to Van Cortlandt Park, accessible from the sidewalk along Broadway.
Mile 3.3/13.8: There are restrooms in Tibbetts Brook Park, located in the park building to your left after you enter the park and descend the hill.

Bicycling Resources

MAPS AND INFORMATION

Bike Smart (www.nyc.gov/bikesmart): Official guide for cycling in NYC.

MTA Bike & Ride (www.mta.info/bike): Information about bicycles and public transportation, bridges, and tunnels in the NYC metro area.

New York City Department of Transportation Bicyclists (www.nyc.gov/html/dot/html/bicyclists/bicyclists.shtml): DOT's website with information about bicycle laws, safety, the city's bike share program, maps, and more.

New York City Department of Transportation Bike Map (www.nyc.gov/html/dot/html/bicyclists/bikemaps.shtml): Current city bicycling map, including detail maps of bridge access points and major intersections. A must for all cyclists.

BICYCLE ADVOCACY

Bike New York (www.bikenewyork.org): Nonprofit bike advocacy organization, with basic biking classes, workshops, rides, and more. The organizers of the Five Boro Bike Tour, among other rides.

Bike NYC (bikenyc.org): A go-to place for all things cycling-related, operated by the nonprofit Transportation Alternatives, with an extensive list of cycling resources on their "about" page.

Citi Bike (citibikenyc.com): New York City's bike share program.

Free Wheels Bicycle Defense Fund (www.bicycledefensefund.org): Nonprofit organization that assists cyclists with legal matters.

New York Bicycling Coalition (www.nybc.net): Nonprofit organization that advocates for bicycle- and pedestrian-friendly policies; includes cycling resources including about laws, safety, legal aid, and more.

Time's Up (times-up.org): Direct-action nonprofit organization that advocates sustainable living through regularly scheduled rides and other cycling events.

Transportation Alternatives (transalt.org): Nonprofit advocacy organization dedicated to promoting cycling-, walking-, and public transportation-friendly infrastructure and more; with a wealth of city cycling resources including maps, rides, and more.

RECREATIONAL BICYCLE CLUBS

Brooklyn Bicycle Club (www.brooklynbicycleclub.org): Brooklyn-based bike group.

Dykes on Bikes (dykesonbicycles.blogspot.com): Queer positive biking group.

Fast and Fabulous (fastnfab.org): LGBT-friendly bike club.

Five Borough Bike Club (www.5bbc.org): Large touring club.

New York Cycle Club (nycc.org): Large touring club.

New York City Mountain Biking Association (www.nycmtb.com): Mountain biking club.

Queens-Long Island Traveling Beginner Bicycle Club (www.meetup.com/TheForestHillsBeginnerBicycleClub): Queens-based leisure bike group.

Staten Island Bicycling Association (www.sibike.org): Touring club.

We Bike New York (webikenyc.org): Female-only bike community.

Weekday Cyclists (weekdaycyclists.org): Weekday cycling club.

Ride Index

About the Author

Mary Staub is a freelance journalist and passionate cyclist who has been exploring the New York City metro area by bike for more than ten years. Biking is part of who she is and always has been. Whether for commuting or for leisure, whether in sub-freezing temperatures or on sultry summer days, whether where she lives or where she travels, biking is what she has always done. Mary's inherent inquisitiveness has led her into various journalistic territories including travel writing, community reporting, mainstream news, and dance writing. Publications she's written for include *Travel + Leisure,* the *New York Sun, Basler Zeitung,* dance journals including *Ballet Tanz* and *Dancer Magazine,* and the technology news site Tech Media Network. She lives in Brooklyn.

IMBA
INTERNATIONAL MOUNTAIN BICYCLING ASSOCIATION

Come Ride With Us!

You've just purchased, or are about to purchase, the mountain bike of your dreams. Where will you take your new steed? Who will you ride with? Joining IMBA's network of chapters, clubs and patrols taps you into a friendly network of experienced mountain bikers. They host rides for all skill levels, build trails and get together before and after rides to share stories and plan the next adventure. Find a local group by visiting imba.com/near-you.

FIVE RECENT ACCOMPLISHMENTS

1) *Built incredible trails.* IMBA's trailbuilding pros teamed with volunteers around the nation to build sustainable, fun singletrack like the 32-mile system at Pennsylvania's Raystown Lake.

2) *Won grants to build or improve trails.* Your contributions to IMBA's Trail Building Fund were multiplied with six-figure grants of federal money for trail systems.

3) *Challenged anti-bike policies.* IMBA works closely with all of the federal land managing agencies and advises them on how to create bike opportunities and avoid policies that curtail trail access.

4) *Made your voice heard.* When anti-bike interests moved to try to close sections of the 2,500-mile Continental Divide trail to bikes, IMBA rallied its members and collected more than 7,000 comments supporting keeping the trail open to bikes.

5) *Put kids on bikes.* The seventh edition of National Take a Kid Mountain Biking Day put more than 20,000 children on bikes.

FIVE CURRENT GOALS

1) *Host regional bike summits.* We're boosting local trail development by hosting summits in distinct regions of the country, bringing trail advocates and regional land managers together.

2) *Build the next generation of trail systems* with innovative projects, including IMBA's sustainably built "flow trails" for gravity-assisted fun!

3) *Create "Gateway" trails* to bring new riders into the sport.

4) *Fight blanket bans against bikes* that unwisely suggest we don't belong in backcountry places.

5) *Strengthen its network* of IMBA-affiliated clubs with a powerful chapter program.

FOUR THINGS YOU CAN DO FOR YOUR SPORT

1) *Join IMBA.* Get involved with IMBA and take action close to home through your local IMBA-affiliated club. An organization is only as strong as its grassroots membership. IMBA needs your help in protecting and building great trails right here.

2) *Volunteer.* Join a trail crew day for the immensely satisfying experience of building a trail you'll ride for years to come. Ask us how.

3) *Speak up.* Tell land-use and elected officials how important it is to preserve mountain bike access. Visit IMBA's web site for action issues and talking points.

4) *Respect other trail users.* Bike bans result from conflict, real or perceived. By being good trail citizens, we can help end the argument that we don't belong on trails.

YOU BELONG WITH IMBA   JOIN

Join IMBA at www.imba.com or call 1-888-442-IMBA